Researching Female Faith

Researching Female Faith is a collection of essays based on recent and original field research conducted by the contributors, and informed by a variety of theoretical perspectives, into the faith lives of women and girls – broadly from within a Christian context.

Chapters describe and recount original qualitative research that identifies, illuminates and enhances our understanding of key aspects of women's and girls' faith lives. Offered as a contribution to feminist practical and pastoral theology, the chapters arise out of and feed back into a range of mainly UK pastoral and practical contexts. While the chapters in this volume will contribute to an enhanced appreciation and analysis of female faith, the core focus is on feminist qualitative research methods and methodology. Thus, they demystify and illuminate the process of research, including features of research that are frequently under-examined.

The book is a first in bringing together a specific focus on feminist qualitative research methodology with the study of female faith lives. It will therefore be of great interest to students, academics and practitioners with interests in faith and gender in theology, religious studies and sociology.

Nicola Slee is Director of Research at the Queen's Foundation for Ecumenical Theological Education in Birmingham, UK, where she oversees the doctoral programme, Professor of Feminist Practical Theology at the Vrije Universiteit Amsterdam, and Visiting Professor at the University of Chester.

Fran Porter is Research Fellow at the Queen's Foundation for Ecumenical Theological Education in Birmingham, UK, where she is involved in supporting and developing research work at the Foundation.

Anne Phillips is a Researcher, Spiritual Accompanist and Retreat Leader, and, a Church of England priest in a Peak District, UK, parish.

'Nicola Slee, Fran Porter and Anne Phillips have done it again, and I am delighted they have! Following their significant volume *The Faith Lives of Women and Girls*, the essays collected in this new book offer fresh insights into research frameworks, gathering and analyzing data, and reflexivity specific to the study of women and girls in contemporary Christianity. Finally, researchers and students in practical, contextual, pastoral theologies and religious feminisms have a resource that speaks to their qualitative approaches, and *Researching Female Faith* will challenge and enrich their methodologies and methods.' – **Dawn Llewellyn**, Senior Lecturer in Christian Studies, University of Chester, UK

Researching Female Faith

Qualitative Research Methods

**Edited by Nicola Slee,
Fran Porter and Anne Phillips**

Routledge
Taylor & Francis Group

LONDON AND NEW YORK

First published 2018
by Routledge
2 Park Square, Milton Park, Abingdon, Oxon OX14 4RN

and by Routledge
711 Third Avenue, New York, NY 10017

Routledge is an imprint of the Taylor & Francis Group, an informa business

British Library Cataloguing in Publication Data
A catalogue record for this book is available from the British Library

Library of Congress Cataloging in Publication Data
A catalog record for this book has been requested

ISBN: 978-1-138-73737-2 (hbk)
ISBN: 978-1-315-18544-6 (ebk)

Typeset in Bembo Std
by Swales & Willis Ltd, Exeter, Devon, UK

MIX
Paper from
responsible sources
FSC
www.fsc.org   FSC™ C013985

Printed in the United Kingdom
by Henry Ling Limited

Contents

Contributors

Jan Berry teaches pastoral and practical theology at Luther King House in Manchester where she is a research supervisor and Principal of Open College. Her research interests are in feminist liturgy and spirituality, and her doctoral research into women creating their own rituals of transition was published as *Ritual Making Women* (London: Equinox, 2009). Many of her hymns and prayers have appeared in anthologies, and she has published a collection of her own liturgical work entitled *Naming God* (London: URC Granary Press/Magnet, 2011). She is co-editor of a publication of new writing, *Hymns of Hope and Healing* (London: Stainer & Bell, 2017). She is a minister of the United Reformed Church, with a commitment to exploring creative forms of liturgy; in addition to her academic work, she is involved in leading workshops, quiet days and retreats exploring feminist and embodied spirituality, and creative writing for worship and prayer.

Helen Collins is an ordained priest in the Church of England and currently works as the Diocesan Director of Ordinands and Vocations in the Diocese of Bristol. Within this role, she also has oversight for support and training of the curates within the diocese. Her PhD was awarded in 2017 from the University of Bristol for her thesis, which analysed charismatic worship from the perspective of early motherhood. Helen has a BA in Theology from Oxford University and an MA in the Social Anthropology of Religion from Kings College, London. She trained for ordination at Trinity College in Bristol where she gained an Advanced Diploma in Ministerial Theology. Prior to ordination, Helen was a teacher in international schools. Her present research interests centre around pioneering new models of selection and training for church ministers.

Janet Eccles gained her PhD on Christian and disaffiliated women in 2010 as a mature student at Lancaster University UK, then worked as research associate on the Young Atheists Project, based at Lancaster. Now an independent researcher, she has published work on Christian women affiliates and disaffiliates, forms of non-religion, multi-faith chaplaincy, Anglican monasticism and insider/outsider issues.

Manon Ceridwen James is the Director of Ministry for St Asaph Diocese and was among one of the first women priests to be ordained in the Church in Wales in 1997. She received her PhD from Birmingham University in 2015 on research into the impact of religion on the social and personal identities of Welsh women. Her book, *Women, Identity and Religion in Wales: Theology, Poetry, Story*, is due to be published by the University of Wales Press in 2018. She has also published her poetry in several literary magazines, including *Poetry Wales*, *Under the Radar* and *Envoi*. She was the consultant for *Parch*, a Welsh language drama about a female vicar shown on S4C, and tweets as @manonceridwen.

Kate Massey is a vicar in Nuneaton and Dean of Women's Ministry for the Diocese of Coventry. Prior to ordination, she worked in the NHS as a doctor, specializing in mental health. She has a Master's in Applied Theological Studies through the Queen's Foundation, and her dissertation looked at the experiences of women combining callings to work and to motherhood. Kate's ongoing research interests are in the silencing and speaking of women in Evangelical Church of England contexts.

Jenny Morgans is a Church of England curate in North Lambeth Parish in south London. Her current research explores the faith and identity journeys of young Christian women amidst the transition of university. She is writing a PhD through the Queen's Foundation for Ecumenical Theological Education (Birmingham) and Vrije Universiteit Amsterdam. Jenny has worked in various church, charity and higher education chaplaincy contexts, including as Convenor of the Student Christian Movement, which prompted her doctoral research. Her research interests include gender, feminist theology, emerging adulthood, and identity. She has an MSc by Research from the University of Edinburgh, which focused on the bridge-building roles of Scottish women converts to Islam.

Sarah-Jane Page is a sociologist of religion and senior lecturer in Sociology at Aston University, Birmingham, UK. Her principal area of research is how gender and sexuality relate to religion. Projects she has worked on include her PhD, which investigated the experiences of Anglican clergy mothers and male clergy spouses, the findings of which have been published in journals such as *Sociological Research Online*, *Feminist Review*, *Feminist Theology* and *Gender, Work and Organization*, as well as the *Religion, Youth and Sexuality* project, which investigated the navigation of sexuality by religious young adults across the UK. Outcomes from this project are numerous and include two books: *Religious and Sexual Identities: A Multi-faith Exploration of Young Adults* (with A.K.T. Yip; Farnham: Ashgate, 2013) and *Understanding Young Buddhists: Living Out Ethical Journeys* (with A.K.T. Yip; Leiden: Brill, 2017).

Anne Phillips is a spiritual accompanist, retreat leader and researcher, now a Church of England priest in a Peak District, UK, parish. She enjoyed careers in education and as a parent, before being ordained and serving as a Baptist minister for over 25 years. After a local pastorate, she joined the staff of Northern Baptist College in Manchester first as a tutor, and then as Co-Principal, where she and her male colleague modelled gender equality in a fully collaborative style of leadership. She taught Christian education and faith development, theological reflection, and pastoral studies with an emphasis on women and children, besides researching, writing and training on issues of justice for women and children within the Baptist Union. Her doctoral research explored the faith lives of pre-adolescent girls, and was published as *The Faith of Girls: Children's Spirituality and the Transition to Adulthood* (Farnham: Ashgate, 2011). An original member of the Research Symposium on The Faith Lives of Women and Girls, she co-edited with Nicola Slee and Fran Porter its first book: *The Faith Lives of Women and Girls: Qualitative Research Perspectives* (Farnham: Ashgate, 2013). She continues to research into the spiritual flourishing of women and girls as they relate to God.

Fran Porter is Research Fellow at the Queen's Foundation for Ecumenical Theological Education in Birmingham, UK, where she is involved in supporting and developing research work at the Foundation. She researches and writes in socially engaged theology, exploring Christian faith, feminism, gender, equality, social diversity and reconciliation. The focus of much of her work is concerned with the churches' mission and relationships to wider society, and for many years she has contributed as an adult educator to the churches sector working with church members and leaders. An experienced qualitative researcher, she contributed to, and co-edited with Nicola Slee and Anne Phillips, *The Faith Lives of Women and Girls: Qualitative Research Perspectives* (Farnham: Ashgate, 2013). Among her other publications is *Women and Men After Christendom: The Dis-Ordering of Gender Relationships* (Milton Keynes: Paternoster, 2015). Fran has a BA in Theology from the London School of Theology, and an MSc and PhD in Women's Studies from the University of Ulster. Born and raised in England, Fran lived in Belfast for 27 years and was involved in church, voluntary and academic sectors in Northern Ireland. Since 2008, she has been living in the Midlands.

Susan Shooter taught languages in a comprehensive school, before being ordained in Rochester Diocese. She served as parish priest for thirteen years, becoming Biblical Strand Leader for Christchurch Canterbury University's Certificate in Theology & Ministry. In 2011 she completed her doctorate at Kings College London about Christian survivors, published as *How Survivors of Abuse Relate to God* (2012: Farnham, Ashgate). Susan's publications include, 'What on Earth Is She Thinking of, Still Attending Church? Action Research in a Southeast London Parish' in *Practical Theology* (December 2013), and 'How Feminine Participation in the Divine Might Renew the Church and Its Leadership' in *Feminist Theology* (January 2014). She has edited book reviews for *Practical Theology*. Currently she lives in North Cornwall and is writing a historical novel, *The Phoenix and the Kingfisher*, about medieval writer Marguerite Porete who was charged with heresy by the Inquisition. Susan's website is www.shooterspen.com.

Nicola Slee is Director of Research at the Queen's Foundation for Ecumenical Theological Education where she oversees the doctoral programme, Professor of Feminist Practical Theology at the Vrije Universiteit Amsterdam, and Visiting Professor at the University of Chester. She was involved in some of the earliest feminist Christian networks and groups in the UK in the late 1970s and early 1980s, contributed to some of the first publications in Christian feminist theology in the UK, and her doctoral thesis, published as *Women's Faith Development: Patterns and Processes* (Aldershot: Ashgate, 2004), broke new ground in the qualitative study of women's faith lives. Since then, she has published widely in feminist theology, spirituality and liturgy, as well as in practical theology. She convenes the Symposium on the Faith Lives of Women and Girls and co-edited with Anne Phillips and Fran Porter *The Faith Lives of Women and Girls: Qualitative Research Perspectives* (Farnham: Ashgate, 2013). She is a poet and belongs to two writing groups, one of them a group of poet-theologians. She is currently working on a book on Sabbath and collaborating on a project on feminist liturgy. She is a lay Anglican and honorary Vice President of WATCH (Women and the Church).

Kim Wasey is the Church of England Chaplain at the University of Salford and Assistant Priest at St Chrysostom's, an inner city parish in Manchester. She is the mother of three young children. She completed her doctorate at Birmingham University, through the Queen's Foundation, in 2012. Prior to this, she read Theology at Manchester University and also has an MPhil by research from Birmingham University on the radical, social and inclusive ministry of Anglo-Catholic slum priests in the nineteenth century. Kim has worked in various church and higher education chaplaincy settings, as well as teaching and mentoring. These contexts prompted her doctoral research into young women's relationships with the Eucharist, and have led her to explore how the extensive use of social media in her chaplaincy work is also able to resource and inform her research.

Alison Woolley has been working as a music therapist with young people with profound and multiple learning difficulties in West Yorkshire for over twenty years. She has a PhD from Birmingham University, and her doctoral research into contemporary Christian women's chosen practices of silence will be published in 2019 by Routledge as *Women Choosing Silence: Relationality and Transformation in Spiritual Practice*. She is Director of the Seeds of Silence project, which supports Christians in developing a spiritual discipline of silence through workshops, training and retreats for people in all kinds of ministries. Alongside her work in spiritual accompaniment, her own practice of silence, photography, 5 Rhythms dancing and walking by the sea or in the Yorkshire countryside are important aspects of her spirituality.

Introduction

Anne Phillips, Fran Porter and Nicola Slee

The nature, contexts and aims of the book

Researching Female Faith: Qualitative Research Methods is the second collection of essays to emerge from the Symposium on the Faith Lives of Women and Girls convened at the Queen's Foundation for Ecumenical Theological Education, Birmingham, England, which has been meeting regularly since 2010. In our first edited collection, *The Faith Lives of Women and Girls,*[1] we narrated the genesis of the Symposium and described its ethos as a collaborative, feminist-inspired network of qualitative researchers engaged in researching female faith lives at postgraduate, doctoral and postdoctoral levels. As in that first collection, the work represented in this volume is based on original field research, informed by a variety of theoretical perspectives, into the faith lives of women and girls – broadly from within a Christian context. We continue our substantive concern to illuminate the still neglected faith lives of women and girls, but in this volume focus on issues of feminist method and methodology – on *how* feminist researchers go about doing their research.

We have been heartened by critical and conversational responses to our first book. Readers – both new and more experienced researchers – valued the self-reflexive, narrative accounts of particular projects that highlighted findings that throw new light on women's and girls' practices of faith. Our aim in that volume of demystifying the research process continues to inform this book by focusing specifically on methods and methodology. We explore explicitly how feminist researchers employ qualitative methodology and methods to study the faith lives of women and girls. Contributors offer both broad reflections on methodology and more focused accounts of particular research methods, with a detail that is still rare in many research methodology texts. Chapters trace different stages of the research process: the initial, sometimes hesitant, idea for a research project; the honing of a proposal; the choices in research design and the creation of an overarching methodology; and the conduct of the research, data analysis and writing up. Contributors describe in detail what they did and why, the challenges or difficulties they faced in developing their research design and how they overcame them or, sometimes, had to change tack and take a new approach. They discuss the variety of methodological frameworks available to them and, in some cases, the development of new methodologies and new variations on well-worn methods.

We consider that this volume makes a valuable addition to the research literature and will be of great benefit to new researchers in the field of gender and faith, demystifying and illuminating the process of research, including features of research that are frequently under-examined. We know of no collection of essays that focuses on feminist research methodology in the study of female faith lives per se. There are, of course, a growing number of texts on feminist research methodology more generally,[2] but none of these addresses the study of religious faith. Conversely, there are texts exploring research methods from a theological perspective and we welcome the growing literature within practical theology attending to the conduct of qualitative as well as quantitative research,[3] but few if any of these address issues of gender or, if they do, only in passing. Our text is the first in the field to combine a specific focus on feminist qualitative research methodology with the study of female faith.

We hope that this text makes a significant contribution to feminist practical and pastoral theology, to the social scientific study of religion, to feminist research methodology more generally, and specifically to feminist-inspired qualitative research on religion. We anticipate that it will be a valuable text for students in theological education (those preparing for various forms of ministry in the churches), for those working in the field of practical/pastoral theology, particularly at master's and doctoral level, and for researchers in the field. While located primarily in a UK context, we believe that the research here may speak to a wider international readership.

A note on method and methodology

It is important to be aware that there are differences in the way writers define 'method' and 'methodology'. After pointing out that the terms are frequently used as if they were synonymous and interchangeable, John Swinton and Harriet Mowat offer helpful definitions, making the distinction and connection between methods and methodology clear:

> *Methods* are specific techniques that are used for data collection and analysis. They comprise a series of clearly defined, disciplined and systematic procedures that the researcher uses to accomplish a particular task. Interviews, sampling procedures, thematic development, coding and recognized techniques and approaches to the construction of the research question would be examples of qualitative research methods.

> *Methodology* is connected to method, but in a particular way. The term 'methodology' has a number of different meanings. Formally it relates to the study of methods. More broadly, the term methodology has to do with an overall approach to a particular field. It implies a family of methods that have in common particular philosophical and epistemological assumptions.[4]

They go on to discuss the ways in which particular methods are employed within the methodological assumptions of specific interpretative paradigms. For example, the philosophical perspective of logical positivism within the natural sciences is based on an objectivist epistemology in which there is a sharp distinction between knower and what is known, and understands the role of science as that of measurement and prediction. This approach tends to employ quantitative methods, which are presumed to be able to measure accurately and objectively the phenomena under investigation. By contrast, what they call the 'hermeneutical/interpretative paradigm' is based on a social constructivist understanding of knowledge in which the boundary between knower and known is blurred, and in which the knower therefore always impacts upon what is known as participant and co-creator. The creation of theory is seen as a heuristic exercise leading to more or less satisfying accounts of reality, and qualitative methods are favoured by this approach because they take far greater account of the porous line between the researcher and the researched.

This understanding of methods and methodology is shared by a number of other British practical theologians, for example Helen Cameron and Catherine Duce,[5] who offer a helpful, simplified summary of Swinton and Mowatt's approach. Cameron and Duce emphasize the ways in which methodologies – what we might call overarching theoretical frameworks that shape and guide the research and give meaning to specific methods – are themselves shaped and guided by the underlying epistemological frameworks of the researcher(s). Methodologies, in other words, tend to enshrine and express fundamental orientations to truth and knowledge, whether these are made explicit in the research or not; and this may be true, to a lesser extent, of research methods. They identify four basic paradigms (objectivist, critical, interpretivist and action research) that tend to be operative in practical theology, each of which operates with different epistemologies, methodologies and, to a certain degree, methods.

Other writers use the language of theory rather than methodology to differentiate between discrete research methods and the larger epistemological frameworks within which research is conducted. Particular paradigms within theology, as well as specific geographical and socio-political contexts, powerfully shape the ways in which it is understood knowledge is derived, including the purpose and outcome of research. For example, emancipatory theory, feminist and womanist theories, narrative approaches, ethnography and participatory action research offer specific approaches to the conduct of research shaped by epistemological, political and practical factors.[6]

Sandra Harding helpfully distinguishes between epistemology, methodology, and method.[7] An epistemology, according to Harding, is a theory about knowledge; a method is a technique for gathering and analysing information, and a methodology 'works out the implications of a specific epistemology for how to implement a method'.[8] Joey Sprague, discussing Harding's clear and useful distinction, suggests that, 'when we decouple the elision of epistemology and method, methodology emerges as the terrain where philosophy and action meet, where the implications of what we believe for how we should proceed get worked out'. She continues:

> Reflecting on methodology – on how we do what we do – opens up pos-sibilities and exposes choices. It allows us to ask such questions as: Is the way we gather and interpret data consistent with what we believe about how knowledge is and should be created? What unexamined assumptions about knowledge underlie our standards for evaluating claims about how things are or what really happened? We can even pose questions rarely considered in rela-tion to methodology, questions about how knowledge fits into the rest of social life: Whose questions are we asking? And to whom do we owe an answer? Thinking about methodology in this way puts the technical details into a social and political context and considers their consequences for people's lives. It gives us space for critical reflection and creativity.[9]

It is precisely to create such a space for critical and creative reflection that we offer this volume.

Feminist approaches to methodology and method

Feminists by no means agree on questions of method and methodology any more than they agree on epistemological commitments or understandings of feminism. Mary Daly is typical of those who hold a scathing antipathy towards method. 'One of the false gods of theologians, philosophers, and other academ-ics is called Method', she opined in *Beyond God the Father*,[10] going on to claim:

> The tyranny of methodolatry hinders new discoveries. It prevents us from raising questions never asked before and from being illumined by ideas that do not fit into pre-established boxes and forms. The worshippers of Method have an effective way of handling data that does not fit into the Respectable Categories of Questions and Answers. They simply classify it as nondata, thereby rendering it invisible.[11]

Nevertheless, Daly went on to develop her own highly distinctive meth-ods and methodology, what she described in *Gyn/Ecology* as 'Gynocentric Method', built on the 'murder of misogynistic methods (intellectual and affec-tive exorcism)' and the 'free play of intuition in our own space, giving rise to thinking that is vigorous, informed, multi-dimensional, independent, crea-tive, tough'.[12] When Daly castigates method, what she is really railing against and rejecting wholesale is androcentric, patriarchal application of methods, rather than method itself.

Following Daly, feminist scholars in every field have sought to develop feminist means of knowledge production commensurate with the emancipa-tory and liberating aims of feminism. Numerous accounts exist of the debates within feminist methodologies and methods over the past two to three decades, and readers are referred to these for wider discussion.[13] Broadly speaking, the debate has centred around the question of whether there are specifically feminist methods and/or methodologies, or simply feminist approaches to method and methodology. In *Women's Faith Development: Patterns and Processes*, Slee categorized three main stages of the debate and, more than 10 years later, we suggest this categorization still holds. The first phase, designated 'the critical stage', was stimulated by contributions from feminist scholars in the natural and physical, as well as social sciences, who called attention to the sexism and androcentrism inherent in generally accepted scientific procedures, for example, in the common use of male-only subjects in studies of human participants, and male activity and male-dominant animal populations in experiments using animals. This phase was also characterized by a wider critique of quantitative methods, 'widely regarded as alienating and inimical to women's experience, rooted in a positivist empiricism which reified objectivity and philosophical neutrality whilst masking its own commitments to such culturally conditioned (and male) values as autonomy, separation, distance and control'.[14] A second, constructivist stage built on this earlier critique and deconstruction by seeking to develop new research methods and methodologies grounded in 'feminist standpoint' epistemologies, 'characterised by the commitment to researching women's experiences, worldviews and meanings using methods grounded in their own social practices'.[15] Participatory methods of research were developed and advocated, in which participants were regarded as co-researchers sharing in the task of knowledge production, rather than as 'subjects' under the critical gaze of the researcher(s). In practice, qualitative methods were favoured by the majority of feminists working in the social sciences 'as the only ones capable of yielding such mutuality of participation'.[16] Feminists made adaptations of existing methods – in particular, the interview, but also oral history and so on – in order to minimize, as far as possible, the power differential between the researcher and researched and to allow for genuine collaboration, even 'friendship', between researcher and researched.[17] There was also a strong commitment to disseminate research findings in non-standard academic forms (for example, popular forms of writing, political and feminist gatherings, and media presentation), which could be more accessible to research participants. The third phase, categorized as one of 'diversification and self-reflective critical sophistication', is still ongoing (although of course there have been significant publications in the past decade and more). This phase has been marked by a move away from the earlier search for exclusively 'feminist methods' towards a broader consideration of the principles and epistemological commitments that shape research practice. The simplistic binary between quantitative and qualitative research approaches, and the assertion that only qualitative research is authentically feminist, have given way to a more inclusive recognition that both qualitative and quantitative approaches and methods can play their part in feminist research and can helpfully critique and enrich each other. Another characteristic of this third, ongoing phase is the recognition and assertion of plurality and diversity within feminist practice and epistemology and the dismantling of singular notions of either feminism or research.

As a result of these debates and contributions to feminist research practice, there is now a widely shared view that the pursuit of specifically feminist research methods or even methodologies is both obsolete and erroneous. It is obsolete because feminists use any and all of the existing research methods that have been used in earlier, androcentric research – albeit with adaptations, applied to new contexts and research questions – so that it is contradictory to declare any method feminist per se. It is erroneous because it is to impose a unitary view and practice upon feminists and to exclude work that does not fit such criteria – an approach that seems inherently anti-feminist in its imperialism. Nevertheless, as Andrea Doucet and Natasha S. Mauthner suggest, 'While it is difficult to argue that there is a specifically feminist method, methodology, or epistemology, it is the case that feminist scholars have embraced particular characteristics in their work'.[18] They suggest the following: first, 'that feminist research should be not just on women, but *for* women and, where possible, with women'; second, 'feminist researchers have actively engaged with methodological innovation through challenging conventional or mainstream ways of collecting, analysing, and presenting data'; third, 'feminist research is concerned with issues of broader social change and social justice'; fourth, feminist research is marked by critical attention to power, exploitation, knowing and representation and aims for 'accountable and responsible knowing'; fifth, feminist research is marked by explicit reflexivity and transparency about such core issues as social location, the co-creation of data and the construction of knowledge.[19] Gayle Letherby shares a similar stance when she asserts:

> although there is no such thing as a feminist method, and there is debate over the usefulness and even the existence of feminist methodology and a feminist epistemology, there is a recognition that 'feminist research practice' (Kelly, 1988) is distinguishable from other forms of research. Feminist research practice can be distinguished by the questions feminists ask, the location of the researcher within the process of research and within theorizing, and the intended purpose of the work produced.[20]

The debates about what makes for good and authentic feminist research practice, and the specific characteristics advocated by Doucet and Mauthner, as well as others, will be evident in the following chapters and form part of the background to this book. In this sense, *Researching Female Faith* contributes to the ongoing debates about feminist methods, methodologies and epistemologies. What is new is the bringing to bear of such methodological perspectives onto the study of female faith – itself as varied and diverse as the perspectives and approaches of the women who have contributed to this book. These chapters constitute only a partial record of such debate and a partial contribution to debate about the best ways for feminists to engage in research and, specifically, the most authentic and empowering ways for feminists to research other women's and girls' faith lives.

We hope what follows will stimulate ongoing discussion and debate and, above all, further research that can enrich both substantive knowledge of female faith and offer new and creative methodological perspectives.

A synopsis of the book

In Part I, we offer some broad feminist methodological perspectives as a way of setting the discussions of specific research methods that follow into a wider framework. These chapters, by Anne Phillips, Nicola Slee, Helen Collins and Janet Eccles, discuss the development of broad, overarching perspectives or frameworks for research, the metanarratives or theories that give meaning to, and shape, specific research methods, although those methods may well also – and do – reciprocally shape the broader methodo-logical framework that emerges generally slowly and gradually out of the trial and error processes of conducting research. If, as Letherby suggests, 'thinking methodologically is theorizing about how we find things out; it is about the relationship between the process and the product of research',[21] then these first four chapters offer theoretical, as well as practical, approaches to the conduct of feminist research and to the production of feminist theory. However, they do so by keeping close to the actual practice of research itself – which is a key aim and intention of the collection as a whole.

Writing on research methodology can become divorced from the detail of the daily practices, choices and dilemmas faced by researchers in the field. We asked all contributors, whatever their stance or approach, to describe as clearly and precisely as possible, what they actually *did* in developing a specific research method or broader methodology; how they did it and why; what this produced by way of knowledge as well as research process; how it impacted on themselves as researchers as well as the participants; what worked and what did not, and what they did then. Throughout, we hope that readers will get the sense of the actual practice of research – its ups and downs, its surprising twists and turns, its frustrations and dead ends as well as its sudden moments of illumination and discovery. Research is a dynamic, active and emergent pro-cess and, however experienced the researcher(s) or well prepared for entering the field, there are always unpredictable factors that cannot be planned or even known beforehand. We believe that the chapters that follow give a real sense of this emergent aspect of research; we are invited into the process as it takes shape, and we join the questioning, questing and experimental journey of each researcher as the research progresses.

It has been a deliberate choice to start this book with Anne Phillips' chapter, which reflects on her research with girls and the methodological choices she had to make in researching the spiritual lives and faith of girls. We start here, not only because, chronologically, girlhood precedes womanhood, but more significantly because the experience of girls is still a neglected site in social scientific research (although this is changing), most particularly where the faith lives of girls is concerned. Phillips' pioneering work in this field is gaining broad, international recognition, and we hope it will stimulate much more research. In her chapter, she describes and reflects on the participative nature of the methodology and methods she used in her interviews with girls in a British Baptist context, a methodology grounded in the commitment to the empowerment of the girls and to advocacy on their behalf. Phillips reflects on the limits, as well as the strengths, of her participative methodology, particularly in light of the constraints imposed by working within a faith community. By comparing and contrasting her study with both adult-led projects and a substantially child-led project, she draws out the particular contribution of her own study. Messy, unpredictable and 'immature' at the same time as being open-ended, innovative and experimental, such participative research has the capacity to create a space in which the newly emergent subjectivities of both researcher and researched can interrelate, in respectful and playful dialogue.

On the face of it, Nicola Slee's discussion of the development of a research methodology using poetry as a means of data analysis, presentation and reflexivity appears to have little in common with Phillips' chapter, but closer scrutiny suggests shared themes of evolving a methodology experimentally, committing to the full participation of research subjects, and understanding research with women and girls itself as practices of solidarity and advocacy. Slee's chapter offers a case study of 'Meg', one of the first cohort of women priests in the Church of England, who Slee had originally interviewed more than twenty years ago. Returning to the transcript and re-analysing it through a range of poetic responses, the chapter charts the ways in which this experimental method enabled the re-opening of a dialogue with Meg, who was gradually drawn into the reflexive scrutiny of the earlier conversation and offered her own poetic response to it. The chapter sheds light on the respective journeys and life choices of two Anglican women – the researcher and the researched, lay and ordained, one of whom has left the church and the other of whom has remained – as well as offering a creative case study of the potential insight poetry can offer to qualitative data.

Helen Collins' chapter is also marked by experimentation, trial and error and the gradual evolution of a novel methodology emerging from and integrating her respective identity markers as feminist, evangelical and charismatic. She describes her endeavours to find an existing methodology that would be suitable for her study of first-time mothers from charismatic evangelical backgrounds and the impact of motherhood on their experience of charismatic worship. None of the existing methodological frameworks – feminist or practical theological – seemed to offer what she needed, although she drew widely on existing models and approaches in the development of her own. The chapter offers a reflexive narrative of her research journey, in which she describes in some detail how she developed a novel methodology of 'web-weaving', drawing on Mark Cartledge's practical theology methodology and enriching as well as critiquing it from feminist perspectives. Having described the creation of this new methodology, she goes on to show how she used it to analyse data from her interviews and how it enabled the complexity of her participants' lives, as well as her own, to find a more adequate expression than would have been the case if she had been forced to choose a pre-existing methodology.

Janet Eccles' research methodology, like Collins', took shape over many weeks and months because pre-existing categories in the sociology of religion did not fit or appeared inadequate to theorize the complex and nuanced accounts offered by her participants as they narrated their religious/spiritual lives and practices. Within her study of older women church affiliates and nonaffiliates in the South Lakeland town where she lives, Eccles hit the problem when she was beginning to search for a typology to enable her to code and categorize the transcripts of interviews with women. Thus, the chapter contains helpful and illuminating insight into the processes of data analysis, and might have gone into Part III; we have placed it here partly to demonstrate how larger methodological issues arise out of data analysis, but also because, in her wrestling with existing categories available from the sociology of religion, Eccles eventually came to develop a new typology. Her work demonstrates, along with the other chapters in this section, how feminists are developing new frameworks for the analysis of female faith: critiquing, adapting, revising and expanding existing models or bringing them into unlikely conversation with each other. These methodologies suggest new ways of doing research at the same time as offering new theoretical perspectives on female faith. Thus, Eccles became dissatisfied with existing typologies that make a hard and fast distinction between 'religion' and 'spirituality', or between Christian and non- or post-Christian believers. Her research participants offered many examples of women who contradicted the categories: women who attended church for many different reasons, by no means all of them obviously devotional; dechurched women who still considered themselves Christian and engaged in practices such as prayer, Bible reading and so on, often more devoutly than some of the affiliates; women who both attended church and other practitioner groups, such as pagan/holistic groups, critiquing both in the light of the other. Thus a new typology gradually developed, through much trial and error, and Eccles offers this as a more flexible and nuanced model that can account for the fact that '[w]omen may be both religious and spiritual whether they "belong" to the institutional church or not'. At the same time, she encourages feminist researchers to 'refuse previously (often male) defined categories', arguing that '[o]ur subjects deserve their own, which reflect their lives as they live them, not a standard off-the-shelf model'.

Part II turns to the stage of data gathering in qualitative research and offers a range of chapters discussing the use of different kinds of data and different ways of generating data. While the focus here is on specific research methods, larger methodological questions and issues are never far away. It is unhelpful and unrealistic to make too sharp a division between discrete research methods and larger theoretical or methodological frameworks, since there is almost always a backwards and forwards iterative process in the development of research methods and the broader methodological framework. Thus the lines between Parts I and II of the book are inevitably blurred (as are the lines between all of our section divisions). What unites the discussions by Fran Porter, Sarah-Jane Page and Kim Wasey in these chapters is their detailed and careful attention both to the minutiae of research practice and to wider theoretical – philosophical, sociological and theological – questions that give meaning to specific research practices. First, Fran Porter discusses a research method much used and favoured by feminists, the interview; unusually, Porter advocates the usefulness and value of a highly structured interview format in contrast to the looser narrative or semi-structured interview schedules adopted by the majority of feminist practitioners. Situating the argument in a review of some of the key debates about feminist interview methods, Porter then goes on to describe two research projects in which she employed highly structured interview schedules to interview women, offering a rationale for this choice based on the desire to cover specific areas and avenues of enquiry that, at that time, had received very little research attention. Porter shows that a highly structured approach can still be used flexibly, and can elicit a very wide range of responses; she counters the contention that a highly structured interview makes the process of data analysis easier, since participants can and do respond in a highly individual manner to standard questions – and this, of course, is part of the fascination and value of the approach. Above all, she demonstrates that a highly structured research instrument can be used to advance feminist aims of empowerment and reciprocity, and can offer to participants opportunities for self-expression and understanding.

The following chapters by Page and Wasey offer contrasting discussions of research methods that employ new technologies and social media unavailable to earlier generations of feminist scholars. Sarah-Jane Page discusses the use of video diaries in a research project exploring young adults' faith lives, offering a nuanced account that acknowledges the complexity of ethical issues arising in such research, especially around issues of consent, voice and power. While Page acknowledges the arguments for inviting research participants to make video diaries on the grounds of giving them more power and enabling research to be more collaborative, she goes on to question the naïve assumption that such methods ensure the balance of power in favour of participants. The discussion of visual methods is set within the framework of the debate about feminist research in which Page problematizes the notion that any specific method can be guaranteed to be non-exploitative and participatory. Page then goes on to review studies that have employed new technologies, such as the smart phone and the video diary, to access the social worlds of vulnerable or marginalized groups, noting the potential strengths as well as pitfalls of such methods. She goes on to describe the use of such methods in a project on young adults' faith and sexuality, arguing that video diaries may be particularly powerful in capturing the everyday religious lives and practices of participants. At the same time, she notes some participants' ambivalence about using video diaries and the operation of class and other forms of privilege that shaped the confidence and ease with which participants were able to construct narrative identities. She argues that the video diary method 'privileges certain ways of knowing', those 'supported by dominant Western norms' and, conversely, is more problematic for members of marginalized and disadvantaged groups. Nor are all narratives equally permissible or supported, and she notes a number of constraints and controls, including gendered ones, that were operative in the study and impacted on participants' sense of voice and agency. This careful and nuanced discussion of new technological methods in research gives the lie to any assumption that new technologies are automatically benign, especially for female participants. Moreover, as a study that included male and female participants, there are some helpful comparative findings that illuminate gender analysis.

Kim Wasey is, perhaps, rather more upbeat about the potential for new technologies in research, agreeing with a number of feminist commentators on the potential for new technologies to create online feminist communities and engage participants in genuinely collaborative dialogue and interaction. After reviewing a number of studies that have employed blogs and social media platforms such as Twitter and Facebook, Wasey describes her own use of social media in a pilot study exploring women's experiences of Holy Communion. She compares and contrasts the research process conducted through a social media platform with her earlier study, which had used more conventional methods of interviews. Using social media enabled her to access a far larger number of research participants from a wider range of contexts more quickly than traditional methods of accessing interviewees (although of course it would be perfectly possible to access interviewees by use of social media – something Wasey did not do in her earlier study). She also notes 'a significant difference in the nature and quality of the data which was generated by this social media method in comparison with data generated through face to face interview and transcription'. Tweeted and posted comments created 'more concise and formed data' than interview transcripts, obviated the need for transcription and all the technical and ethical issues involved in transcribing verbal data, and thus speeded up the process of analysis considerably. Acknowledging legitimate concerns that can be raised about the functioning of on-line spaces, Wasey nevertheless argues for a number of benefits of using social media 'for engaging with marginalized, dispersed and isolated groups in a reflective, transparent, practical and collaborative research process'.

Whether the reader sides more with Wasey in her optimism about the use of new technologies, or Page in her more qualified view, these two chapters between them shed significant light on the development of new research methods and raise a range of philosophical, ethical, practical and methodological issues, which helpfully move the debates in feminist methodology on.

In Part III, Susan Shooter, Kate Massey, Alison Woolley and Manon Ceridwen James each offer chapters on various aspects of, and approaches to, the task of data analysis. This is usually the point at which the researcher needs to bring together and integrate theoretical perspectives from their reading of the literature with the mass of collected data. Research methodology textbooks offer a wide variety of possible methods of data analysis, and many existing models and methods are available from the field. Yet, as we have seen with Janet Eccles' account of her data analysis, existing methods and models are by no means unproblematic and do not always serve feminist goals or data from women's lives. Thus feminist researchers often revise or reject existing approaches and develop their own unique methods of data analysis. In these chapters, we find a range of approaches and methods, some researchers sticking more closely to tried and tested methods than others, and some evolving new methods or at least new approaches to well-tried methods. Each of these studies employed interviews as their basic data collection method, but used a variety of approaches to analysing the data.

Feminist and other qualitative researchers often favour grounded theory approaches to data analysis, although some use this term rather loosely, with minimal reference to the original principles and approach as developed by Barney Glaser and Anselm Strauss. Susan Shooter offers a careful and nuanced description of grounded theory, highlighting a discrepancy in the views of Glaser and Strauss concerning coding. She discusses her use of Glaserian grounded theory to analyse data from women survivors of abuse, favouring his approach because of his commitment to allowing categories to emerge from the data rather than forcing data into predetermined categories. This was as much a moral as a methodological commitment for Shooter, based on a determination to allow her participants' voices to be heard and to frame a theology *of* survivors rather than *for* them. Following a careful tripart coding of the data, she goes on to discuss her use of NVivo computer software as the next stage of enabling her to store and sort efficiently the vast amount of data resulting from the coding process. She describes the ways in which NVivo can be used to build up models of complex and advanced relationships between the various codes and, eventually, to identify core categories – higher level concepts that offer hypotheses about the data.

Kate Massey discusses her use of a voice-centred, relational analysis in reading data from a study of mothers' dual sense of calling (i.e. their sense of vocation to some kind of professional or creative work alongside their sense of vocation to motherhood). She sought an approach that would do justice to the complex interactions between motherhood, vocation and spirituality within each of the women's narratives at the same time as allowing her to pay attention to each voice (including her own) in a multi-faceted group interview of four women. The voice-centred, relational methodology advocated by Mauthner and Doucet,[22] developed from the interview studies of Carol Gilligan, provided the key to such an approach. In her chapter, Massey describes this approach and gives an insightful account of how she adapted it to her own study in ways that enabled her to practice reflexivity and transparency. She highlights and discusses three particular aspects of the method: the value of the method in paying attention to the voices of both researcher and researched;

the benefits and limitations of using the method in a group interview situation; and the significance of the use of indirect speech by the women in the study. Her skilful use of this method enables her to offer a perceptive theological reading of the relationship between faith, work and mothering in her small research group that enhances other contemporary studies of motherhood.

Alison Woolley's chapter, like Massey's, focuses in detail on the process of analysing interview transcripts, but in this case she is particularly concerned with the methodological, substantive and theological significance of *silences* in the interview encounter. She describes how she developed a particular approach to interviewing women about their chosen practices of silence, which, rather than regarding pauses in the interview as problematic, held them as an intrinsic part of the meaning-making. Challenging negative notions of silence in feminist theology, Woolley offers an alternative reading of silence in the interview exchange, arguing that it may be something the interviewer offers to her interviewees as a space for reflection, contemplation and recognition, and as a way of being more fully present to the other. Woolley's work is an important corrective to approaches to interviews in which the focus is on words as the sole carriers of meaning. It also points towards one of the myriad ways in which researchers who pursue their scholarship within a context of faith may seek to discern the activity of God in their participants' lives, by paying acute attention to the relational process of the interview encounter – of which silence is one important dimension.

Manon Ceridwen James discusses her use of poetry in a study of Welsh women's identity and religious belonging (or lack of it), in a way that both connects with and stands in contrast to, Slee's earlier chapter. James takes the work of one of the most prominent female poets writing in Welsh, Menna Elfyn, and brings it into conversation with data from her own interviews with Welsh women about their social and personal identities. After identifying key themes and tropes in Elfyn's work (offering fascinating analysis of religious faith in Welsh society in its own right), James brings these into dialogue with similar themes in her interview transcripts. In particular, she explores how the women in her study, and Elfyn, approach religious faith both more personally and in the contexts of public liturgy, motherhood and the trope of the 'Strong Woman', highlighting issues of voice and voicelessness. The result is a rich and textured probing of her interviewees' experience and ordinary theologies and a case study of how an individual poet's work can be used to triangulate and illuminate qualitative data.

The final part of the book, Part IV, offers two reflections on reflexivity in feminist qualitative work. Although questions of reflexivity and the use of the self in research are woven throughout this book – arguably, this is a key characteristic of feminist research – it becomes the main focus here. Jenny Morgans and Jan Berry discuss feminist understandings of reflexivity and illustrate some of the issues – including tensions and problems – which can arise in the researcher's use of self in the research enterprise.

Situating herself as a younger researcher nearing the completion of doctoral studies and growing in an awareness of the complexity of her own investment in research, Jenny Morgans offers a reflection on her own journey of reflexivity. She writes with painstaking honesty about a number of incidents in her encounters with first-year female undergraduates in the context of university Christian societies, as she began her study of young Christian women's transitioning to university. From her very first interview, Morgans found many of her assumptions about her professional and personal identity and her role as a researcher confused and shaken. She narrates both the emotional intensity of the resulting reflexive process and its intellectual, as well as personal, demands. She describes the work of reflexivity as 'useful, ongoing and hard', demonstrating how crucial it was to her own growing understanding of herself and of her participants. More than being a matter of ethical care of self and other, or of mere transparency about the research process, Morgans renders reflexivity as a vital and embodied means of thinking and knowing that contributes core insights to the research. She discusses the use of a research journal as well as the practice of prayer, as sites for working through the complex and sometimes confusing emotions arising from research encounters.

Finally, Jan Berry offers distilled wisdom on the use of self in feminist qualitative research from her own research experience but also, significantly, from her experience of supervising doctoral students from a range of cultural contexts. Drawing on literature in feminist research methodology, practical theology as well as published and unpublished accounts of research by women from the Symposium on the Faith Lives of Women and Girls, Berry writes autobiographically and reflexively on her understanding of the self as research instrument, problematizing the notion of the self as fluid, constructed and culturally located. What she calls the trajectory of using self in research is complex and unique for each researcher, and her many examples of researchers' struggles to locate their selves in their research, as well as the creative ways in which they do so, illuminate the thickness of research accounts that take seriously the dialogical nature of research. Berry's insights into the use of self in the supervisory relationship between doctoral student and supervisor(s) will be helpful to supervisors and students alike. Her strong affirmation of the positive theological significance of the female self also offers a distinctive perspective to broader methodological discussion of reflexivity from the faith perspective shared by contributors to this book.

Some key themes and issues arising

Without wanting to impose uniformity on the varied contributions in this volume, there are a number of recurring motifs which are worth noting. Some of these themes are familiar from the literature and practices of feminist and qualitative research studies, but they take on new significance by the focus of each contributor on the study of (female) faith. If there is something new and distinctive about this volume as a whole – which we believe there is – it is precisely in this intersection between feminist and qualitative research methodology and methods, on the one hand, and the focused research on lived religious faith in the experience of particular groups of women and girls, on the other.

First, we note a strong emphasis on the convergence of the research process with the content, values and the outcomes of research. One of the defining characteristics of feminist research – and we could say the same about research that is explicitly theological – is that the means of research must be commensurate with the topic of research and the core values of the researcher. Feminist theological research is not defined merely by its subject – the faith lives of women and girls – but by the ethical norms of its practices: the openness and transparency of its aims and procedures; the relational and collaborative approach to its participants; the honesty of its self-involvement; and the intentional openness of its orientation and methods to a faith perspective. Where feminist research would endorse most of these characteristics as axiomatic, what is novel about the discussion in this volume is the deliberate contextualising of the debate in the environment of faith, where qualitative and feminist approaches are employed to shed light on and to expose the quality of women's and girls' faith lives. Another way of expressing this is to say that the research methods and methodology described by the contributors to this book are a core expression of their own lived convictions as they pursue more thorough, complex and rigorous accounts of the lived faith of women and girls. Thus ethical considerations – or what might also be described as spiritual and theological considerations – run as a current through all of the chapters, rather than being compartmentalized into one or two specific sections.

Second, the chapters each highlight in different ways the experimental and creative nature of feminist research, whether on the macro or the micro level. While there is nothing new under the sun and no such thing as an entirely novel research method or methodology, most of the research studies described here narrate the development of fresh approaches to or particular adaptations of existing methods or methodologies, on the grounds that none of the existing approaches could be applied wholesale to the particular fields of study and/or to the particular research participants without development or revision. The scale of the adaptation varies, from Helen Collins' endeavours to create a broad, overarching model of doing a piece of practical theology informed by evangelical, charismatic faith, to the apparently more microscopic attention of Alison Woolley to the significance of pauses within the interview process or Kate Massey's adaptation of a voice-centred method of data analysis to a particular research group of mothers with dual callings. Perhaps because the qualitative study of women's faith is still relatively new, the field is marked by an experimental approach characterized by innovation, playful and metaphoric creativity, trial and error. Or perhaps it is of the nature of all qualitative research that the specificity of the context and the focus of each research study requires a new approach that, while drawing on existing studies, cannot simply copy them. Each of the contributors to this volume stands on the shoulders of preceding feminist qualitative and theological researchers, but works that legacy into new patterns, configurations and methods. Thus, it would not be in the spirit of this volume to expect its readers to do anything different, that is, not to copy what we have done, but to learn from the dialogue each of us has engaged with existing literature and methodologies, and to be creative in the development of their own.

Whether the scope of methodological innovation is at the macro or the micro level, the interaction between discrete research methods and larger methodologies is interrogated throughout – and this is another broad theme that emerges across the book. A researcher may start from the big picture of the epistemology which will shape her research and from there work out the overarching methodological framework and thence to discrete methods. Alternatively, she may begin from the other end, with the detail of specific methods of data collection, transcription and analysis, working from the ground upwards to more generalized and abstract principles. The choice of where to start may be a matter of temperament, training, preferred learning style and any number of other matters. Either way, the design of a robust research study needs to consider the same questions: How do discrete research methods contribute to, and shape, the overarching methodology, and vice versa, and how do both serve the basic aims of the research? Is there a fundamental coherence and compatibility between research aims, questions, epistemology, methodology, methods and outcome, or are there gaps and tensions between any of them? What larger frame of reference is capable of holding and interpreting best the diverse ingredients, intentions and concepts engaged by the research, and does such a larger frame of reference already exist somewhere or must it be created out of a range of disparate disciplines and theoretical concepts? Of course, there will always be gaps between the larger research agenda and the small-scale nature of qualitative research, but these gaps need to be attended to and addressed in the research design so that readers can perceive and evaluate what it is legitimate to claim on the basis of the research methods and methodology, and what goes well beyond the grounds of the research itself. In other words, we hope that by our contributors' careful and honest descriptions of their unique research methods and their discussion of how these methods evolved and what these methods permitted to be known, readers will come to an enhanced appreciation of the complex and nuanced interrelationship between method, methodology and epistemology (and indeed, theology). Such an enhanced understanding will contribute both to the shaping of readers' own research methodologies and a greater appreciation of the subtle and creative work involved in designing even the most small-scale qualitative study.

Research design, as well as execution (and perhaps these are not two separate things), is more of an art than a science, and this emerges from many of the chapters. This is hardly a novel insight within the qualitative paradigm, and it may be one primary reason why individuals from an arts and humanities background (as most of our writers are) are drawn to the qualitative, rather than the quantitative approach (although some writers espouse both and indeed, as editors, we commend a triangulated approach that makes use of both qualitative and quantitative methodologies). A large part of the pleasure and insight in reading these chapters lies in their artistry and creativity. They demonstrate, in a wide variety of ways, the skill that is involved in asking good research questions, in designing robust as well as politically and ethically sensitive research methods, and above all, in entering into relationship with the issues and the persons they seek to engage. The book as a whole suggests that all research is more a matter of reading and writing reality than of 'discovering' it (hence some prefer to speak of 'constructing' rather than 'collecting' data, on the grounds that data do not exist independently of the perceiving researcher). Each chapter exemplifies in different ways the qualitative and feminist axiom that the researcher is a primary tool, or means, of knowledge, co-creating the new wisdom offered by research. For many of our contributors, this methodological commitment rests on an epistemological conviction that the nature of reality is inherently dynamic, processional and relational rather than fixed and static. The researcher shapes, probes, reads and interprets the field of research even as she interacts with it. That process changes her, as well as her participants, and changes – even if only minutely – the state of knowledge and understanding that exists in the field. We see this in each of the chapters, as writers chart the ways in which their own pre-commitments and theological convictions shaped the topics they wanted to study and their approach to that study while, at the same time, being themselves challenged and changed in the process. Research participants, too, participate in that process of transformation – and this is evident in a number of the chapters where we eavesdrop on participants engaged in conversation and can almost hear and see them in the process of thinking and of coming to fresh realization about themselves, the nature of faith, God and so on, which would not have been elicited without the research.

Finally, then, we hope that this volume demonstrates how research itself may be an agent of change – for the individuals concerned but also, through the many interconnections of individuals with larger groups, institutions and political structures, for academic disciplines and for lived faith in churches and in wider society. The process of research changes those who engage in it, either as researchers or participants; but it also has the capacity to change those who read about it and who take the insights and knowledge of ongoing research into the field in new studies and applications of knowledge. And, when we speak about 'change', we do not only mean change to existing concepts, practices and research methods – though we certainly do mean that (we hope, for example, that future research into the faith lives of women and girls will be enriched by the methodological offerings of this book); we also mean change in the sense of ethical, political change. We hope for research that challenges and changes invisibility, injustice and inequality in faith communities, educational institutions and wider society. This is an ideal to which any one individual research study may only contribute a small amount, but the whole is greater than the sum of the parts. The impact of any of the studies described in this collection on the lives of women and girls might be deemed to be small (which does not lessen the significance of such an impact on those lives) but collectively, we hope that the body of work represented in this volume adds up to more: more visibility for the research that is already going on and adding to the quality of our knowledge and understanding of lived faith; more transparency about the challenges and creativity of the research enterprise; more energy and encouragement for those beginning research and wondering about its relevance; and more stimulus to conversation and dialogue among all those around the world who are committed to the nurturing and support of the faith lives of women and girls.

Notes

1 Nicola Slee, Fran Porter and Anne Phillips (eds), *The Faith Lives of Women and Girls: Qualitative Research Perspectives* (Farnham: Ashgate, 2013).
2 For example: Jane Ribbens and Rosalind Edwards (eds), *Feminist Dilemmas in Qualitative Research: Public Knowledge and Private Lives* (London: Sage, 1998); Caroline Ramazanoglu with Janet Holland, *Feminist Methodology: Challenges and Choices* (London: Sage, 2002); Sharlene Nagy Hesse-Biber (ed.), *The Handbook of Feminist Research: Theory and Praxis*, 2nd ed. (London: Sage, 2012).
3 For example: Elaine Graham, Heather Walton and Frances Ward, *Theological Reflection: Methods* (London: SCM, 2005); John Swinton and Harriet Mowatt, *Practical Theology and Qualitative Research* (London: SCM, 2006); Mary Clark Moschella, *Ethnography as a Pastoral Practice: An Introduction* (Cleveland, OH: Pilgrim Press, 2008); Helen Cameron et al., *Talking About God in Practice: Theological Action Research and Practical Theology* (London: SCM, 2010); Helen Cameron and Catherine Duce, *Researching Practice in Ministry and Mission: A Companion* (London: SCM, 2013).
4 Swinton and Mowatt, *Practical Theology*, 74–75.
5 Cameron and Duce, *Researching Practice*, 29.
6 These, and other approaches to method and methodology are outlined in Bonnie J. Miller-McLemore (ed.), *The Wiley-Blackwell Companion to Practical Theology* (Malden MA and Oxford: Wiley Blackwell, 2014), part 2.
7 Sandra Harding, 'Introduction: Is there a Feminist Method?' in *Feminism and Methodology: Social Science Issues*, ed. Sandra Harding (Milton Keynes: Open University Press, 1987), 1–14.
8 Joey Sprague, *Feminist Methodologies for Critical Researchers: Bridging Differences*, 2nd ed. (Lanham, ML: Rowman & Littlefield, 2016), 5.
9 Ibid., 5.
10 Mary Daly, *Beyond God the Father: Towards a Philosophy of Women's Liberation* (London: Women's Press, 1986), 11.
11 Ibid., 11.
12 Mary Daly, *Gyn/Ecology: The Metaethics of Radical Feminism* (London: Women's Press, 1979), 23.
13 For example, Ramazanoglu with Holland, *Feminist Methodology*; Hesse-Biber, *Handbook of Feminist Research*; Sprague, *Feminist Methodologies for Critical Researchers*.
14 Nicola Slee, *Women's Faith Development: Patterns and Processes* (Aldershot: Ashgate, 2004), 44.

15 Ibid., 44.

16 Ibid., 44.

17 For example, Ann Oakley's advocacy of a 'friendship' model of interviewing in 'Interviewing Women: A Contradiction in Terms', *Doing Feminist Research*, ed. H. Roberts (London: Routledge, 1981), 30–61.

18 Andrea Doucet and Natasha S. Mauthner, 'Feminist Methodologies and Epistemology', in *21st Century Sociology: A Reference Handbook*, Vol. 2, ed. Clifton D. Bryant and Dennis L. Peck (Thousand Oaks, CA: Sage, 2007), 40.

19 Ibid., 40–41.

20 Gayle Letherby, *Feminist Research in Theory and Practice* (Buckingham: Open University, 2003), 4–5.

21 Ibid., 5.

22 Natasha Mauthner and Andrea Doucet, 'Reflections on a Voice-Centred Relational Method: Analysing Maternal and Domestic Voices', in *Feminist Dilemmas in Qualitative Research: Public Knowledge and Private Lives*, ed. Jane Ribbens and Rosalind Edwards (London: Sage, 1998), 119–146.

Part I

Developing feminist methodologies

1 'Come as a girl'

Exploring issues of participative
methodology for research into the spiritual
lives and faith of girls-becoming-women

Anne Phillips

Introduction

Across the Western world in recent years, multiple reports from statutory and
voluntary bodies based on interviews with girls and young women reveal the
effects of the gender-based pressures in their everyday experience, physical,
social and psychological.[1] In one response, Laura Bates, founder of the *Everyday
Sexism Project*[2] in 2012, reminds girls that: 'You're not defined by your gender,
your body, or what anybody else says about you. Only you get to decide who
you are'.[3] When I conducted my research with girls aged 11–13 in churches
during 2004–2005,[4] issues of body image, discrimination and sexualization
were concerns that they raised spontaneously. Georgia observed how girls
'were "hardly ever happy" about their body image', upset there was something
wrong, and thinking they were 'either a bit too short or a bit too big'.[5] Hannah
reflected on gendered peer stereotyping: 'sometimes boys say if you want to
play football, "you're not a boy, you don't know how to play"', and on the
injustice of staff discrimination: 'in class, when the teachers ask you to go and
get boxes, they never ask girls, but girls are as strong as boys'.

Lucy, approaching teen years, was conscious of the increased and constraining sexualization suggested by adults over mixed friendships: 'there's quite a
few boys in my class who I get on really well with, but if you're seen with boys
it's considered straight away that it's girlfriend/boyfriend and it's not!'[6]

I open my chapter with these accounts to illustrate the reality of the world girls
inhabit to the increasing detriment of their flourishing. Where girls are involved
in the life of faith communities, there is both the need and the opportunity
to work with them to connect life and faith, and to draw on the resources of
spirituality to help build their resilience and gendered self-confident awareness.
Obsession with body image, and low self-esteem, are not only psychological
and health issues, they are profoundly spiritual.[7] In working with girls, it is
inadequate for adults to determine programmes and support structures claiming to understand their lives based on their own memories and perceptions of
adolescence, for 'their souls dwell in the house of tomorrow, which you cannot
visit, not even in your dreams'.[8] Only those living in that liminal place in each
discrete generation can tell it as it is for them in its particularity. The role of their

adult accompanists is to enable them to voice and reflect on their experiences, to listen and learn from their thoughts and feelings, and to offer informed support and advocacy through all aspects of their growth towards full flourishing. This must rest on good qualitative research engaging girls as participants, requiring researchers to adopt creative and reflexive methodologies. In this chapter, I will examine the participative nature of the methodology and methods I used, within the constraints of a faith community, and in conversation with other examples of research methodologies demonstrating varying levels and models of participation.[9]

Girls within childhood research: the contemporary scene

I begin with a summary of the current state of research with girls/boys,[10] which from early years to adulthood is flourishing: normatively now employing feminist and liberation methodologies, methods are increasingly participatory. Most research is, however, conducted in the fields of education, health, psychology or the social sciences, fields where significant funding is forthcoming, and takes place almost exclusively in institutional settings. Inclusion of young people as active participants reflects their acceptance not only as research subjects but also in some instances as researchers. These issues, along with their corresponding philosophical and epistemological bases, are well represented in the contemporary literature on research with children and young people.[11]

Underpinning the trend towards greater participation is the political impetus enshrined in the 1989 UN Convention on the Rights of the Child, followed in the UK by the Children Act (1989) and Every Child Matters (2003), which underlies the Children Act (2004) and all of which promote both the empowerment of children and young people to make a positive contribution to society, and also their rights among which is that to impact the issues and services that affect them.[12]

Participation in research ranges from being simply an active subject in a pre-determined process to full adherence to the principles of Participatory Action Research (PAR), an umbrella term for a variety of action-oriented research whereby researcher and participants 'work together to examine a problematic situation or action to change it for the better'.[13] Using context-specific methods researchers seek to engage participants in 'genuinely democratic and non-coercive research with and for, rather than on, participants'.[14] Seminal texts defining the concept and examining the construction of theoretical participatory frameworks with girls/boys, models by which social research is both informed and evaluated, are Hart's 'Ladder of Children's Participation', which traces it through hierarchical stages from tokenism to full participation, and Shier's alternative model focusing more on adult roles. Both are designed to assist practitioners to explore different aspects of the participation process.[15] Girls/boys are now seen as broadly competent agents, their competence being different from but not lesser than adults', and their knowledge as rooted in lived experience, so a research methodology in which they are engaged in some way as partners is the most appropriate.

Since most childhood research is conducted in social and political contexts, discussion of the methodological framework of participatory research takes place almost exclusively in relation to institutions and services that govern the lives of young people, and most commonly focuses on cognitive skills and functional outcomes in the social or built environment. Empowerment of young people in these areas has, potentially, far-reaching consequences in capacity building as they engage with social and political structures and contribute to community enhancement. Through being enshrined in a very broad sense in legislation and good practice guidelines, *spirituality* has gained some acceptance as contributing to a girl's/boy's well-being, and has been the subject of some research mainly in educational and medical arenas. However, confessional *faith* as an application of spirituality, and *gender* specificity or differentiation within the spiritual life, have received scant attention. So, despite the prevalence of *childhood* research and some research into *spirituality*, girls' inner relational worlds and their faith lives in the context of their places of worship, have largely been neglected as subjects for empirical study.[16] In studying the *faith of girls*, I am therefore breaking the silence in two areas of research.[17]

Participation within my research methodology

All research is participative in that it requires the acquisition of data from consenting subjects. However, as a qualitative methodology participative research indicates active engagement with the process by the subject, including in the research design, determination of topic and methods, conduct of the enquiry, data analysis and in some cases active pursuit of named goals. It is also imprecise and contested in its meaning and practice: strongly advocated at different levels by practitioners in child research, its claims as well as its epistemology and ontology are also challenged, as in the work of geographers Lesley-Anne Gallacher and Michael Gallagher.[18] On the grounds that participatory methodologies retain power imbalances, they propose an alternative model, or rather attitude, of 'methodological immaturity' on the part of the researcher and the child, to which I shall return later.

I have briefly outlined participative methodology's parameters as the framework within which to evaluate my own practice: while following much good practice in childhood research, my work also illustrates some of the questions raised by Gallacher and Gallagher particularly as it relates to the conduct of research with girls/boys in the voluntary sector, and specifically in a faith community, a context imposing restraints as well as opportunities not found in formal or state institutions. The researcher in a faith community usually has limited choice in levels of participation, and my chosen methodology necessitated some compromises, but for me the key ontological and epistemological tenets mirroring those fundamental to current theories of childhood theory were non-negotiable. The aim of my research was both to contribute to girls' empowerment within the adult-constructed community, and to exercise wider advocacy on their behalf. The girls I worked with had their own unique appropriation and practise of faith, and this I aimed to explore in its particularity,[19] while also in my analysis seeking commonalities within the age range across different churches both to inform, and to instigate debate among, church leaders working with girls in their personal and developmental transitions. These research goals, then, guided the development of my methodology, the desire to identify and advocate new and potentially transferable knowledge, and create an opportunity for empowerment by encouraging new thinking and gendered spiritual awareness. Since I also had an ethical responsibility to be respectful of the norms and beliefs of their current ecclesial heritage, it felt at times like walking a methodological tightrope.

The methodology in practice

In my empirical research, then, conducted in churches with varied demographic profiles, ecclesial style and theological stance, I planned for girls to be active participants as far as was practicable working within the social constraints consequent on church attendance being a voluntary pursuit, and the institutional constraints arising from my 'intrusion' into the privately organized and controlled space of a church. My own active participation required careful negotiation and practise of reflexivity, both with the churches' leaderships and within myself as researcher, educator and faith practitioner.

The research took place in the girls' normal meeting times in their churches, usually on a Sunday, so scope for extensive contact and complex engagement was limited. There are other difficulties intrinsic to working in the voluntary sector not encountered in statutory or public settings: these further challenge and frustrate researchers. Finding a sufficiently varied set of churches with enough girls in my chosen age range to form a viable group was one problem, another that I was working full-time as a minister alongside part-time research, and self-funding so distance of travel affected the choice of geographical location. The churches I recruited held their own programmes with young people, and time available with them was both precious and pressurized; to gain their release from their planned programme was part of the negotiation with the gatekeepers. The maximum time allocation agreed upon was four or five weekly sessions of up to an hour each, while on two occasions the research took place on one Sunday only and consisted of shared congregational worship, a meal together and an afternoon session. Despite this variation, each was comparable in the level of participation, relationships built, ground covered and data collected.

To what extent, though, could the girls become active research participants under these conditions? Without preparatory access to the girls to engage them in any advance planning, and to maximize use of the time available, I prepared a structure for each session to create immediate momentum as well as some comparability across my resulting data for analytical purpose. I drew inspiration both from my previous experience as a secondary school teacher and from interactive models used in other research projects into childhood spirituality consistent with my epistemological framework.[20] The girls knew the broad area of my research, so after playful introductions to each other, we set ground rules and I offered to hand to them the control of the tape recorder. I opened the conversation by asking what they enjoyed, and later disliked, about being a girl, in order to help them centre on their own gendered identity as the standpoint from which they were thinking and speaking. As I re-read the transcripts now and analyse my role as interviewer to assess how far I encouraged the girls to exert influence on the direction of and agenda for discussion, I see there was usually a balance between giving space for their chatter[21] on a tangential topic onto which they deviated and my own seizure of openings to move the conversation on; otherwise my interventions were largely for clarification and to facilitate inclusion. I was constantly alert to and learning from the themes that were of significance; these were largely predictable, dominated by school, friendships and family, but I noted the mature way they were reflecting on these subjects particularly in the light of changes taking place over time in themselves and their contexts.

As I had no prior relationship with the girls, and couldn't predict how the conversations might flow, I had devised a 'worksheet' of questions and activities to use if necessary.[22] Thankfully, I didn't need it: to do so would have introduced a pedagogical tone that would have affected adversely my relationship with the girls, and the delightful freedom of thought they demonstrated. They entered enthusiastically into the activities, and as a direct result of our interaction, I was able to tweak some in subsequent research locations to greater effectiveness. The most significant activity was visual as they responded to images they selected from a range I had prepared, and through which we began to engage more deeply with overtly existential and spiritual issues. On one occasion these gave rise to further spontaneous 'faithing' conversation when the girls gathered of their own accord round a pool table where I'd placed the pictures, but I was unable to draw on this later, they having decided to switch off the recording equipment. Participation doesn't always work to the researcher's advantage! With some girls, in group activities and in personal interviews, God-talk came more readily than others and although sometimes formulaic at the outset, given time and careful listening both within the group and individually, many moved significantly beyond verbal and conceptual dependence and came to a freedom of expression on matters of faith that I consider demonstrated original thinking and modes of believing. It was where we discussed biblical characters and narrative that I had to exert a strong level of reflexivity, endeavouring to remain in research mode and resisting the temptation to turn educator especially where knowledge, most notably of biblical women, was lacking.

How participative does participative research need to be?

The extent to which my methodology was participative is the question I now address, as I engage in dialogue with other participative childhood research projects. I have selected examples whose methodologies, on the continuum of participation, might be described as 'less' and 'more', although that might be too simplistic a differentiation.[23] They address two questions raised by my methodology: can a predominantly adult-led process of activity and interview such as I used encourage genuine self-disclosure, reflection and empowerment; and can the constraints of research in the voluntary sector, specifically in faith communities, enhance the potential for participative research? The first two examples compare levels of participation, one adult-led, the other shared between researcher and participants; my third example discusses participative research in a faith community.

Two adult-led research projects

The first example is part of a wider project by Anna Lipscomb and Irvine Gersch to develop a 'spiritual listening tool' to explore girls'/boys' understanding about spiritual and philosophical meaning in their lives and enhance their 'spiritual questing'.[24] It was fully adult designed and led, which appeared at first sight to minimize the potential for the subjects' participation. In individual interviews, the girls/boys aged 10–11 from local schools chose, in their own order, to talk about one-word concepts (such as 'happiness', 'destiny') from among six cards set in front of them. The interview proceeded through a highly structured process within which the interviewer's role was limited to checking participants' understanding of words and offering prompts to stimulate their thinking. Thus the young people exerted choices and to a significant degree controlled input within the process, the interview being time- not completion-bound. On this basis the researchers claim the elicitation of valid and original data, facilitated but uninfluenced by adult intervention; power of expression lay with the subjects, the researcher having no relational engagement with them, while respecting their being and agency. Examples from the research findings demonstrate positive outcomes for the girls/boys as well as the researchers, who concluded that the 'children appeared to make a link between concrete or "*visible*" elements of their life (e.g. behaviour or lived experience) and metaphysical or "*hidden*" elements (underlying beliefs or world view). The children could then reflect on these new understandings'.[25] They documented how within the space offered by a spiritual listener, change and growth had taken place in the participants, including in Evren who, reflecting on the session, said: 'After I said all these things and I can't believe that I really said it, there's change in me'. The aim of this on-going project is to develop the listening tool and 'explore links between children's spirituality and measures of self-esteem and happiness'.[26]

Although here the interviewer plays an apparently minimal role and the process is highly structured and unbending, its positive outcomes are the result of carefully constructed guidance through the 'probes' and questions, alongside space and affirmation through attentive listening; together they develop participants' thinking in an unhurried and individual way. The researchers' analysis demonstrates a growth of participants' meaning-making skill helping to foster spirituality as it contributes to holistic living. I see a parallel here with the positive contribution to my research of my own listening, and careful prompts to encourage deeper thought, while also allowing my participants to take some control of the pace of the process. Perhaps there is a greater level of participation in the 'spiritual listening' approach than I initially judged.

I now turn to a second research project similar in its adult construction because, like mine, it was conducted in leisure space, and the researchers faced similar hurdles to my own in setting it up. It also demonstrates a different and more contestable means of encouraging free thought on the part of young people. In their study with an inter-faith youth project, Catherine Harris and her colleagues experimented, alongside more conventional research methods, with a videoed diary room on the model of that used in the TV reality show 'Big Brother', with minimal evident presence of the observing researchers.[27] In this private space an unseen researcher led a conversation on designated topics chosen randomly by each individual participant speaking only to a camera: all were keen to take part through its novelty, yet on-screen familiarity. Despite there being no rapport between the mysterious 'voice' and the participant, in itself a learning experience for the researcher engaging with an interviewee without non-verbal codes, the resulting video showed that the young people expressed more honest opinions than they had done in other activities in the public space. Although the power of questioning was in the adult's hands, the researcher felt a greater degree of *dis*empowerment as the young people took control of the apparently vacant diary space, trusting its confidentiality to express themselves freely. Unlike in the TV version, the interviewer was a complete stranger having had no prior contact with any of the young people nor involvement with the other activities in the club so although representing adult 'authority', their invisibility appeared to level the playing field of power and not to inhibit the interviewee, whereas a pilot study in the club using traditional methods had, they said, been unsuccessful. By comparing the diary room data with that from semi-structured interviews and other more conventional activities of the evening, Harris *et al.* affirm its value for increasing the knowledge gained. Whether such a method would enhance research within a faith community would depend on whether the quality of adult/child relating around a shared belief and value system created a more positive environment for openness and honesty than in a secular organization. This is where the totality of the context, some ethnographic awareness, may assist the construction of an appropriate methodology. Nonetheless it offers an interesting complement to the previous example, and I concur with Harris *et al.* that there is potential here for further experimentation. Of importance too is evaluation of this method within the wider debates about the influence of social media on, and its use by, young people, a discussion that is outside the scope of this chapter.

A project modelling shared participation

For contrast, I turn to a project employing a methodology in which the subjects participated fully from inception right through to data analysis and public presentation. Based on an established Scandinavian 'study circle tradition with democratic ideals', Jeanette Åkerström and Elinor Brunnberg developed a 'research circle' method,[28] which documents the learning nine girls aged 15–19 undertook to become full partners in a research project: this included topic identification, interview and analytical skills, and research ethics. Foundational to the project was the conviction that young people are able to acquire the necessary skills to conduct valid and rigorous research, an issue contested on the grounds that age and cognitive development determine competence. 'Reflecting on the skills needed to undertake research it is apparent that these are not synonymous with being an adult; they are synonymous with being a researcher': this is the view of Mary Kellett who, through extensive work with the UK-based Children's Research Centre (CRC) she founded to facilitate child-led research, offers plentiful evidence for her conclusion that 'a barrier to empowering children as researchers is not their lack of adult status but their lack of research skills' and that, as for any new researcher, these skills can be learnt.[29]

Like the CRC's work, the Scandinavian research circle justifies this claim. It was substantially child-led, the girls equipped to conduct it from start to finish with varying levels of input from the researchers. The girls became research partners under the guidance of two academic researchers, a circle leader (responsible for the conduct of the meetings) and a research leader (holding an overview of the process). Instigated and explained by researchers, the project was then progressed principally by the partners (the girls) who selected a topic using multiple methods of enquiry, engaged in discussion and collected their data, all in mutual interaction with the research leaders. For example, as they reflected on their data, the partners were helped to try out different forms of interpretation, while in return the partners helped the researchers to identify generational issues and perspectives that challenged their adult understanding of the topic. Learning was thus two-way, and a body of knowledge was being created from the perspective of the girls. The partners received training in methodological and analytical processes influenced by Lev Vygotsky's two-pronged theory that: a) in a 'zone of proximal development' (ZPD) cognitive development occurs in the space opened up by social learning, and b) social development is supported by the 'more knowledgeable other' (MKO) who provides and adapts the 'scaffolding' as the partner becomes more skilled. In the process, empirical learning becomes earthed in theoretical knowledge acquired through exploratory activity, and transferable skills are learned. Åkerström and Brunnberg confirm the reciprocity within this process as the girls were correspondingly able to act as MKOs for the researchers when they shared their contemporary experiences and perspectives.[30]

Fully aware that overall power remained in adults' hands, Åkerström and Brunnberg bring strong reflexivity to bear on the asymmetric nature of the relationship with the girls, recognizing the fragile balance between partners and leaders at every stage, and the ease with which the researcher, with an eye to the eventual 'audience' for the research findings, might compromise the young people's perspectives, for example, by 'a tentative categorization in the conceptualization stage of the research process'.[31] The girls' ownership of the project, engendered in no small part by their participation in design and execution, was illustrated by their willingness to devote significant leisure time to it: not only were they fully committed but showed an impatience with the adult timescale, arranging extra meetings to speed up the process, reflecting a 'here-and-now' attitude made possible by social media. The report of the project validates the interactive process where participation is built into the methodology, demonstrating the social learning and capacity building that resulted for the young people, and the building of respectful inter- and intra-generational relationships despite asymmetry.

Could I have emulated a model such as this, to engage the girls more substantially in the research process? Here again context plays a key role. Such research requires extended contact between researcher and researched, and 'extra-curricular' time commitment by the participants. I was reluctant to add to the pressures on them particularly from schoolwork, considerable even at that age, by requesting 'homework' between sessions such as took place in Åkerström and Brunnberg's project, although this might have increased their participation and ownership of the research, and the breadth or depth of the level of enquiry. When it came to my analysis, I was conscious of a time lag after the interviews during which the girls' memories of what they said would have dimmed or become a cause of embarrassment, and any subsequent participation would have been influenced by changes to their thinking and believing beyond the research data gathering. It would not, therefore, have been productive to have reflected with the girls on my analysis as in other circumstances I might have done. I had captured a snapshot of immense research value at a particular point in time, and had to preserve the credibility of my outcomes. Although this is also a consequence of part-time academic research, it also reflects the necessity for immediacy if young people are to be full participants. This is not to say that, as the research circle experience shows, where girls seize the initiative themselves, they might not engage fruitfully with all levels of the enquiry.

Researching in a faith community

A faith community context offers circumscribed opportunities for conducting academic research, yet there are positive factors too that can enhance the project.

As with most research with young people, initial contact is made in negotiation with gatekeepers who retain the power of access. These youth or church leaders can be valuable assets as resource people. I interviewed one or more in each location, and they provided insightful background to each context. Physical constraints are often imposed by limited time-allocation and sometimes less than optimum research spaces, in my case a minister's vestry, or side rooms with furniture ill-suited to either comfort or activity. These are factors I accepted and accommodated to as researcher since the faith *community*, the location in which girls absorb, learn and practise their faith, can offer strong support to the quality of the research despite any material limitations. It is also where any outworking of the research by the girls takes place, outcomes hopefully resulting in their further empowerment, and enhanced application of critical skills to their faithing. For me to spend time with the girls in worship, learning and leisure served a purpose beyond the gathering of ethnographic data: it engaged me as participant in the girls' faith lives not just as a prelude but as integral to mutual participation in the research activity. Hence, the level of participation in structuring and executing my design is not the only measure by which to assess my methodology for its participative strength. A personal relationship had been established that, while inevitably retaining asymmetry, had lessened the effect of the power imbalance. This was aided in no small way by the fact that I was interviewing the girls in their own spaces whether in church or a home: I was thus a visitor submitting to their unknown customs and rules, and by so doing ceding more power to them. The importance of this is not often recognized but should not be underestimated for its enhancement of a research process with young people, maybe especially girls. Eleanor Nesbitt is an advocate of this practice in places of worship, to ground the process in 'observation and incipient insights from the field, . . . ease the relationship between interviewer and interviewee . . . and encourage children's confidence in speaking about these areas of their experience'.[32] In considering the importance of spatial context, Harris *et al.* note that the club premises in which they operated was one 'in which the children and young people have more agency than at school. . . . In this setting the young people were to some extent "in charge"'.[33]

A working example of the benefit to researching in this way is supplied by Cathy Ota who, in the course of her work with the Children and WorldViews Project team, describes her own journey of learning at the hands of three 6-year-old girls. In this particular project, she was engaging with school teachers to explore ways of addressing spiritual, moral and emotional development through the potential offered by story-telling.[34] Admitting she had 'no fixed model of what we were going to do or what was going to happen' with such young girls, Ota met weekly with them and their teacher to hear the personal stories they were eager to tell. The project achieved its aim of developing narrative skills, but more pertinent to this discussion is Ota's account of her own move from visiting researcher to genuine participant, on the girls' own terms. Attempting to remain within her comfort zone as the dispassionate outsider, she became 'as much a part of the dialogue and relationality as the girls', drawn in by them to share her own story through which the power imbalance was lessened: 'this' she says, 'was fast becoming a very different kind of ball game – not the kind of participation that I was used to'. Through the experience Ota learnt that despite her theoretical regard for children's voices, she had still seen them as 'other', yet they, sensing her 'otherness', strove to draw her into a caring relationship with them. She argues that this contributed to the achievement of the research goal, the growth in their narrative skills. An unforeseen by-product of her research design was therefore the 'impact of all participants in such a process' which 'revealed what to me are important lessons about meeting beliefs, values and community, about engaging with difference and diversity'.[35] These younger girls, by taking power upon themselves to extend participation, played an active role in creating a more mutually participative methodology. Although the example here was of a different age group and culture from that of my research where there was a cultural consonance between researcher and researched, there was still diversity between myself and the participants through age and experience. Ota's project contributed to my reflection on the influence of the wider context on my research when I shared games, a family lunch, a barbecue and worship both formal and informal with the girls. I argue, then, that integral to a successful operation of a participative methodology with young people, especially girls, is an investment of 'downtime' as a guest in their space as a strategy not just to counter power asymmetry but to build relationships that become an unquantifiable factor in creating quality data from all activities within the research programme.

This also concurs with the reminder from Gallacher and Gallagher that 'knowledge is thoroughly relational' and created, or co-created, through narrative and conversation. Rethinking the current paradigm of children's agency, and reflecting on their respective experiences of childhood research, they propose that methodological immaturity allows the freedom for researchers to recognize their own incompleteness, without which they would not be undertaking the research. 'For us', they say, 'research is fundamentally a process of *muddling through*, sometimes feeling lost and out of place, asking stupid questions, being corrected and having our preconceptions destroyed. In this way, we cannot deny our incompetence and vulnerabilities: our immaturity. And we do not want to'. Their concern is not with methods, but with the methodological attitude of the researcher: my somewhat messy research experience resonates with their view that 'good research cannot be reduced to ingenious techniques, planned in advance and carefully applied. Research is inherently unpredictable: the best laid plans are liable to go awry. Methodological immaturity privileges open-ended process . . . offering experimentation, innovation and "making do"'.[36] Each participant, researcher and researched, are players in this game, creating a newly emergent but vulnerable subjectivity, an insight that resonates with my own experience, and opens my methodological approach to further study and debate.

These reflections on my methodology also suggest that in addition to facilitating research by an outsider such as I was, a faith community is well positioned for appropriately trained and skilled youth leaders also to introduce research-based learning into their programme. Focusing on existential or practical issues relevant to young people and to the community, this could enable girls/boys to integrate critical skills already part of the school curriculum with their spiritual lives, supporting their informed growth in faith and thus empowerment. Such capacity building for young people, taking their place as participants at the centre of community life rather than at the margins many currently inhabit, could represent an investment in the community's future.

Conclusion

My commitment to growing my own understanding of the specificity of being a girl in a rapidly changing world, and encouraging others to do likewise, is born out of my own long experience of voicelessness, sexism and discrimination as woman, feminist, mother and Christian minister. Evidence from the reports with which I opened this chapter reveals that varieties of oppression of girls have increased and intensified in the ten years since I conducted my empirical research. Spirituality is recognized as a component of healthy living; faith communities are in a position to offer substantial interventions in support of girls as they negotiate adolescence in the hostile environment of the Western world where race, dress, class, sexual orientation and gender become means by which they are demeaned and often bullied, subjected to what can justifiably be described systemic oppression.

The projects that have resourced my critique all encourage participation on a variety of models, and when set in dialogue with my research shed fresh light on aspects of participatory methodologies as they apply to faith communities. All methods were shaped by conversation, some highly relational, others barely so. Gendered data analysis of research among girls/boys is sadly rare, and does not feature explicitly in any of the reports cited. Even among the projects in which girls alone were the subjects, their gender was coincidental. That the girls Ota studied were Asian, a little researched demographic group, and that her work may 'go some way to redress this situation',[37] is seen as a by-product of a project where the girls participated in and changed both research and researcher by enacting a traditionally female 'ethic of care'. This feature is not discussed. It would be enlightening to undertake a gendered analysis of the data from the 'Spiritual Listening' project, additionally to assess whether there were variables according to gender in the responses to the method: this would contribute to an appreciation of the scope of its applicability. The Big Brother experiment does not record the ratio of male to female participants, this in spite of it being part of an international research project studying difference across a range of social categories.[38] More analysis is needed, then, of gender differentiation in the responses to particular methodologies, to aid our understanding of the degree to which research methods lend themselves not only to eliciting meaningful data from girls, but contributing positively to the growth of their gendered self-awareness, of the distinctness and validity of their faithing, and in their confidence to identify gender-based oppression as they meet it.

My research was a beginning: there is much still to be developed in this field. Appropriately gathered, original data from girls and its analysis with and by researchers, is an offering to faith communities to enable their voices to be heard, to encourage those communities to support them in their resistance and engender their resilience, to the enrichment of girls' faith journeys as they get to decide who they are becoming on their way to womanhood.

Notes

1 Examples of such reports can be found in: American Psychological Association, *Report of the APA Taskforce on the Sexualization of Girls, Executive Summary*, accessed 1 November 2016, www.apa.org/pi/women/programs/girls/report-summary.pdf; *Girlguiding Girls' Attitudes Survey*, accessed 6 December 2016, www.girlguiding.org.uk/social-action-advocacy-and-campaigns/research/girls-attitudes-survey; NHS Confederation, accessed 6 December 2016, www.nhsconfed.org/news/2016/09/the-adult-psychiatric-morbidity-survey; and in journals, e.g. Lin Bian, Sarah-Jane Leslie and Andrei Cimplan, 'Gender Stereotypes about Intellectual Ability Emerge Early and Influence Children's Interests', *Science* 355, no. 6323 (January 2017): 389–391, accessed 27 January 2017, doi: 10.1126/science.aah6524.
2 http://everydaysexism.com/, accessed 1 November 2016.
3 Laura Bates, *Girl Up* (London: Simon & Schuster, 2016), 374.
4 Anne Phillips, *The Faith of Girls: Children's Spirituality and Transition to Adulthood* (Farnham: Ashgate Press, 2011). All names used are pseudonyms.
5 Ibid., 89.
6 ibid., 76.
7 As in Lisa Isherwood, *The Fat Jesus: Feminist Exploration in Boundaries and Transgressions* (London: Darton, Longman & Todd, 2007).
8 Kahlil Gibran, *The Prophet* (London: Heinemann, 1926), 20. Discussion of the issue from an academic perspective can be found in, for example: Catherine Harris and Gill Valentine, 'Childhood Narratives: Adult Reflections on Encounters with Difference in Everyday Spaces', *Children's Geographies* (2017): 1–12, accessed 4 January 2017, doi:10.1080/14733285.2016.1269153.
9 Although writing from a Christian perspective, I cite examples from research with young people of other religions: this chapter has relevance for most mainstream faith communities.
10 Except in quotations and unless sense demands otherwise, I adopt this term, as in *The Faith of Girls*, in preference to 'childhood' to highlight the significance of gender in childhood. Although my research, and the focus of this chapter, is on girls, my discussion on research methodology could also be applicable to boys, and under-18s identifying as LGBTI or (increasingly among young people) gender fluid.
11 See Alison Clark *et al.*, *Understanding Research with Children and Young People*, (Oxford and London: The Open University and Sage, 2014).
12 The terminology, and implementation, of policies regarding children and young people in the UK are subject to regular change by successive governments: at the time of writing, information can be found at www.gov.uk/government/organisations/department-for-education, accessed 1 February 2017.
13 For an account and evaluation of PAR particularly in the social and environmental sciences, see Sara Kindon, Rachel Pain and Mike Kesby, *Participatory Action Research Approaches and Methods: Connecting People, Participation and Place* (Abingdon: Routledge, 2007).
14 Ibid., p 2.
15 Roger Hart, *Children's Participation: From Tokenism to Citizenship.* (Florence: UNICEF, 1992): Harry Shier, 'Pathways to Participation: Openings, Opportunities and Obligations', *Children and Society* 15 (2001): 107–117.
16 Some related studies from the USA can be found in Evelyn L. Parker, ed. *The Sacred Selves of Adolescent Girls: Hard Stories of Race, Class, and Gender* (Cleveland, OH: The Pilgrim Press, 2006), and Dori Grinenko Baker, *Doing Girlfriend Theology: God-Talk with Young Women* (Cleveland, OH: The Pilgrim Press, 2005).

17 I use 'spirituality' here to refer broadly to 'human meaning-making' in the context of perceived or experienced 'otherness', and 'faith' to denote trust in and relationship with a divine 'Other', usually lived out in some connection with a faithing community. A full discussion of the terms, and of 'faith' as an active verb, will be found in Phillips, *Faith of Girls*, 9–13.
18 Lesley-Anne Gallacher and Michael Gallagher, 'Methodological Immaturity in Childhood Research? Thinking through "Participatory Methods"', *Childhood* 15, no. 4 (2008): 499–516.
19 Found, for example, in detailed reflections on the faith of Lucy and Rosie; Phillips, *The Faith of Girls*, chapters 5 and 7.
20 Models inspired by research methods of David Heller, Kalevi Tamminen, David Hay and Rebecca Nye can be found in Phillips, *The Faith of Girls*, 569.
21 This is not to dismiss their chatter as irrelevant: Rebecca Nye, 'Psychological Perspectives on Children's Spirituality' (PhD thesis, University of Nottingham, 1998), 229.
22 As I held myself fully accountable to the church leaders who had entrusted the girls to me, it was also available for their perusal.
23 Space does not permit detailed presentation of each project, so I refer readers to the original research reports. In some examples, there were male and female participants.
24 Anna Lipscomb and Irvine Gersch, 'Using a "Spiritual Listening Tool" to Investigate how Children Describe Spiritual and Philosophical Meaning Making in their Lives', *International Journal of Children's Spirituality* 17, no. 1 (2012): 5.
25 Ibid., 11. Authors' emphases.
26 Ibid., 2.
27 Catherine Harris *et al.*, '"Big Brother Welcomes You": Exploring Innovative Methods for Research with Children and Young People Outside of the Home and School Environments', *Qualitative Research* 15, no. 5 (2015): 583–599.
28 Jeanette Åkerström and Elinor Brunnberg, 'Young People as Partners in Research: Experiences from an Interactive Research Circle with Adolescent Girls', *Qualitative Research* 13, no. 5 (2002): 528–545.
29 Mary Kellett, 'Small Shoes, Big Steps! Empowering Children as Active Researchers', *American Journal of Community Psychology* 46 (2010): 195–203. There are many examples of child-led research through the CRC. Projects engage girls/boys to the maximum extent as participants and tend primarily to be quantitative. Some examples of qualitative research are to be found among older age groups, but in analysis of their data younger girls/boys can be seen to exert a high level of independent reflection. www.open.ac.uk/researchprojects/childrens-research-centre, accessed 3 February 2017.
30 Åkerström and Brunnberg, 'Young People', 531.
31 Ibid., 540.
32 Eleanor Nesbitt, 'Researching 8- to 13-year-olds' Perspectives and their Experience of Religion', in *Researching Children's Perspectives*, ed. Ann Lewis and Geoff Lindsay, (Buckingham & Philadelphia: Open University Press, 2000), 143.
33 Harris *et al.*, 'Big Brother, 590.
34 Cathy Ota, 'Stories Told and Lessons Learned: Meeting Beliefs, Values and Community through Narrative and Dialogue', *Journal of Beliefs and Values* 21, no. 2 (2000): 191.
35 Ota, 'Stories Told', 200. Author's emphasis. The group comprised one Sikh and two Muslim girls from different nation communities.
36 Gallacher and Gallagher, 'Methodological Immaturity', 512–513. Authors' emphasis.
37 Ota, 'Stories Told', 197.
38 Project entitled 'Living with Difference in Europe', accessed 3 February 2017, http://livedifference.group.shef.ac.uk.

2 Poetry as feminist research methodology in the study of female faith

Nicola Slee

Introduction

Elsewhere, I have written of the ways in which I employ poetry as a means of theological exploration and reflection,[1] but until now I have not reflected on the use of poetry within qualitative research methodology. In this chapter, I reflect on my use of poetic forms of analysis in my study of women's faith lives[2] (conducted some twenty years ago) and discuss how I am developing new forms of poetic analysis as an interpretative lens to re-read the original data. The discussion is focused around a pilot study of one specific case, that of Meg,[3] a participant in my original study with whom I have maintained intermittent contact and whose transcript offered rich potential for analysis. One of the first cohort of women accepted for training for ordination in the Church of England, Meg's transcript provides a fascinating glimpse into the power dynamics operative in the church at that time, as well as the costly personal journey of women seeking recognition of their priestly calling. This case study thus combines methodological innovation and reflection with commentary on a significant moment in recent feminist history, particularly within English Anglicanism. While the primary focus is on research methods and methodology – specifically, how poetry may contribute to analysis of and engagement with women's faith lives – the data is also of significance in its own right for the light it sheds on recent feminist struggles within the church.

Despite a resurgence of academic and popular interest in the relation between theology and poetry,[4] Heather Walton notes that 'poetics and practical theology do not enjoy an easy relationship'.[5] Practical theologians, Walton suggests, tend to distrust poetics' attention to 'the exotic, the beautiful, the tragic, the unknown, and the unnameable'[6] in favour of a commitment to the values of rationality, order, morality and practical forms of wisdom and action. Walton evidences exceptions to this mutual suspicion, however, noting how feminist practical theologians in particular have been advocates for poetic modes of reflection, recognizing poetry's capacity for prophetic speech that can help to dismantle the power structures of patriarchal religion. She refers to Bonnie Miller-McLemore's 'poetics of resistance',[7] Rebecca Chopp's 'poetics of testimony'[8] and Riet Bons-Storm's 'unstories', which abused women have not had heard or validated[9] as examples of such use of poetics to 'express unique events or experiences outside the representation of modern rational discourses',[10] and thus make the unspeakable speakable. Walton's own work should also be added to the list. Employing 'experimental forms of pastoral poetics through writing that is deeply metaphoric and reflexive',[11] Walton draws on life writing, journaling and other forms of creative writing to revision both academic and religious traditions in prophetic and liberating ways.[12] My work joins forces with these, and other, feminist practical theologians in the pursuit of prophetic and resistant discourse.

Qualitative researchers as poets

While few qualitative researchers describe themselves as poets (some do), a growing number are employing poetry as a method of research, and there is a flourishing literature on poetry as research method.[13] Poetry may be used during data collection as a stimulus for focus groups or individual interviews,[14] as a means of organizing, presenting and analysing data at transcription and writing up stages,[15] and as a medium in which to reflect on findings and practise reflexivity.[16] Poetry has been used in a wide range of research studies, particularly to give prominence to the voices and experiences of participants in marginalized groups, settings or contexts.[17] The poetic medium enables a condensed and accessible summary of content in the presentation of research findings to audiences who may not respond well to academic discourse, and can permit an ongoing dialogue with research participants in a medium more accessible than scholarly writing. The concern in such research to foreground previously ignored individuals and groups resonates with classic feminist concerns to hear into speech the voices and lives of women.

Poets as ethnographers and researchers of the human spirit

While social scientific researchers make use of poetry as a means of examining human and social life, poets employ techniques that come close to ethnographic and qualitative methods of research, though they may not recognize the similarity. Many poets utilize the so-called 'found' poem[18] – taking text that already exists in the world (in newspapers, street signs, graffiti and so on) and turning it into poetry, in similar fashion to the work of ethnographers who take what already exists in the social world and turn it into text.[19] The dramatic monologue, used by many contemporary poets, presents the voice of a character, real or imagined, as authentically as possible, in poetic form. A number of poets have engaged in more extended ethnographic projects, in ways that blur the boundary between art and social science. Muriel Rukeyser's 1938 *The Book of the Dead* represents an ethnography of a West Virginia mining town where the miners were dying of lung disease due to unsafe working conditions.[20] Rukeyser interviewed miners, their families, union and company officials, and wrote a suite of poems widely regarded as one of the major sequences of

American modernism. More recently, the English poet Alice Oswald travelled the length and breadth of the river Dart in her native Devon for three years, interviewing people who lived on or by the river, weaving their stories alongside mythic narratives of dyads and naiads into her long narrative poem, *Dart*.[21] In the variety of these forms, there is a shared commitment to represent the other as faithfully as possible, in their own words and voices, and a concern to create empathy, even for the most unlikely or alien other.

Employing poetry to revisit data from my study of women's faith

In my earlier study of women's faith development,[22] I drew upon my interests and skills as a poet in a number of ways when transcribing and analysing the data, though at the time I was not aware of other studies employing poetry as research methodology. When transcribing, I adapted Chase's[23] method of setting out the verbal data in 'speech spurts' as a way to 'reflect the original richness and complexity of the data',[24] recognizing that 'nobody talks in prose'[25] and that converting interview data to prose is, to some degree, to do violence to it. In analysing the data, I paid particular attention to linguistic features of the interviews such as metaphor, voice, hesitation, repetition and so on, in order to bring to light the artistry of the data and to 'invite new levels of engagement that are both cognitive and emotional'.[26] Nevertheless, I was conscious of the potential within the interview data for a much more extensive analysis than I was able, at that time, to accomplish. More recently, in the light of my discovery of the use of poetry within qualitative research, I have returned to the original data in order to experiment with new methods of poetic analysis. Whereas in the original research, I employed a largely thematic, cross-sectional approach to analysis (while seeking to remain alert to differences, tensions and contradictions within the data), I am now using a case study approach, going back to individual transcripts and examining the depth and detail of the material in each woman's narrative. I am still at an early stage of analysis and this chapter therefore represents work in progress, reporting on a pilot study aimed at testing out the potential for poetic analysis and engagement.

In what follows, I report on the development of a series of poetic analyses of material from one interview transcript in an endeavour to demonstrate the potential of poetic analysis in researching female faith.[27] While I selected Meg's transcript as the first participant whose material I decided to re-analyse initially for the practical reason that I knew how to re-establish contact with her and seek permission to revisit the old data, I have since come to recognize that there are deeper motives at work in my choice to re-engage with this particular narrative. Meg and I attended the same university (where we met), studied with many of the same teachers and were both involved in similar Christian societies and activities. While both committed Anglicans and feminists, we made different life choices. Where Meg went on to train for priestly ministry, I have remained an active lay member of the church. Where Meg married and had children, I remained single for many years and childless. I suspect that, in returning to her narrative, I was making an unconscious decision to revisit some of these life choices and to examine them in the company of someone who had made a parallel but different journey. At a later stage in the process of data analysis (described below), I wrote a series of poems in response to Meg's narrative, and pondered:

> What brought me back to your story
> amongst all the others I could have chosen?

The poem continues:

> I am reading for sameness and also acknowledging difference
> looking for a bridge across the shared story that separates us

It goes on to ask:

> Could we find a way to connect and distinguish
> our mutual but separate ministries and misery?

This excerpt from one of my poems demonstrates the way in which I began to use poetry to interrogate the data and my own re-engagement with it, and to bring myself more overtly into the frame of the research. But this is to anticipate a later stage of the analysis. Let me now describe the various sequences of the data analysis.

In my original study, I set the transcripts out in speech spurts, largely without punctuation, in order better to approximate patterns of speech. The text thus resembles poetry more closely than prose. In returning to Meg's transcript, I took this process a stage further by selecting a number of smaller episodes, narratives and voices within the transcript and turning them into poems, or perhaps more accurately, 'poem-like' representations or 'research poems'.[28] The intention in doing so was to stay with Meg's own words, using only what she had spoken within the interview, but to select, edit out and shape particular narratives into discrete poems, in an effort to allow the data to speak more directly and fluently on the page. For example, here is a section of the original transcript, from the beginning of the interview in which Meg talked about her present experience of faith in light of a recent move to a new parish:

> 4   M   having moved here
>   things are very much in transition really
>   but for the last four years
>   as you know
>   have been incredibly
>   a very dry period
> 5   N   Right

6 M and that I mean
      actually working
      to provide a spiritual focus
      for a group that was dwindling and
      literally dying
      in a *building* that was literally dying
      was very kind of *stripping* really
      Um [p] and I suppose the kind of
      Mother Julian thing of 'all shall be well'
      you know actually just holding on
      to something at the centre
      and thinking
      'There's something' but you know
      not always sure what
7 N Right
8 M Emm [p] so that it's
      it's felt like kind of being underground and [p]
      you know when is this bulb going to emerge?
      Like when you plant snowdrops
      and you don't see anything for about three years
      and then suddenly you get this little
      tiny little snowdrop and I think I feel like I'm
      I'm the green shoot at the moment
      that's actually beginning to come up[29]

The transcript seeks to remain as close to the verbal data as possible, recording every spoken word (including speech fillers such as 'um', 'you know' and 'I mean', repeated words, incomplete sentences and pauses). This was important for the original analysis so that I could study the quality and process of the exchange, as well as the content, paying attention to such features as hesitation, repetition, stammering or emphasis as a clue to Meg's narrative. While staying close to the living speech-act, however, such transcription methods may impede the power and immediacy of the narrative and detract from the accessibility of the data; hence the endeavour to convert sections of the data into research poems, which would make a more immediate impact. A number of writers have argued, with Richardson, that 'poetry can re-create embodied speech in a way that standard sociological prose does not'.[30] I experimented with taking extracts of Meg's transcript and, while using only her words, deleting potentially distracting features such as the para-linguistic 'umms', 'ahhs' and repetitions. I chose excerpts from the transcript that appeared to possess strong thematic cohesion, arranged the text in a format approximating to poetic form (for instance, using lines of similar length arranged in couplets), and gave each 'poem' a title. Here is a poem composed of transcript material from the beginning of the interview (including some of the above transcript excerpt):

Snowdrop emerging: reflections of a woman priest

The last few years – a very dry period
the dryness of being alone

Working to provide a spiritual focus
for a group that was dwindling and dying

Still get up on a Sunday morning and
preach the Easter stuff

Moments of getting to the brink
'What are you doing with your life?'

I'm not experiencing it but the truth never deserted me
That was the call

Like being underground
when is the bulb going to emerge?

Like when you plant snowdrops
and don't see anything for about three years

Suddenly you get this tiny little snowdrop
I'm the green shoot beginning to come up

Even in the most negative and dry absence
there is still a presence

There's a core at the centre of me
something very deep like a seed

Will it wither before it blooms?
I am trusting it but there's always fragility

In returning to Meg's transcript, I was newly struck by her use of the metaphor of the underground bulb that puts out life several years after it has been planted, as an analogy with her own fragile but resilient faith. A persistent theme in her interview was the struggle to maintain hope and faith amid adversity, gender discrimination, suffering and despair. This poem seeks to capture the struggle, the sense of forces of life and death weighed in the balance, the precariousness yet persistence of Meg's own faith and the triumph of hope represented in the emergence of the snowdrop.[31]

Having composed the above poem, I was immediately aware of the selectivity and partiality of its representation of the data. This is an issue faced by all qualitative researchers in their analysis, selection and representation of data, regardless of how they present the data. In selecting excerpts of transcripts to quote against other excerpts that do not receive attention, the researcher is exercising the power of choice and using data to make a case or highlight one feature over another. This is no less true when the means of data analysis is poetic; indeed, the use of poetic means of analysis may concentrate the selectivity in a heightened form. A poem takes its power and meaning from myriad choices the poet makes, either consciously or unconsciously. Where the poem begins and ends, the system of images and metaphors employed, the metre and rhyme scheme, the choice and combination of particular word sounds, the voice of the poem – all of these contribute to the overall impact and meaning. Thus in the above poem, I endeavoured to reflect the delicate paradox and tension of hope and despair, resilience and fragility, that seemed to be at the heart of Meg's narrative. Yet it would be quite possible to represent the same data in a different form in order to convey a different outcome, to tip the balance one way or the other towards hope or despair, triumph or failure. Here is a reworking of the same material, compressing and omitting some of the material from the first poem and adding in some data from later in the interview:

Under siege: the experience of ministry

Working to provide a spiritual focus
for a group that was dwindling and dying

Still get up on a Sunday morning and
preach the Easter stuff

Moments of getting to the brink
'What are you doing with your life?'

I'm not experiencing it
but the truth never deserted me

Having to hold the experience myself
holding on to something

Like being underground
when is the bulb going to emerge?

I was the go-between, containing
[doing] the motherhood thing

Under siege, dried out
going through the motions, keeping it going

Living on a shoestring
keeping each other sane

years of resources dragged out of us

While this poem retains the image of the underground bulb, it omits the development of that metaphor in the extended reflection on snowdrops emerging years later after their original planting. In addition, the image of the bulb is now set within a wider frame of harsher, less obviously hopeful images such as 'getting to the brink', being 'dried out', 'living on a shoestring' and so on. The poem ends on a bleak note and the title, 'under siege', suggests something very different from 'snowdrop emerging'.

Which of these poems more authentically reflects Meg's sense of vocation, ministry and faith? Both poems are composed entirely of Meg's own words drawn from the interview, yet arranged in different ways by the researcher-poet (me). Whereas the first poem uses material from the beginning of the interview, the second poem draws more widely on material from across the transcript. I have given only two examples of reworking the data, but the possibility of representing data in different poetic forms is potentially endless. The point is that there is not one, or even two narrative voices or interpretative lenses at work in this transcript, but several. In the interview, Meg was working with her own questions about how far she could continue to hold on to her sense of self and faith, as well as her commitment to marriage and family life and a meaningful priestly ministry, in the context of prolonged struggle and in the face of opposition from church hierarchy and parishioners. At times she spoke hopefully and at other times there was a sense of weariness and exhaustion. By creating a series of poems, I tried to give voice to the diverse perspectives and narrative lines that exist in uneasy tension within the one transcript. It would be perfectly possible to do this in prose, but the poetic form may concentrate and intensify the different narrative voices in a peculiarly effective fashion. As Jean Rath has argued in her use of poetry to script meaningful research texts with rape crisis workers, the poetic scripting

> resists the desire for analytic certainty, decentering both the texts of researcher/author and the texts of participants. It foregrounds the negotiation of meaning between researcher and participants, and invites the reader into the text in order to take part in this.[32]

At the point of my interview with Meg, the Church of England had only just endorsed women's priestly orders and remained highly ambivalent towards women priests – particularly young, clever women such as her. Meg's story was one of repeated experiences of gendered discrimination, exclusion, infantilization and abuse, whether intentional or, more frequently, the result of unconscious bias and centuries old androcentrism. As one of the first cohort of women accepted for training for priesthood in the Church of England, her dilemma was not merely personal, but mirrored the situation of a whole generation of women who went on to become pioneering priests (or, in some cases, left the church and priesthood altogether). The interview contained many reflections on and readings of gender, rooted in her personal, familial experience as well as the processes of selection, training and ordination she had undergone. She had been introduced to the church by her grandmother and associated church with a warm, feminine, familial space that provided an alternative to her chaotic and disruptive family. On the other hand, many of her experiences of selection, training and seeking a first curacy were governed by androcentric norms, and were associated for her with coercive male power, reinforcing a problematic and abusive relationship with her father. These various gendered associations with church, pulling in opposite directions, were scattered throughout the interview rather than focused in any one place. I brought them together in two brief poetic statements, using Meg's own words, representing feminine and masculine associations with church and priesthood respectively:

Feminine associations with church/priesthood

My first memory of being in church
going with my grandmother

Going into that building was going into somewhere good
I associated her with that building

Church was a very important place
because my home was a disruptive and chaotic place

A very abusive place
church became a safe place, my safe haven

The woman superintendent of the Sunday school
half adopted me

She took me to a Deanery Synod meeting
I remember her saying 'This is for you'

They were debating the ordination of women
'This is for you'

I hadn't ever met a woman who worked in church
women weren't even allowed to dust in the sanctuary

Masculine associations with church/priesthood

There was a calling
but it was like being menaced by something

A Selector asking questions like
'Why wasn't a woman like me at home having babies?'

Living on a shoestring
trying to beg borrow from charities

Didn't look like I was going to get a job
interview after interview

One emotional trauma after the next
there were no resources – we were down to peanuts

The morning of the cesarean when Sophia was born
my parents came in – there was something in my father's look

I'd repressed a lot of the stuff that had gone on
between me and my father as a child

Having employed poetry as a means of analysing and representing the different voices and perspectives present within her transcript, I then used poetry as a means of interpreting and 'talking back' to Meg's story. At this point, I began using my own poetic voice to give shape to questions and hunches about the narrative and to continue a dialogue that I might have engaged face to face but did not have the opportunity to do so. This process represents a more upfront personal dialogue with the interview data than I had engaged in my original study where, although my own experience and concerns were by no means absent, they were less overtly expressed. The use of poetry to engage with Meg's narrative now permitted a more direct, emotionally engaged and interrogative style of commentary that would not have been appropriate in the earlier study. This style of more personal engagement may have been elicited because a case study approach in itself reveals far more of the life story and personal reflections of the interviewee than a more thematic approach, and thus may invite a more sustained personal response.

I found myself writing poems that were attempts to bring to the surface some of the gendered dynamics at work in the transcript, bringing to voice and visibility the discrimination, misogyny and abuse (psychological and possibly physical/sexual, although this was not made clear in the interview), which ran like underwater currents throughout the entire interview but were not always directly named. At the same time, I wanted to endorse and applaud the courage, resilience and determination that were evident in Meg's narrative and that kept her engaged in the struggle to be accepted for priestly ministry in the church as the person she was. 'Wanting it all' affirms the largesse of Meg's vision for priestly ministry and the resistance she faced from the institution of the church:

Wanting it all

As if being young, female and pretty were not enough
As if being working class and bright were not enough
(first generation of women to read theology at Cambridge)
                              you wanted more

You wanted marriage, motherhood and ministry with your PhD
You insisted on producing babies one after the other
parading your leaky maternal body
in the hallowed cloisters of Cambridge
in the chaste spaces of the sanctuary
in the theological college lecture rooms
in the studies and church halls and sherry-drinking parlours
of clerics who'd carved out the rules over generations
who'd demarked the spaces
your body and mind defied

You took them all on, the rules that said

Women shall not be priests
Women shall not preside at the eucharist

Women cannot be academics (minds too flimsy, distractable)
Women shall not work outside the home
taking the authority away from their husbands
If women wish to be mothers
let them fulfil their God-ordained role quietly at home
out of the sight of the public assembly

You would not obey their strictures or accept their authority
you wanted it all
you were greedy, unholy
your desires spurted out with your milk
fouling their snow white cassocks

The following poem, 'Punishment', reworks the same territory but is written in the voice of the male authorities that Meg frequently experienced as constraining, controlling, withholding and punishing. While doubtless, as individuals, many of these male authorities perceived themselves to be merely doing their jobs and exercising appropriate pastoral care and discernment, the cumulative impact upon Meg of a whole series of impediments, put-downs and exclusionary practices was devastating. The poem is an attempt to name the systemic power of patriarchy that was operative, according to Meg's understanding, in the church, and that transcends while subsuming the actions and intentions of individual actors (some of whom could, of course, have been women – although in the main they were not).

Punishment

We had to contain you.
You were a danger to everything we hold most sacred
masquerading as innocent female piety.

We had to constrain you.
As Adam mastered Eve, curbing her insatiable curiosity,
binding her voluptuous sensuality,

we put you in the basement with the nursing mothers
where no light would reach you,
your fertile bodies hidden.

We had to restrain you,
clawing back the resources we'd promised you,
threatening to withdraw your grant.

We had to punish you,
compelling you to travel hundreds of miles, pregnant, in winter,
chasing unsuitable appointments.

We had to make you wait, wear away your persistence
through a war of slow attrition,
death by a thousand qualifications,

watch the men you'd trained with enter first incumbencies,
while you held on through the humiliations and deprivations,
damp houses, low-paid, low-status curacies.

These poems of course represent *my* interpretations of Meg's narrative. In many ways, the poems 'big up' or write large what were often implicit or partially expressed thoughts and feelings within the transcript. Talking from her present experience of priestly ministry, still wrestling with challenges to her own authority and trying to find a way of expressing her priesthood authentically, Meg's narrative was full of the tension of needing to name the powerful forces that resisted her priestly ministry and of hopeful determination to withstand them. I am conscious that I responded to her narrative with a certain 'outsider/insider' ambivalence, which perhaps enabled me to name things I saw more directly and unambiguously than it may have been possible for Meg, at the time, to do. I was the researcher hearing her story but standing outside it, identifying strongly with many aspects of it, knowing at least some of the contexts she described quite intimately since they had also formed me. As a lay woman who had worked very closely with others over many years to campaign for women's priestly orders in the Church of England, I both identified with her journey and was conscious that I had taken a different path. In effect, I was reading between the lines of her narrative – as all data analysis must do – and bringing to consciousness and visibility things that were present in the data but, by being foregrounded and expressed in a particular voice, had a greater force and clarity than when embedded within the narrative itself.

The next poem makes this 'reading between the lines' explicit:

Reading between the lines

You didn't say your father abused you
But 'there was something in his look'
when he came into the recovery room.
You were on a drip and pinned down.
You spoke of flashbacks for months afterwards.

You didn't say your mother failed you
but you felt like a freak, a zoo piece on show,
a money-maker who could look after her in old age.
That plan fell apart when you married
and took your potential earnings elsewhere.

You didn't say the church abused you
but charted one incident after another
of calculated control, withdrawal of funding,
living under siege, getting to the brink,
one emotional trauma after the next.

You couldn't say what it was doing to you
but calmly told how you put your hand through the window

one morning, blood everywhere,
your husband bearing the brunt of your unspoken rage.
You tore up identical Valentine cards.

You didn't say God had abandoned you
but something worse:
'There was a kind of calling
but it was like being menaced by something'.
'What kind of a God is this?' you asked me.

I didn't reply:

> This God is a tyrant,
> This God is an abuser,
> This God wears the face of your father
> and all those priests who hold the reins of power.

You didn't say you could not withstand the violence,
you were going to have to get out.
That would come later
after being held at knifepoint by a desperate addict
after being held hostage by a second attacker

after being thrown into broken glass that could have severed an artery
after months of sickness of the body
and the terror unto death
until one day like any other you walked out the door
and never went back up the grave-strewn path.

I am aware that this poem raises ethical as well as methodological issues and that it is only permissible to publish such a poem with the full and explicit consent of my interviewee. The poem is mine, the voice is mine (though it makes use of a great deal of Meg's narrated reflections), the interpretation is mine – and some might question whether it is legitimate for me, as the researcher, to bring into the limelight aspects of her story that Meg (deliberately?) kept in the shadows. By writing the poem, I have brought to consciousness aspects of Meg's psychological and spiritual struggles that, at the time of the interview, might have been profoundly damaging to articulate. That I have done so many years later, and in the knowledge that Meg has moved on from these earlier struggles and stands in a completely different relation to them (having left the church and active priestly ministry a good number of years ago following a physical attack in the church and having established herself in a new community and professional role as a writer), does not entirely resolve the issues. Even if Meg herself is now in a place where it is safe for her to receive my poem, do I have the right to displace her own narrative by this formulation of my own?

Perhaps the only person who can answer this question is Meg herself. My own hope and intention is that, in so naming the realities that seemed to me to be at play in Meg's narrative (and in that of countless other women priests), the poems may have an empowering impact, not only on Meg herself, but on other readers. There is both rage and disbelief in my own voice in this poem as I chart the unspoken violence and abuse that Meg experienced at the hands of the church she longed to serve and to which she gave years of her life in a costly outpouring. The poem is offered as a protest against abusive patriarchal power and a witness to the women, such as Meg, who have paid dearly for their efforts to combat that power and model something different. Thus I offer it as an act of solidarity and advocacy, an attempt to share and bear – as little as I can – the suffering that Meg and other women priests of her generation have experienced. As poets themselves may exercise the priestly ministry of naming, bearing and witnessing to profound human experience – including suffering – so I see these poems as priestly offerings back to one courageous, wounded and transformed woman priest who is herself now also a poet (and perhaps would never have become one had she not left the church). Established as a writer and someone who works with others to encourage and bring to birth their creative gifts, Meg's priesthood has metamorphosed into new forms and finds expression in alternative communal contexts – yet is no less real for that.

While this is my interpretation and reading rather than hers, Meg herself both accepted and endorsed my interpretation when I sent her an earlier draft of this chapter. She responded with a poem of her own, a poem that picks up some of the imagery in her original interview and that I had used in my poems quoted above. This gift of a poem from Meg in response to my work was an unexpected development in my process of employing poetry as a means of data analysis, and suggests the possibility of giving the poetic voice and authority back to our research participants. The (almost) final word, then, belongs to Meg:

Holding to the light

for N, Christmas Eve, 2016

I'm the shoot still greening
wondering if I'll wither
before I bloom

Christmas Eve
and the light has gone by three
no petals on the fragile stem

And I no longer preach
the Easter faith
yet Advent's here – the hope, the fear

If there's a bridge
it stretches from your spiel to mine
– those shared and separate ministries

and misery –
it's the story's arc across
dry river bed

The call is silent now
No menace there
but absence –

yet your witness waits
holds tight the fear
bears hope

Conclusion

By their careful observation and listening, their painstaking work to represent the lived experience of the human other in all its 'thickness', particularity and nuance, the poet and qualitative researcher both testify to the value and significance of human life and experience, holding up to the light lives that otherwise might remain hidden, unnoticed and marginalized. The very work of poetry and ethnography (broadly understood), when well done, is a witness and sign of the sacramental quality of human experience, an out-working of the Christian doctrines of creation and incarnation, the conviction that God is present in creative and redemptive fashion in every human story, in the concreteness and mundaneness of life as it is lived. In honouring Meg's story, finding poetry within it, turning it into poetry and responding in poetry, I hope to have highlighted and affirmed its sacramental nature. Meg's answering poem does more than triangulate and enrich my own reading of her story; it recognizes the poetic analysis as a work of 'witness' that holds the continuing ambivalence in her own story, balancing the fear with a hope contained in the story's arc.

I hope to have demonstrated how poetic analysis allows a dynamic and deepening conversational engagement with the lived experience of the other, offering the potential for genuinely collaborative and participative research encounters. Poetic analysis highlights and upholds the complex, shifting and multivocal nature of qualitative enquiry, resisting closure or singular analysis. Poetic analysis offers both a frame and a lens on experience that is focused yet capable of multiple refraction, enabling the many-layered texture of the conversations engaged between research participants to be both held and analysed. The use of poetic analysis by the researcher and the offering of the fruits of such analysis back to the participant can invite further poetic response, which opens up new dimensions of insight and enquiry. The conversations are multiple and varied: between different narrative lines and voices within the one story; between the different selves of the researcher and the participant; between different readings of the research transcript. Every poem is an offering rather than an assertion, an opening into multiple meaning rather than a closing down into fixity. Poetry, no less than ethnography, can make a vital difference to the lives of women and other marginalized groups.

Notes

1　Nicola Slee, '(W)riting Like a Woman: In Search of a Feminist Theological Poetics', in *Making Nothing Happen: Five Poets Reflect on Faith and Spirituality*, ed. Gavin D'Costa *et al.* (Farnham: Ashgate, 2014), 9–47.

2　Nicola Slee, *Women's Faith Development: Patterns and Processes* (Aldershot: Ashgate, 2004).

3　'Meg' is a pseudonym; data from the transcript is presented here with her permission, and she has had an opportunity to read and comment on this article.

4　See, for example, Malcolm Guite, *Faith, Hope and Poetry: Theology and the Poetic Imagination* (Farnham: Ashgate, 2010); Francesca Bugliani Knox and David Lonsdale (eds), *Poetry and the Religious Imagination: The Power of the Word* (Farnham: Ashgate, 2015), and subsequent volumes; The Association for Theopoetics Research and Exploration at http://theopoetics.net; as well as popular texts such as Mark Pryce, *Literary Companion to the Lectionary* (London: SPCK, 2001); Janet Morley, *The Heart's Time* (London: SPCK, 2011); Malcolm Guite, *Word in the Wilderness* (Norwich: Canterbury Press, 2014); and Mark Oakley, *The Splash of Words* (Norwich: Canterbury Press, 2016).

5　Walton defines poetics as 'concerned with the construction of literary texts and the conventions employed by creative writers in the making of these works'. Heather Walton, 'Poetics', in *The Wiley Blackwell Companion to Practical Theology*, ed. Bonnie J. Miller-McLemore (Malden, MA and Oxford: Wiley-Blackwell, 2012), 173. See also p. 178, where Walton outlines Aristotle's distinction between *phronesis* and *poesis*.

6　Walton, 'Poetics', 173–182.

7　Bonnie Miller-McLemore, 'The Subject and Practice of Pastoral Care as a Practical Theological Discipline: Pushing Past the Nagging Identity Crisis to a Poetics of Resistance', in *Liberating Faith Practices: Feminist Practical Theologies in Context*, ed. D. M. Ackerman and Riet Bons-Storm (Leuven: Peeters, 1998), 175–198.

8　Rebecca Chopp, *The Power to Speak: Feminism, Language, God* (New York: Crossroad, 1989) and *Saving Work: Feminist Practices of Theological Education* (Louisville: Westminster John Knox Press, 1995).

9　Riet Bons-Storm, *The Incredible Woman: Listening to Women's Silences in Pastoral Care and Counselling* (Nashville: Abingdon, 1996).

10　Rebecca Chopp, 'Theology and Poetics of Testimony', in *Converging on Culture: Theologians in Dialogue with Cultural Analysis and Criticism*, ed. Delwin Brown, Sheila Greeve Davaney and Kathryn Tanner (Oxford: Oxford University Press, 2001), 56.

11　Walton, 'Poetics', 175.

12　Heather Walton, *Writing Methods in Theological Reflection* (London: SCM, 2014) and *Not Eden: Spiritual Life Writing for this World* (London: SCM, 2015).

13　See, for example, Monica Prendergast, Carl Leggo and Pauline Sameshima, ed. *Poetic Inquiry: Vibrant Voices in the Social Sciences* (Rotterdam: Sense, 2009), accessed 1 May 2017, www.sensepublishers.com/media/765-poetic-inquiry.pdf; Carol Grbich, *Qualitative Data Analysis: An Introduction*, 3rd ed. (London: Sage, 2013), 129–142; Patricia Leavy, *Method Meets Art: Arts-based Research Practice*, 2nd ed. (New York: Guilford Press, 2015), 77–120.

14　See Robin Mark Pryce, 'The Poetry of Priesthood: A Study of the Contribution of Poetry to the Continuing Ministerial Education of Clergy in the Church of England' (DProf thesis, University of Birmingham, 2014), accessed May 10, 2017, http://etheses.bham.ac.uk/5772.

15　For example, Laura Brearley, 'Exploring the Creative Voice in an Academic Context', *The Qualitative Report* 5, no. 3/4 (2000), accessed 1 May 2017, www.nova.edu?ssss?QR/QR5-3/brearley.html; Laurel Richardson, 'Poetic Representation of Interviews', in *Postmodern Interviewing*, ed. Jaber F. Gubrium and James A. Holstein (New York: Sage, 2003), 187–201.

16 For example, Carol L. Langer and Rich Furman, 'Exploring Identity and Assimilation: Research and Interpretive Poems', *Forum: Qualitative Social Research* 5, no. 2 (2004), accessed 1 May 2017, www.qualitative-research.net/index.php/fqs/rt/printerFriendly/609/1319.

17 For example, C. C. Poindexter, 'Meaning from Methods: Re-Presenting Narratives of an HIV-Affected Care-Giver', *Qualitative Social Work* 1 (2002): 59–78; C. Langer and R. Furman, 'The Tanka as a Qualitative Research Tool: A Study of a Native American woman', *Journal of Poetry Therapy* 17 (2004): 165–171.

18 See www.foundpoetryreview.com for definitions and examples.

19 See Elaine Graham, Heather Walton and Frances Ward, *Theological Reflection: Methods* (London: SCM, 2005), chapter 1, for a discussion of turning life into text as a method in practical theology.

20 Available at http://murielrukeyser.emuenglish.org/writing/the-book-of-the-dead/, accessed 25 April 2017.

21 Alice Oswald, *Dart* (London: Faber & Faber, 2010). See www.poetrysoc.com/content/archives/places/dart/, accessed 25 April 2017.

22 Slee, *Women's Faith Development*.

23 S. E. Chase. 'Taking Narrative Seriously: Consequences for Method and Theory in Interview Studies', in *Interpreting Experience: The Narrative Study of Lives, Volume 3*, ed. Ruthellen Josselson and Amia Lieblich (London: Sage, 1995), 1–26.

24 Brearley, 'Exploring the Creative Voice', 2.

25 Dennis Tedlock, *The Spoken Word and the Work of Interpretation* (Philadelphia: University of Pennsylvania Press, 1983), in Richardson, 'Poetic Representation', 189.

26 Brearley, 'Exploring the Creative Voice', 2.

27 The stages I describe are similar to those employed by Langer and Furman, 'Exploring Identity'.

28 For a discussion of research poems, see Rich Furman, Cynthia Lietz and Carol L. Langer, 'The Research Poem in International Social Work: Innovations in Qualitative Methodology', *International Journal of Qualitative Methods* 5, no. 3 (2006): 1–8, accessed 1 May 2017, www.ualberta.ca/~ijqm/.

29 Italics indicates emphasis by the speaker; [p] indicates a pause in the interview; 'M' = Meg and 'N' = 'Nicola', i.e. myself as interviewer.

30 Laurel Richardson, *Fields of Play: Constructing an Academic Life* (New Brunswick, NJ: Rutgers University Press, 1997), 143.

31 This is a classic poetic metaphor of renewal employed by generations of poets such as George Herbert in 'The Flower' – see www.poetryfoundation.org/poems-and-poets/poems/detail/50700, accessed 25 April 2017.

32 Jean Rath, 'Poetry and Participation: Scripting a Meaningful Research Text with Rape Crisis Workers', *Forum: Qualitative Social Research* 13, no. 1 (2012): 13, accessed 25 April 2017, www.qualitative-research.net/index.php/fqs/article/view/1791/3312.

3 Weaving a web

Developing a feminist practical theology
methodology from a charismatic
perspective

Helen Collins

Introduction

My research interests have arisen out of my own personal experience of
becoming a mother. Despite years of fruitful engagement with the Charismatic
Movement before having children, once I became a mother I felt isolated from
this spiritual tradition. Previously enriching methods of worship and prayer felt
deeply divorced from my embodied experiences of motherhood and childcare.
Essentially, I found that I could no longer be totally absorbed in the expected
'abandonment' model of charismatic, sung worship – epitomized by closed
eyes and arms raised in an ecstatic moment of divine encounter – when the
baby's needs were felt to be all-consuming. Cut adrift from a felt encounter
with God and overwhelmed by the seemingly endless demands of new mothering, I felt confused, guilty, frustrated, isolated and forgotten by God.

While the initial motivation of my research was to find personal reconciliation, I wished to model an approach that could equally be described as 'feminist',
'charismatic', and 'evangelical' in its practical theological method, in order to
remain faithful to my personal convictions.[1] I found that none of the existing
methodological approaches within practical theology were entirely compatible
with this aim. Also, many works I read describe the valuable insights of feminist
practical theology,[2] but did not always make explicit the step-by-step process
taken by the researcher to produce those insights. Issues of feminist methodology in relation to researching women's faith are addressed within the field,[3] but
they are mostly in tension with an evangelical or charismatic approach. This
is because feminist approaches ordinarily foreground women's experiences as
a legitimate basis for constructing renewed theology, whereas an evangelical
approach consistently looks to scripture as the authoritative foundation for the
theological task, and a charismatic perspective prioritizes the authority of the
Holy Spirit's inspiration. Attempting to hold together these different epistemological perspectives was the impetus for developing a new methodological
approach that was appropriate for my context and research question.

This chapter offers a reflexive narrative of my research journey, describing
the process of developing a new methodological approach. Such a chapter
would have been invaluable to me at the start of my research as an aspiring

feminist practical theologian. Therefore, while the web-weaving methodology is described here so that it may be used by other researchers, I also seek to offer other researchers the inspiration to pioneer their own methodologies, and to map out how they might do so.

This chapter begins by outlining the focus of my research with a reflexive narrative of how I approached the research question and the methodological choices I made. This leads into an explanation of the web-weaving methodology I developed, which draws on the metaphor of a spider weaving a web as an image of how the research process unfolds. I outline the theory for this approach and show how it was applied to my particular research question. Finally, I conclude with an illustration of how the methodology was employed within my data analysis.

The background

My research question was: *How and why might a woman's transition to motherhood affect her experience of charismatic sung worship?* and my intention was to reflect theologically upon the experiences of charismatic mothers in the hope of discovering a more life-giving praxis. The academic field of practical theology was an obvious context for the research, since practical theology is a confessional discipline where the research question emerges from a position of faith within the service of the wider Christian community. Swinton and Mowat define practical theology as a 'critical, theological reflection on the practices of the Church as they interact with the practices of the world with a view to ensuring faithful participation in the continuing mission of the triune God'.[4] Thus it is praxis-orientated, seeking to bring about change and make a significant and relevant contribution to the performance of faith.

The pastoral cycle model is commonly used in theological education to frame the dialogue between tradition and experience.[5] The cycle begins with an 'experience' and then enters into a deeper 'exploration' of that experience before drawing in resources from the faith tradition for 'reflection'. The final stage of the process is formulating renewed 'action', which feeds back into 'experience' to complete the circle. This method of theological reflection developed out of Kolb's experiential learning cycle, which offers a model for adult education.[6] Liberation theologians such as Segundo developed a similar model, which allowed praxis to critique theological tradition.[7] Lartey's version of the pastoral cycle emphasizes the mutual interrogation between 'exploration' and 'reflection', such that both perspectives can critique each other. Tracy describes this process as 'mutually critical correlation'[8] between theory and practice, while Pattison calls it a mutual critical conversation.[9] According to Lartey, what is common to all these approaches is 'a concern to relate faith (or doctrine) with practice (or life) and to do so in ways that are relevant and useful'.[10]

Influenced by Kolb and Segundo, Green proposes a 'Doing Theology Spiral',[11] which explicitly acknowledges that the pastoral cycle produces a new situation and is therefore not a circle but a spiral that develops through time. Green observes that despite the orderly nature of a cycle or spiral diagram, 'experience can play a very significant role in all the phases of the cycle and not only in the first phase'.[12] My experience of doing theological reflection is that every phase plays a significant role in every other – and it is this principle that inspired the development of my own web-weaving methodological approach outlined below.

The foundations

Initially, I chose to follow the pastoral spiral model proposed by Green as the framework for structuring my unfolding research. This was because the spiral reflected my personal experience of the evolving nature of my spirituality as my children grew. I found that my mothering experiences changed through-out the course of my research, and occasionally these changes were the result of my reflections. The spiral therefore seemed a good methodological fit.

In order to broaden and deepen the 'experience' stage of the process beyond my own personal experiences, I conducted semi-structured interviews with twelve women within eighteen months of giving birth to their first, second, or third child. The majority of the mothers were accessed through my existing networks. My status as 'mother' and 'charismatic' was instrumental in securing access to the specific context of my research and provided a clear rationale for my chosen topic of study.[13]

Each of the twelve participants was white, middle class, and married, while ten of them were tertiary educated. This sample is reflective of the traditional demographics of the British Charismatic Movement and therefore appropriate for my research question.[14] Six of the women worshipped at different char-ismatic Anglican churches, four attended different Vineyard churches, and the final two were from non-denominational churches. Each interview lasted between sixty and ninety minutes and was conducted in the mother's home, usually without their baby being present. I asked them about various aspects of their spiritual lives – prayer, singing, church attendance, the bible, other peo-ple, intimacy, emotions, embodiment – and how these might have changed or developed with having children.

Once all the interviews had been completed, I visited the women's churches in order to research their particular charismatic worshipping contexts. While I could have used the mothers' accounts of their charismatic traditions, I wanted to triangulate their reflections by independent observation. If they were experiencing the same alienation I felt, their accounts of their tradition could be unhelpfully influenced by their recent experiences. I contacted the eight churches represented by the women in the sample, and received per-mission from five of them to conduct my research. They were considered to be charismatic churches due to their affiliation to a well-known international charismatic network of churches. I also chose to include two conference meet-ings of this network within my sample. This was to reflect the significance that these larger-scale gatherings have upon charismatic worship in the local church. Ward notes that the charismatic worship subculture is grown and sustained through such large-scale gatherings,[15] and so it was important to include this perspective in the data. I attended two consecutive worship services in each context in order to get an illustrative picture of their worship styles. For each service observed, I recorded the audio output while also noting my observations and impressions of what I saw and experienced.[16] These recordings of what was spoken or sung throughout the service were transcribed using discourse analysis notations.

Once the data was collected and I was in the throes of laborious transcription work, I realized the spiral model did not offer an accurate description of my approach. It felt as if I had got stuck between 'exploration' and 'reflection' on the cycle model as I repeatedly moved backwards and forwards between them, trying to establish patterns between my diverse data. I started to wonder if there was a better way to represent what I was doing. Furthermore, I realized that I needed a methodological approach that more closely reflected my charismatic, evangelical convictions and could be firmly rooted within that community.

The framework

I began to look for a framework on which to structure my developing methodological approach, which was more reflective of the iterative process I found myself involved in, and more faithful to my evangelical and charismatic commitments. I discovered Cartledge's method of practical theology, which he employed in his study of charismatic spirituality.[17] The model's dialectic approach and its rootedness within the charismatic, evangelical tradition gave it significant appeal and relevance to my thesis.

Cartledge's charismatic perspective recognizes that God is an active agent in the process of theological construction, through the Holy Spirit. Cartledge describes theology as a holistic enterprise that involves not only right doctrine and right action, but incorporates the human affections. It is therefore focused on the divine 'encounter' between Creator and creature. This divine/human theological relationship is dialectical, orientated towards personal transformation for the purpose of faithful participation in the *missio Dei*. This dialectical understanding of theology informs Cartledge's practical theology method, which is based upon two intersecting axes. The horizontal axis of his model represents the relationship that exists between the practical theologian, on the one side, and their faith community, on the other side, which in Cartledge's case is charismatic spirituality. The horizontal axis indicates that a dialectic exists between the theologian and their spirituality as they negotiate their own identity within the tradition. This horizontal dialectic intersects a vertical axis that represents a second dialectic between theory at one end, and practice at the other end of the axis. Cartledge describes the two ends of the vertical axis as the 'lifeworld' (concrete reality) and the 'system' (theological identity).[18]

A research question can arise from either end of the vertical axis; however Cartledge explicitly gives priority to the 'system', because the whole process is orientated toward theology.[19] The dialectic then moves backwards and forwards along the vertical axis, within the context of the horizontal axis, in order to generate insights, which may bring greater revelation to scriptural interpretation or change the praxis of faith. This whole process is understood to be the work of the Holy Spirit, encountering the practical theologian in the process of enquiry and inspiring individual and communal transformation.

This model resonates with the values of the charismatic tradition in which I am rooted, and also does so from an evangelical perspective by giving priority to scripture. Furthermore, it reflects the backwards and forwards movement I was engaged in between my two distinct sets of data. However, I desired to nuance Cartledge's model to incorporate a more consciously feminist perspective and to align my research with feminist practical theology.

The structure

Despite the strengths of Cartledge's model for my methodological approach, the concept of a dialectic between distinct poles did not wholly resonate with a feminist approach, and so I began to explore the concept of a web. Gilligan makes use of the web metaphor to demonstrate how women's development happens within the context of relationships and interconnection, as opposed to the more individualistic and separation-based frameworks that characterize men's development.[20] A web model is therefore more appropriate for understanding women's experiences than the linear, dialectic model Cartledge proposes. Miller-McLemore similarly makes use of the web concept to argue that pastoral care should not see people only as individuals, but rather treat them within their complex web of relationships.[21] Furthermore, Couture discusses the limitations of individual approaches to pastoral care and argues that it should rather be enacted within a web model, which takes seriously the socio–political realities of individual lives, as opposed to a narrow focus on psychological resources. Finally, Procter-Smith uses the metaphor of a spider spinning a web as a model for feminist spirituality, which is characterized by interconnection and creativity.[22]

The web metaphor highlighted for me the complementary metaphor of 'weaving' as a useful description of the iterative process of my data analysis. Weaving is widely employed within feminist studies of religion, and while it is occasionally employed alongside a web metaphor,[23] 'weaving' brings out a different focus. Christ describes how the term symbolically connects women with the labour, creativity, and power of their foremothers, for whom weaving was a central domestic activity.[24] The metaphor of weaving is also used by Plaskow and Christ to reflect the diversity of women's experiences and the heterogeneous approaches to feminist spirituality.[25] Smith describes the weaving metaphor as expressing actuality and possibility, describing how things are and imagining how they are becoming, as 'weaving' embodies the wholeness and integration of all things.[26]

I therefore employed these significant metaphors of 'weaving' and 'web' to ground my research within the feminist tradition and to highlight the fundamental interconnection of ideas and people. My approach sought to combine and extend these metaphors into a systematic and transferrable methodology. My research was initiated by and continued through my own mothering and spiritual journey, and therefore my experiences infiltrated every part of the process. As such, I became the spider, weaving the web of understanding. Nothing happens within the research project that is not filtered through the researcher's own experiences, interpretations, and agendas, and so the spider metaphor reflects the embodied nature of the work. Smith describes the spider's web making connections between unrelated objects and this became particularly significant for my research. Smith describes how spiders: 'deliberately span environments with intense energy and work. They give birth to threads of connectedness, somehow creating out of their own bodies a substance that will bring together separate edges, walls, and space'.[27]

This quotation describes the research process as I experienced it, and furthermore, it highlights the connections between the processes of web-weaving and birthing, which relates to my particular focus on mothers. As my research sought to connect the distinct and hitherto unrelated academic fields of motherhood and charismatic worship, the metaphor of a spider 'birthing' her web and weaving the strands together to join unconnected areas felt particularly apt.

In describing my web weaving methodology, I shall initially use vocabulary from Cartledge's dialectic model to show how I have adapted it. In my research, I was seeking to occupy two 'lifeworlds', which are in conversation with each other as well as with the theoretical 'systems' I was employing. The two main 'lifeworlds' were the experience of mothering and the experience of charismatic worship. Also, I was trying to navigate multiple 'systems', which included not only the witness of scripture, filtered through charismatic, evangelical and feminist perspectives, but also the theological literature informing these interpretations *and* the theological and sociological literature on motherhood and charismatic worship. Again, these systems are in conversation with each other as well as with the lifeworlds. This gave me four main poles around which I framed the dialogue, which I entitled: scripture (system 1) and reason (system 2), experience (lifeworld 1), which, in the case of my research was the mothering experience, and tradition (lifeworld 2), which was the charismatic worshipping tradition I observed.

Stage 1

A spider begins to weave her web by sending out a single strand, or bridge thread, in the hope that it will catch onto something secure, and this strand forms the basis for the whole structure.[28] In my model, this strand originates from scripture, God's self revelation, reaching out in the hope of taking root in an individual life – which I have described as one's 'reason'.[29] A bridge thread between scripture and reason is formed which is the foundation of the whole structure.

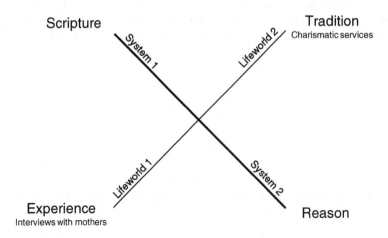

Figure 3.1 Stage 1: anchor points

The spider then moves to the centre of her main thread and creates further anchor points from which to weave. On my model, the secondary anchor points of tradition and experience set the revelation-response account (system 1–system 2/scripture–reason) within its particular context (lifeworld 1–lifeworld 2/experience–tradition). Already, a dialectic is created between each of these anchor points, as the researcher moves backwards and forwards between them in an attempt to establish their methodological framework (Figure 3.1).

Stage 2

Once these anchor points have been established, a spider will create scaffolding between them. This scaffolding is a temporary connection between the anchor threads, providing a tentative stability to the structure in order for her weaving work to be carried out. This is where the identification of key themes or the formulation of tentative hypotheses fits into the overall process of research. These key themes emerge through the interaction between reading, reflection and personal experience, which takes place early on in the process and comes to influence the later data collection and analysis.

This method is similar to thematic networks as proposed by Attride-Stirling, and is particularly linked to that method through the shared use of a web-like diagram to organize and represent the interpretation. A thematic network approach begins by coding the data in order to generate 'basic themes'. These basic themes are grouped together to form 'organizing themes' that 'summarize abstract principles'.[30] Finally, the organizing themes combine to generate 'global themes' that are the 'principle metaphors' in the text. My web-weaving approach is the reverse of this. It acknowledges the reality that the researcher never comes to the data 'empty', but is informed by their own experiences and the concepts and ideas of others, obtained through reading. These inherited concepts inevitably influence how the researcher will understand and interpret the data, and the web-weaving approach makes that explicit. I therefore used 'global themes' that emerged from the literature and applied them to the data, allowing these to guide the generation of basic themes.

Within my research, the scaffolding I employed was a model proposed by Cartledge, which offers a systematic process for charismatic worship, described as search–encounter–transformation (Figure 3.2).[31] Cartledge suggests this three-stage process is a framework for understanding the spirituality of the Charismatic Movement and I found that it gave coherent expression to my experiences. During early motherhood, I tried repeatedly to follow the formulaic process of search, encounter and transformation in worship without the expected 'success' of a felt, transformative experience of God. Furthermore, the three-stage process is significant in that it directly relates to feminist concerns. Search, encounter and transformation are values inherent to a feminist cause: searching relates to the discovery and uncovering of women's stories; encounter is linked to relationality; while personal and societal transformation is the explicit goal of feminism. Thus in trying to offer a feminist critique of charismatic worship, I was able to use a scaffolding framework, which expresses shared values of each field.

I took these three global themes of 'search', 'encounter' and 'transformation' and applied them to the data. I worked through the whole data set looking for and recording any evidence of how 'search' was understood and articulated, first in the data from the charismatic services observed, and second in the interviews with mothers. This generated numerous basic themes that were systematically recorded and categorized. I then went back to the beginning and worked through the whole data again looking for evidence of 'encounters'. I went through this process a third time for evidence of 'transformation'. This process generated six 'groups' of basic themes ('searches' in motherhood,

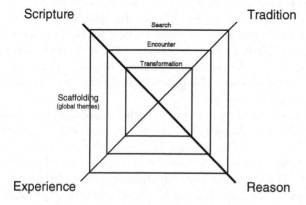

Figure 3.2 Stage 2: scaffolding

'searches' in charismatic worship; 'encounters' in motherhood, 'encounters' in charismatic worship; 'transformations' in motherhood, 'transformations' in charismatic worship), which provided the structure on which to weave.

Stage 3

Finally, the spider works her way between the anchor points of her web doing the intricate work of weaving it all together within the scaffolding structure she has created. This corresponds to the intricate task of data analysis, moving backwards and forwards between the two different lifeworlds for increased mutual understanding. Significantly, once the spider has completed a section, she eats up the scaffolding as it has no further use. The weaving, or analysis, therefore produces fresh insight, which can redefine the global themes and thus may require their 'eating up' in order to formulate new themes and concepts. This therefore reinforces the provisionality of the framework employed.

In the context of my thesis, the weaving relates to the development of organizing themes, which happened by comparing and contrasting all of the data that emerged from the application of the scaffolding. As described above, each time I went through the data looking for evidence of a global theme, it would generate two 'groups' of data: all the occurrences of search-related utterances from the charismatic data and all the search-related utterances from the motherhood data. This process generated a variety of basic themes within each group. For example, some of the basic themes in the search-related utterances on charismatic worship were: searching for unexpected encounters; searching for 'more of the same'; search as enjoyable/uncomfortable; search as safe/unpredictable, and so on. Examples of the basic themes within the search-related utterances in the mothering interviews include: divine search as positive/negative; divine search and emotions; divine search at church; divine search with/without child. Whenever an utterance corresponded to one of the basic themes, it would be coded as such and grouped with the others. Whenever a new basic theme emerged from the data, I would go through all the data again to see if there was other evidence for this new theme. These two groups of basic themes related to 'search' were then placed side by side as I went backwards and forwards between them looking for patterns, correlations, and inconsistencies between the two accounts. The goal was to identify and define organizing themes that would reveal how the global themes were experienced by charismatic mothers. This process was repeated for 'encounter' evidence and 'transformation' evidence.

The organizing themes exposed the ways in which the global themes caused tensions for women trying to inhabit the roles of 'mother' and 'charismatic worshipper'. For the final stage of the process, I therefore chose to return to the bridge thread of scripture-reason, in the same way a spider would return to the centre of her web. This process involved interrogating the global themes in the light of the witness of scripture in order to test whether the exposed tensions were biblically justifiable, or whether the global themes needed revising

in light of the women's experiences. This 'eating up' of the scaffolding therefore foregrounds scripture in line with my evangelical commitments.

The application

I shall give a brief example of how I used this methodological approach in the
data analysis to demonstrate how it works in practice. I have chosen to focus on
one organizing theme within one of the three global themes, which equates to
one revolution around the web.[32] For each stage of the data analysis, I offer a
diagram to relate the methodological theory explicitly to the practical application, and to orientate the reader within the process.

Effortful search: a charismatic perspective

The second organizing theme of a charismatic 'search' through sung worship
is that worshippers are expected to fully engage in the worshipping experience
in order to derive enjoyment from it. Here is an example of a call to worship
given by a worship leader at the beginning of a block of singing which indicates the expected level of personal effort to engage in the singing required
from those gathered.

1   So we're just going spend a bit of TIME in <u>worship</u> (1.0)
2   Whether the songs are <u>new</u> to you (0.2)
3   Or they're FAMILIAR (0.4)
4   Erm (0.2) our heart is that we just (0.2)
5   press into the PRESENCE of God (0.8)[34]

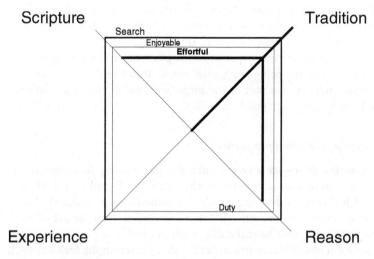

Figure 3.3 Weaving 'effortful'[33]

The worship leader is saying that whatever songs they are singing as a church, it is the worshippers' role to use them to engage with God and strive for that encounter with God (note emphasis on 'presence' in line 5). It is clearly within the act of singing that this is expected to happen, as 'worship' (line 1) is intimately connected to 'songs' (line 2). Also, the emphasis upon 'TIME of worship' in line 1 indicates that it is understood to be the intentionality of extended time that facilitates the expected encounter. In line 4, the worship leader reveals 'our heart', which Ward suggests is a key metaphor in charismatic worship that communicates the deepest truths.[35] Therefore, by using the plural 'our heart', the leader is implying that everyone's deepest desire is to 'press into the presence of God' (line 5). Significantly, his hope is not just that people will be in the presence of God or experience God's presence, but that they will 'press into it'. 'Press into' is a phrase that invokes the use of force, such as 'press something into a mould' or 'press into service'. Hence there is a sense of pushing or forcing oneself into God's presence, regardless of how one feels and whatever songs are being played. Elliot similarly describes the goal of charismatic worship as being to 'break through to the presence of God'.[36] These forceful concepts place a significant amount of pressure upon the worshippers as they are expected to expend whatever effort is necessary in order to 'break through' to God. The weight of responsibility for an encounter with God is therefore placed upon the worshippers' ability to search for it. While this reminder to make the choice to engage might be entirely appropriate and helpful for some members of the congregation, it is also potentially alienating for those who are unable to exert the necessary effort to 'press in' due to their circumstances.

This emphasis on the individual effort required in the search for a divine encounter was also evident within the worship songs. Many of the song lyrics describe the activity of singing, and further emphasize this by using highest notes or slower pace on the word 'sing',[37] for example, in the chorus of the song '10,000 Reasons'.[38] These songs often encourage worshippers to sing louder, harder and higher, with more passion, feeling, and commitment than previously. This is a significant expectation to place on the worshipper, particularly if these songs are being sung each week. It demands a high level of effort and engagement on the part of the singer and implies that a lack of such effort would result in less acceptable worship.

Effortful search: a mothering perspective

I will now examine the concept of exerting effort in worship from the mothering perspective to demonstrate how mothers can be affected by this theme. The levels of individual effort expected of worshippers, as outlined above, mean that mothers (and indeed others) may be excluded from the act of worship because they are unable to make the required effort.

In the quotation below, Lucy articulates the disconnection she feels between her mothering experiences and the expectations to engage in sung worship.

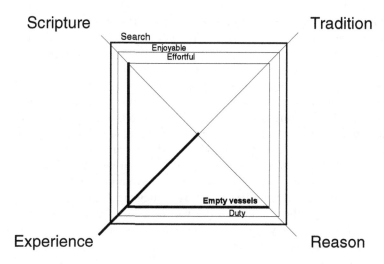

Figure 3.4 Weaving 'empty vessels'

When asked about how her feelings of intimacy with God have changed due to her mothering, she responded,

1 I find it VERY difficult to (0.4)
2 sort of lose myself as it were (0.2)
3 kind of in (1.4) in worship
4 coz I'm out of practice (0.8)
5 so even when I DO get to do it (.) I find I'm like (0.2)
6 a bit fidgety (1.6)
7 some people are just (.) you know (0.4)
8 the worship band strikes up and they're like
9 [mimes eyes closed, arms raised]
10 you know straight away (.)
11 whereas I'm like (.) [groan]
12 takes me a while to get going (.)
13 coz I'm (0.2) I'm so used to having to (0.4)
14 you know (0.2) juggle (0.6)
15 I can't just (0.2) switch it on

Here, Lucy is contrasting herself with other worshippers who seem able to engage and enjoy the experience of worship (lines 7–10) whereas the prospect of it causes her to groan (line 11). This indicates that she is not eagerly anticipating the opportunity to 'press into the presence of God' as expected above, instead, she finds it very difficult (line 1, note her emphasis). She attributes her lack of engagement to her prolonged withdrawal from participation in worship due to mothering (line 4), such that now, after five years of mothering three children, it is difficult for her to engage in worship even when the children are not there (line 13–15). Her phrase in line 2, 'sort of lose myself as it were', expresses what she understands to be happening in sung worship encounters. Although she does not explain this phrase, her mime of 'ideal worshipper' as someone with eyes closed and arms outstretched in the air suggests abandonment. The closed eyes symbolize a shutting oneself off from the world while the raised, outstretched arms symbolize a letting go. Thus Lucy understands acceptable worship to be the kind during which the worshipper can transcend themselves and abandon their temporary situation in order to focus their concentration on God. Elliot describes this worshipping position as ideally symbolizing the charismatic belief that 'the individual is an axis mundi between heaven and earth'[39] and thus the ability to adopt this position is of vital symbolic importance. In contrast, what Lucy and other mothers are doing is 'juggling' (line 14) the needs of their children within the confines of the worshipping space. Years of this juggling have left Lucy 'fidgety' (line 6) and unable to 'lose herself' or 'press in' even when the children are not present.

The comparison of these two sets of data reveals that concepts of 'search' in charismatic worship assume that the worshipper must assert their effort in order to experience an encounter with God. The difficulties that Lucy describes offer a critique of these assumptions and expose the potential for worshippers to experience alienation from charismatic worship as a result. It therefore raises the question of whether such a charismatic 'search' is an appropriate or necessary category for understanding worship. These questions – and the others that emerged from the similar comparisons – were gathered together in the penultimate chapter and assessed from a biblical perspective in order to give scripture the definitive voice in the discussion.

Conclusion

I found that this web-weaving methodological approach worked particularly well within my thesis, as the section above demonstrates. I found that the web model more faithfully reflects the complexity of the process I was engaged in of bringing together two distinct areas of scholarship. The method demonstrates and celebrates the interconnected nature of the thoughts that emerge, it makes reflexivity central to the whole process through the metaphor of the spider, and it is strongly rooted within a feminist perspective through the metaphors of 'web' and 'weaving'. It is very labour intensive, through the numerous revolutions around the structure, but it provides a clear process to follow, especially when distinct data sets are being compared.

A potential risk of the model occurs at Stage 2, when the scaffolding is established, in that one's choices here will significantly affect how the data is interpreted. However, this is always true in any research project at every stage; decisions around research questions, key texts, participants, interview questions, interpretation and write-up all alter the outcome. The principles of reflexivity advocate for an honest and open account of the choices made, to act as a 'map of the research decisions'[40] for those seeking to follow. I consider that the scaffolding stage makes explicit what often happens in the practice of research, which is that during the compilation of the literature review key themes emerge for the researcher that inevitably influence their choices around data collection and analysis. Indeed, this is understood to be the purpose of engaging with the relevant literature. The scaffolding stage acknowledges that the researcher is influenced by ideas that emerge from her reading, and allows her to make use of them in a transparent way. Furthermore, I found that the repeated movement around the anchor points of the web and between the sets of data was instrumental in exposing my prior assumptions about terminology or concepts that I had taken up without critical reflection. The iterative process allowed themes to be continually revisited from different perspectives and this significantly sharpened my own capacity to be reflexive about my prior assumptions. Finally, the process of returning to scripture and 'eating up' the scaffolding prevents a self-serving circulatory in the findings.

A significant contribution of this methodology is to foreground the place of scripture and the Holy Spirit in the practical theological task, and to attempt to do so from a feminist perspective. There is little encouragement or precedence for being an evangelical, charismatic feminist either in the church or in the academy. However, this approach shows that it is possible, if not always easy. I hope that my web-weaving methodology might encourage other evangelical feminists that one can carry out theological research in a way that is faithful to both identities. However, more than that, I hope this chapter will inspire a new generation of researchers boldly to pioneer new methodological approaches that best fit their contexts and faithfully reflect their own theological identities.

Notes

1 I do not have the space within this chapter to discuss or define these terms, or show how I have attempted to hold these positions together. However, I address this in detail within my thesis and I refer the reader there for further information: Helen Collins, 'Weaving Worship and Womb: a Feminist Practical Theology of Charismatic Worship from the Perspective of Early Motherhood' (PhD diss., University of Bristol, 2017).

2 For example, Elaine Graham and Margaret Halsey, ed., *Life Cycles: Women and Pastoral Care* (London: SCM Press, 1993); Bonnie J. Miller-McLemore and Brita L. Gill-Austern, ed., *Feminist and Womanist Pastoral Theology* (Nashville: Abingdon Press, 1999); Nicola Slee, Fran Porter and Anne Phillips, ed., *The Faith Lives of Women and Girls* (Farnham: Ashgate, 2013).

3 Nicola Slee, *Women's Faith Development: Patterns and Processes* (Farnham: Ashgate, 2004); Elaine Graham, Heather Walton and Frances Ward, *Theological Reflection: Methods* (London: SCM Press, 2005); Dawn Llewellyn, *Reading, Feminism and Spirituality: Troubling the Waves* (Basingstoke: Palgrave Macmillan, 2015).

4 John Swinton and Harriet Mowat, *Practical Theology and Qualitative Research* (London: SCM Press, 2006), 25.

5 Judith Thompson with Stephen Pattison and Ross Thompson, *SCM Study Guide to Theological Reflection* (London: SCM Press, 2008), 50.

6   David Kolb, *Experiential Learning: Experience as the Source of Learning and Development* (Englewood Cliffs, NJ: Prentice Hall, 1984).

7   Juan Luis Segundo, *The Liberation of Theology* (Maryknoll, NY: Orbis Books, 1982).

8   David Tracy, 'The Foundations of Practical Theology', in *Practical Theology: The Emerging Field in Theology, Church and World*, ed. Don S. Browning (New York: Harper & Row, 1983), 76.

9   Stephen Pattison, 'Some Straw for the Bricks: A Basic Introduction to Theological Reflection', *Contact* 99 (1989): 2–9.

10 Emmanuel Lartey, 'Practical Theology as a Theological Form', in *The Blackwell Reader in Pastoral and Practical Theology* ed. James Woodward and Stephen Pattison (Oxford: Blackwell, 2000), 129.

11 Laurie Green, *Let's Do Theology: Resources for Contextual Theology* (London: Bloomsbury Academic, 2012).

12 Ibid., 26.

13 For reflection on 'insider' status, see Jacqueline Watts, '"The Outsider Within": Dilemmas of Qualitative Feminist Research Within a Culture of Resistance', *Qualitative Research* 6, no. 3 (2006): 385–402.

14 Tom Smail, Andrew Walker and Nigel Wright, *Charismatic Renewal* (London: SPCK, 1995), 40.

15 Pete Ward, *Selling Worship: How What We Sing has Changed the Church* (Milton Keynes: Paternoster, 2005), 77.

16 See Robert Emerson, Rachel Fretz, and Linda Shaw, *Writing Ethnographic Fieldnotes* (Chicago, IL: Chicago University Press, 2011).

17 Mark Cartledge, *Practical Theology: Charismatic and Empirical Perspectives* (London: Paternoster, 2003).

18 Ibid., 27.

19 Swinton and Mowat, *Practical Theology*, 86–91 similarly argue for the 'logical priority' of theology within the dialogue, following Barth.

20 Carol Gilligan, *In a Different Voice: Psychological Theory and Women's Development* (Cambridge, MA: Harvard University Press, 1982), 24–63.

21 Bonnie Miller-McLemore, 'The Living Human Web: Pastoral Theology at the Turn of the Century', in *Through the Eyes of Women: Insights for Pastoral Care*, ed. Jeanne Stevenson-Moessner (Minneapolis, MN: Fortress Press, 1996), 9–26.

22 Marjorie Procter-Smith, *In Her Own Rite: Constructing Feminist Liturgical Tradition* (Nashville: Abingdon Press, 1990).

23 For example, Pamela Couture, 'Weaving the Web: Pastoral Care in an Individualistic Society', in *Through the Eyes of Women: Insights for Pastoral Care*, edited by Jeanne Stevenson-Moessner (Minneapolis: Fortress Press), 94–106.

24 Carol Christ, 'Weaving the Fabric of our Lives', *Journal of Feminist Studies in Religion* 13, no. 1 (1997): 131–136.

25 Judith Plaskow and Carol Christ, ed., *Weaving the Visions: New Patterns in Feminist Spirituality* (New York: Harper Collins, 1989).

26 Christine Smith, *Weaving the Sermon: Preaching in a Feminist Perspective* (Louisville: John Knox Press, 1989), 15.

27 Ibid., 19.

28 See David Attenborough, (Presenter) and Bridget Appleby (Producer), 'The Silk Spinners' [Television series episode]. In M. Salisbury (Series Producer), *Life in the Undergrowth*, (London: BBC, 2005) for details of how a spider weaves a web.

29 My choice of the term 'reason' is to explicitly relate the model to the four sources for theological reflection often known as the Wesleyan Quadrilateral: Alister McGrath, *Christian Theology: An Introduction*, 5th ed. (Oxford: Blackwell, 2011), 146. I use the term here to represent a holistic human thinking, reflection and interpretation of events.

30 Jennifer Attride-Stirling, 'Thematic Networks: An Analytical Tool for Qualitative Research', *Qualitative Research* 1, no. 3 (2001): 388.

31 Mark Cartledge, *Encountering the Spirit: The Charismatic Tradition* (London: DLT, 2006): 25–27. Charismatics begin their worship with a 'search' for God, which is enabled through the singing of lively praise songs. This 'search' for God transitions to an intimate 'encounter' with God where worshippers feel the presence of God and then experience a 'transformation', which is often emotional and therapeutic in scope.

32 In total, there were nine revolutions around the structure. Within the first global theme of 'search' I identified three organizing themes of 'enjoyment', 'effort' and 'emotional arousal', each of which represented a revolution of the web. Within the second global theme of 'encounter' the organizing themes were 'fulfillment', 'location' and 'extended time', and within the third global theme of 'transformation', the organizing themes were 'realization', 'homogeneity' and 'efficacious'.

33 This diagram focuses on the second organizing theme and shows the organizing theme that preceded it to show how it is built up with each section. The dotted line of 'search' is to indicate that it is temporary scaffolding. The 'tradition' anchor is in bold because this is the section being focused on.

34 I used discourse analysis notations within my transcriptions, based upon the conventions in Maxwell Atkinson and John Heritage, 'Jefferson's Transcript Notation', in *The Discourse Reader*, ed. Adam Jaworski and Nikolas Coupland (London: Routledge, 1999), 158–166. The number in brackets indicates the length of pause in seconds; capital letters indicates a louder utterance; an underlined word shows that emphasis is placed – sometimes accompanied by an upwards or downwards arrow to show the shifting intonation; a colon shows that the sound is elongated.

35 Ward, *Selling Worship*, 152.

36 Esther Elliot, 'Worship Time. The Journey Towards the Sacred and the Contemporary Christian Charismatic Movement in England' (PhD thesis, University of Nottingham, 1999), 191.

37 David Montgomery, *Sing a New Song: Choosing and Leading Praise in Today's Church* (Edinburgh: Rutherford House and Handsel Press, 2000), 55.

38 Matt Redman, *10,000 Reasons* (Integrity Music UK and Hillsong, 2011).

39 Elliot, *Worship Time*, 207.

40 Llewellyn, *Reading, Feminism and Spirituality*, 170.

4 Living religion

Collapsing (male constructed?) boundaries between the religious and the spiritual

Janet Eccles

Religious or spiritual? An overview

In this chapter I offer a new typology within the sociology of religion for understanding women's faith lives that accommodates diverse relationships between the religious and the spiritual. The meaning of 'religious' is often understood to involve conventional religious institutions, rituals and systems of belief, whereas 'spiritual' often connotes a more individualized search for the transcendent, which gives meaning to one's own particular life, regardless of where others may be on that journey. However, my research suggests that a distinction cannot so easily be drawn between the two categories. It is true that people have often claimed they are spiritual but not religious,[1] as if this was possibly a more desirable position to hold in the, arguably, more secularizing Western world of recent decades. Hay and Hunt suggest, 'spiritual awareness is a necessary part of our human make-up, biologically built into us, whatever our religious beliefs or lack of them', so still suggesting a marked distinction between the two.[2] Could it be, alternatively, that 'entrenched scholarly categories for understanding religion' pose a challenge to the 'polar (+/−) single and exclusive' understanding of religion, as Beaman and Beyer remark, of people who cross boundaries between the religious and spiritual?[3] Might there not be other ways in which we could examine religiosity and spirituality that more accurately portray how people actually live and practise their faith stance? Bowman, for example, writing of what she calls 'vernacular' or 'folk' religion, suggests that, realistically, religion should be viewed in terms of three interacting components: official religion (meaning what is accepted orthodoxy at any given time within institutional religion, although that is subject to change), folk religions (meaning that which is generally accepted and transmitted belief and practice, regardless of the institutional view) and individual religion (the combination of received tradition, folk and official, and personal interpretations of this 'package' in response to personal beliefs and insights gained from experience).[4] Similarly, Shakman Hurd, in describing what she calls everyday religion, sees it 'as that which is practiced by ordinary people as they interact with a variety of religious authorities, rituals, texts, and institutions and seek to navigate and make sense of their lives, connections with others, and place in the world'. She considers it a diverse field of activity, relations, investments, belief, and practices that 'may or may not be captured in the set of human goings-on that are identified as religion for the purposes of generating expert knowledge or meeting the aims and objectives of governance'.[5] Everyday or lived religion may be indifferent, opposed, supportive or inassimilable to the terms of both official religion and that defined by 'experts'. If this is true, we need seriously to reconsider how we research the religious and spiritual and how it actually is lived in the everyday lives of those we seek to study.

Much has already been written, including the various sources quoted above, to show that spirituality most certainly does not reside simply within institutional boundaries.[6] But my own research indicates that the same can be said of Christian faith, as practised by the women in my study, and that it can be found outside the church among those who no longer attend. Moreover, even within those institutional boundaries I found there existed a wide range of faith stances and practices among women, some of which might be considered more orthodox expressions of faith and belief than others. I should also add that what I found, through empirical research, also coincided with a number of observations I had privately noted over a period of 60 years and more of church attendance, off and on, and what led, partly, to my interest in this subject. In this chapter I suggest it is time to consider new methods for examining faith lives, women's in particular, since so often it is men's faith lives that have been taken to constitute the norm when examining behaviours, belongings and beliefs. Such novel methods will allow us to think outside the box and no longer straitjacket faith lives/worldviews into neatly (often male determined) traditional categories.

I begin by describing my study of older women, in which it became clear that a new typology needed to be created to reflect my actual findings. I then go on to discuss the usefulness of the terms 'lived religion' and 'fuzzy fidelity' and whether (or not) they help us understand what is going on in women's faith lives. Finally, I argue on the basis of my research, for a methodology that enables new categories to be developed for describing the faith stance/worldview of women subjects, since they are ill served by the old ones.

Blurring the boundaries

In 2001, Callum Brown, a social and cultural historian, asserted that it was women who had lived through the cultural revolution of the 1960s who were responsible for what has become the considerable and continuing decline in Christian affiliation, practices and beliefs.[7] This time of significant cultural, social and religious change gave women permission to cast off the patriarchal and hierarchical church's long-standing constraints on their behaviour, he claims, and huge numbers left. He sees the cultural revolution causing the 'depietization of femininity and the defeminization of piety',[8] implying, thereby, that only churchgoing women are likely to be 'pious', that is, devoted to their church and its hierarchical norms and values, naturally assuming the role of 'angel in the house' and setting a shining example of good (womanly) Christian behaviour to all around them. The second implication of such a statement is that those who have left have cast off those notions of 'piety'.

If Brown was correct, I argued at the beginning of my study, I should expect to find a clear boundary between the 'pious' affiliates and non-pious disaffiliates. I should be able to find, therefore, two distinct groups of women who had, apparently, each emerged with quite different beliefs, values and behaviours as a result of the cultural revolution. Finding suitably aged affiliates and disaffiliates proved relatively easy as I had several connections with churchgoers, through attendance at a Free Church myself, being secretary of a Churches Together group in my town in South Lakeland (UK) and through visiting various churches related to this (voluntary) post. I also knew a number of disaffiliated women through my various leisure activities in the town and through both groups used the snowball method, which involves asking those who have already agreed to be part of the study if they know of anyone else who might care to participate. I carried out semi-structured interviews sometimes in my home, usually in the participant's home, lasting around two hours each, taping each encounter and transcribing it afterwards.

Recording and transcribing conversations with the women, I soon realized that what I had long suspected was correct, and that the terms affiliate and disaffiliate needed much more amplification. Affiliates had a range of beliefs and practices, were not necessarily more 'pious', in the sense that Brown described, than some disaffiliates, and those who had given up official 'belonging' to a church might be more 'orthodox', more 'pious' in some practices and beliefs, than affiliates. Moreover, these were not necessarily Davie's 'believers without belonging',[9] or those who relied on 'vicarious belonging', since not all necessarily admired what the church (the one they had left) was doing or wanted it to speak and practise on their behalf as Davie suggests of vicarious belonging.[10]

An emerging typology

As I set about data analysis and despite pressing my supervisor several times on the issue, she suggested I let any typology emerge naturally from the data themselves. I found this quite daunting, as I had very limited experience, apart from what I had done for my master's degree, and there were a number of false dawns before a viable approach emerged. I began by making two lists, affiliates on one side, disaffiliates on the other, trying to determine to what extent any of my informants fulfilled the requirements of piety, following Brown's definitions. After I had interviewed each one, I had written a short summary profile, to help me assess their 'piety'. Yes, the affiliates attended church regularly and the disaffiliates did not, not regularly at least. But many disaffiliates continued with a number of practices and beliefs showing they had remained both religious and spiritual (of which more below). So this became more and more confusing as I found 'pious' women on both lists. Clearly the pious/non-pious divide was not going to be helpful. Indeed, it became apparent that all these women practised what has been termed 'the ethic of care',[11] regardless of affiliation or disaffiliation, as a voluntary but necessary, loving expression of who they were. If this was a necessary aspect of piety, then all the women were, to some degree, pious.

So, what did distinguish the two lists if not 'piety'? I returned to my first principle for devising the lists: the attenders and the leavers. Why did it matter to attend to thirty-eight women and not the other thirty-two? And why had some changed the type of place in which they worshipped and yet others had been happy to stay in the same church or find another one like it, if they moved house? Pondering these questions led me to look for further subdivisions in my original two lists, further markers in the women's conversations that pointed to possible differences between forms of 'belonging' to their respective institutions.

Exploring the affiliates

Beginning with the attenders, I began to see that all their 'belongings' were not identical. There were those who had remained more or less attached to the same type of community all their lives, those who had switched to a different community and those who had left and returned. What had prompted the differences in their behaviours?

The ones who really stood out, initially, were the switchers. They had changed denominational affiliation because they had changed their beliefs and type of practice and this *did* coincide with a desire to shake off certain hierarchical norms as Brown had suggested. It did not, however, result necessarily in women leaving the church, contra Brown. It was the words of a Quaker friend of mine who I interviewed that gave me the key to this type of belonging. She had left the Anglican community because she felt it no longer welcomed her presence when she came out as a lesbian. As a single woman with no family members left and only her ageing partner for support, she needed, she said, a community, a place where she could talk of things of value to her and where others shared the same values. Reading through the words of most of the switchers, it was apparent to me that the new community of shared values was profoundly significant in engendering a sense of belonging and self-worth, which had been lacking in their previous place of worship. The affirmation of their new identity had given them an entirely new sense of purpose and direction in their life, had 'turned them round', made them whole again.

It was a somewhat different, far less self-conscious, sense of shared values that also bound the lifelong belongers together. I asked most of the women, regardless of affiliation status, if they felt the church valued them as women, as I tried to probe Brown's thesis and the notion of piety. The switchers were clear the church did not and could articulate that clearly, especially as some had been involved in the Movement for the Ordination of Women (MOW). Most switchers evinced a total rejection of a male God and saviour and one or two were even uncertain if they believed in a transcendent deity at all. By contrast, it seemed the lifelong attenders had never thought about the question of male dominance and even when I pressed further, this was clearly a perplexing question for which they had no answer. What bound them together was forms of embodied practice carried out through the church year, such as preparing the church for Advent or Easter, sitting on church committees, singing in the choir, fund-raising events, sitting alongside each other in times of stress and turmoil, rejoicing at the birth of a new baby or the success of their children. Male vicars/ministers/priests may come and go but the community of women to which they belonged was enduring, there for them whenever they needed it. Their faith was in this community and its enduring reliability and to which they each made a significant contribution.

The returners had initially turned their backs on (or simply drifted away from) this kind of embedded belonging earlier in their lives, often in adolescence, but at a time of crisis years later, they had come to realize, usually through a churchgoing friend, that they had lost something of value. When invited to return alongside their friend, they had gladly done so, becoming the same kind of committed belonger as those who had never left. Thus emerged three ideal types of affiliates or belongers: the embedded belongers, a group who had maintained a constant church affiliation throughout their entire lives; the rehabilitated returners, a group who had left and then returned; and those who had taken issue with the beliefs and some of the practices of their original congregation and had become reflexive switchers.

Caring disaffiliates

Turning to my list of disaffiliates, again I found one group standing out distinctly from all the rest: women who exhibited neither spiritual nor religious leanings and had become thoroughly secular/nonreligious in their outlook. The interesting feature of this group was that although they claimed no Christian belonging, behaviours or belief, asserting they found belief intellectually incredible, and hence why would they practise, they maintained this same sense of caring for others, the ethic of care. One woman, for example, the wife of a non-stipendiary minister, worked full-time, brought up two children, cared for the house and still ran round to support elderly in-laws everyday with very little help from her husband. So while thoroughly 'depietized' in almost all the senses outlined by Brown, these women were indistinguishable from the other women. So, even here, the ethic of care is not a useful trope for characterizing distinctions between churchgoers and non-religious leavers.

This left twenty-four disaffiliates remaining. Why had they left? Had they given up on belief as well as belonging and practice as the secular women had? Did they still care about things spiritual? Did they refer to a transcendent other? Did they maintain any practices from their earlier churchgoing days? Were they caring women or had they left in order to be free to pursue their own ends entirely? In fact, these women also maintained aspects of piety that had not been cast off with their churchgoing. There were differences, however. Some women maintained only Christian expressions of faith, while others might combine elements from various (particularly pagan) traditions.

While these two groups of leavers overlapped in their practices to some degree, the Christian dechurched women continued to pray, might sometimes turn to the Bible for guidance, spoke of God or Christ being behind them in their daily activities, lit candles in church, listened to church music as a spiritual experience and certainly cared for family, friends and neighbours, as the need arose. They no longer sat in church Sunday by Sunday, they no longer joined with other women in active participation throughout the church year but in many other respects there was little to distinguish them from a number of embedded belongers. When they sought community it was often through some activity in their town or village, engaging with some kind of charity work or being active in a local club or group, say. Originally, I had styled these women explicit/implicit believers, but 'belief' is inadequate to encapsulate what is important about their faith for these women. They continue to seek embodied forms of practice in relationship, even though not within the church. Hence, I've now come to think of them more accurately as dechurched practitioners.

This leaves the final group who combined traditions in their practices and beliefs. Some of these women did tell me that the Christian church was damaging to them in its patriarchal attitudes and values but, again, they had not left off all things religious and spiritual, contra Brown, but had sought community within various pagan/holistic practitioner groups. This did not necessarily, however, mean they never engaged with Christian beliefs and behaviours. One had become an interfaith practitioner, for example, and had found that a friendly local vicar was willing for her to hold ceremonies – naming a child, handfastings, celebrations for a life well lived – in the church building. Quite often these had Christian elements, she said, if that's what her clients wished, and she was happy to comply if that was what was needed to make the ceremony meaningful and of value to the participants.

Thus emerged a second threefold typology, for disaffiliates: the secularists/religiously indifferent who had no interest in things religious or spiritual but still practised the ethic of care; the dechurched practitioners who maintained many Christian beliefs and practices outside of the church; and the holistic switchers who still sought significantly religious and spiritual experiences but combined in a number of faith traditions. In all, this represents a six-fold typology of affiliation and disaffiliation: embedded belongers, rehabilitated returners and reflexive switchers on the one hand and dechurched practitioners, holistic switchers and secularists, on the other. This constitutes as good an assessment as I can make of the types of beliefs, belongings and behaviours of the women I spoke to. I do not argue it is representative of all women but it is illustrative of what I found in this particular context and opens up the way for others to build on this by further research.

Putting labels on people is quite a difficult process for me, but producing a typology when working in the sociology of religion helps in the process of analysis and for drawing out distinguishing features that may be common to a sub-group. Typologies can, however, describe no more than Weberian ideal types[12] and do not fully describe how an individual woman's faith stance plays out in her everyday life. As Stringer notes of such a process in anthropology,[13] it is a question of creating models and models are inevitably simplifications of reality, but without some simplification it is almost impossible to proceed to any kind of analysis of the complex human subject. So my typology does not represent hard and fast divisions but particular sets of practices, beliefs and belongings falling along a continuum.[14] From this continuum, it became clear to me that the religious are not always so easily distinguished from the spiritual as Heelas and Woodhead claim. Rather, as Cheruvallil-Contractor *et al.* argue, the terminology of 'religion' and 'non-religion' is imprecise and contested, while that of 'spiritual' and 'spirituality' may be even less clear.[15]

Lived religio-spirituality

Work on 'lived religion'[16] leads me now to consider that, apart from the secularists who specifically defined themselves as being neither religious nor spiritual, all the other women pursued forms of religio-spirituality, regardless of their particular (dis)affiliation. Their conversations centred on three dominant themes: those of practice, embodiment and relationship, rather than propositional belief. Belief was part, but only part, of the story for some women. Also important is the way they sometimes find themselves accommodating to the challenges posed by inequalities within their religious traditions, sometimes negotiating ways round them and sometimes simply switching to other forms of religio-spiritual practice in an effort to feel comfortable and to be able to 'own' what they are doing. Studying lived religion, therefore, necessitates a reconceptualizing and broadening of what counts as religion and what does not, and may involve considerable rethinking of categories for determining religio-spirituality. Some forms of Christian expression are not necessarily to be found in ecclesiastical circles or those 'approved' by the church but outside. My research has shown that deeply held religio-spiritual beliefs and behaviours can be found far from church congregations and that all disaffiliates do not become non-religious or religiously indifferent. It is important that the methods of investigation we choose for our research, therefore, allow us to listen carefully to what participants tell us, giving them space to challenge previous assumptions, as I found.

As McGuire notes of lived religion, there is no boundary between sacred and profane time and place.[17] Thus women were to be found praying in many different circumstances, even crossing the road was accompanied by prayer for one long-standing, churchgoing woman. A dechurched practitioner prayed while visiting in prison or doing her shift with the Samaritans, needing guidance for some of those she had encountered. 'I may not be in church', she said, 'but I see Christ behind me in all I do'. Another dechurched practitioner still referred to Christ as 'an incredible force for good in the world', in a somewhat similar fashion and sees prayer as 'a wish (really), of goodness . . . to help that situation through vibrations in a way . . . or wavelengths'. She firmly believes in the resurrection because of certain spiritual manifestations or 'presences' she experienced as a younger woman at times of family bereavement. Having consulted a spiritualist medium, she is convinced these are her guardian angels.

For a church returner, the Anglican liturgy was becoming increasingly hard to accept, and being told what she might and might not believe, but hers was also very much an embodied faith.

> Spirituality is important (to me). I find difficulty with the actual words of the service because I can't say the Creed, so chunks of that I'm not happy with. I'm much happier with the family communion which is a different liturgy. (Sometimes) I have this desire to be in the church alone and flatten myself on the ground and so my own ritual ... with nobody looking at me, I could do some very strange things.

Some of the reflexive switchers had often moved from more mainstream congregations to join the Religious Society of Friends or Unitarians, for example. They welcomed the silent worship on Sunday mornings, where no position is privileged, compared with (particularly male) priests and bishops, and no one is divided from another by class, race, gender or sexual orientation. Some of these women might not believe in God at all but valued common humanity, seeing us all having something of the light within, in interdependent relationships with other human beings. As one (theistic) Quaker put it, speaking of the need for tolerance of difference and diversity:

> We need to listen to each other and that's part of our spiritual development, too, and I've just been reading some of the testimonies of our own groups, you know of our own Quaker meeting. We have so much to learn from each other ... we don't need to agree ... we just need to listen: 'So where do these words come from? What is it that makes this person hold that belief so strongly even if I can't?'

Following the work on lived religion it seems appropriate, therefore, to apply to them Aune's suggestion that we collapse the (artificial) distinction between the religious and spiritual and refer to these stances of faith as religio-spiritual.[18]

A problem with the dechurched?

The dechurched – but not atheist – represent, according to demographers David Voas and Ingrid Storm, about half the population of the UK.[19] They term them the 'fuzzy faithful' or 'woolly middle', which I would argue gives the wrong impression, suggesting they are not quite bona fide, a slippery group, and in some ways uncountable: they are neither one thing (having a religious affiliation) nor the other (quite explicitly nonreligious/atheist).[20] However, although this rarely seems to be explained, 'fuzzy' is a technical term taken from set theory.

In classical set theory, what goes into a set is assessed in binary terms: an element either belongs or does not belong to the set, so the religious and the atheists. By contrast, 'fuzzy set theory' is a concept of which the boundaries of application can vary considerably according to context or conditions, instead of being fixed once and for all. A closer definition can be arrived at by examining the context or conditions in which the concept is used. Thus, we need to examine more closely the context that has given rise to the women becoming dechurched practitioners. Coming at this slightly differently, Chandler argues we should not simply see dechurched spirituality as something that is just a personally held stance by a particular individual, based on what she feels is right – a common assumption made of dechurched spirituality. Rather, we should also look at the cultural context from which it emerges.[21] For the dechurched, their religio-spirituality is comprised of a number of elements, very much as Bowman claims.[22] There are elements of official religion – reading the Bible for guidance, praying to a recognizably Christian God; there is something of the folk element – belief in guardian angels, for example, and personal interpretations of particular, intense experiences, aided by a spiritual medium. All of these constitute a personal response, as Bowman says, to particular beliefs and insights gained from experience. They are fuzzy in the classical set theory sense of the word but they are not fuzzy in the more popular sense. They are coherently held views, arrived at through mature reflection, and situated in the particular context of historical time, place, age group, social class and race in which these women find themselves. As Bowman also argues: 'Nobody lives a religious life in a "pure" unadulterated form', and possibly nobody ever did.[23] Bowman includes both the churched and dechurched here.

Conclusion

Women may be both religious and spiritual whether they 'belong' to the institutional church or not. As we see from the example above, dechurched women as well as churchgoing women, may exhibit a number of religio-spiritual beliefs and behaviours. The term 'fuzzy fidelity' may describe these women as far as the large quantitative studies of Voas and Storm are concerned, since they do not tick all the traditionally (often male defined) 'religious' boxes in terms of belongings, beliefs and behaviours. They are only fuzzy in terms of set theory in which it is a neutral term. That is not the point here, however, since we are looking for, and have created, a methodology that enables new categories to emerge that more accurately define women's religio-spirituality, in their own terms, as my data demonstrate, not those of box-ticking exercises. Old rigid formulations do not serve our purpose well and certainly inaccurately reflect religio-spirituality as lived, encompassing as it does the unquantifiable, namely the need for warm relationality and the opportunity for embodied practices. The results of my research method, following Beaman and Beyer suggest it is time to stop viewing 'religion' or 'spirituality' as if it were 'polar (+/−) single and exclusive': indeed, it finds more nuanced approaches to what constitutes the religious and spiritual in a human life. Hence when exploring suitable methods to research women from a broad range of traditions and even, perhaps I should add, from none, we should refuse previously (often male) defined categories. Our subjects deserve their own, which reflect their lives as they live them, not a standard textbook off-the-shelf model. Shakman Hurd argues that 'everyday kind of religion' is the religion of much of the world, where it is often difficult to classify individuals as believers or nonbelievers in a single and stable religious (or spiritual, I would argue) tradition.[24] Dissidents, doubters, those who practise multiple traditions, 'nonorthodox' versions of protected traditions, or no (recognizable) tradition at all, struggle for representation on the faith-based stage. We should also note that the 'theatre' in which this stage is set has been constructed by men (more often than not) who hold the power to decide what may and may not be represented on that stage. Everyday practitioners (churched and dechurched) know, and do/embody, things differently.

Notes

1 Robert C. Fuller, *Spiritual But Not Religious: Understanding Unchurched America* (New York: Oxford University Press, 2001); Leigh Eric Schmidt, *Restless Souls: The Making of American Spirituality. From Emerson to Oprah* (New York: HarperCollins, 2005); David Tacey, *The Spirituality Revolution: The Emergence of Contemporary Spirituality* (Hove and New York: Brunner-Routledge, 2004).

2 David Hay and Kate Hunt, *Understanding the Spirituality of People Who Don't Go to Church: A Report on the Findings of the Adults' Spirituality Project at the University of Nottingham* (Nottingham: University of Nottingham, 2000), 3.

3 Lori G. Beaman and Peter Beyer, 'Betwixt and Between: A Canadian Perspective on the Challenges of Researching the Spiritual but Not Religious', in *Social Identities: Between the Sacred and the Secular* ed. Abby Day, Giselle Vincett and Christopher Cotter (Farnham and Burlington, VT: Ashgate, 2013), 127.

4 Marion Bowman, 'Christianity, Plurality and Vernacular Religion in Early Twentieth-Century Glastonbury: A Sign of Things to Come?' in *Christianity and Religious Plurality: Volume 51: Studies in Church History*, ed. Charlotte Methuen, Andrew Spicer and John Wolffe (Woodbridge: Boydell, 2015).

5 Elizabeth Shakman Hurd, *Expert Religion: The Politics of Religious Difference in an Age of Freedom and Terror* (Badia Fiesolana, Italy: RSCAS, 2015), 3.

6 See also Paul Heelas and Linda Woodhead, *The Spiritual Revolution: Why Religion is Giving Way to Spirituality* (Malden, MA and Oxford: Blackwell, 2005).

7 Callum G. Brown, *The Death of Christian Britain: Understanding Secularization 1800–2000* (London and New York: Routledge, 2001).

8 Ibid., 192.

9 Grace Davie, *Religion in Britain Since 1945: Believing without Belonging* (Oxford: Blackwell, 1994).

10 Grace Davie, 'Vicarious Religion: A Methodological Challenge', in *Everyday Religion*, ed. N. Ammerman (Oxford and New York: Oxford University Press, 2007), 21–35.

11 For discussion of 'ethics of care', see Eva Feder Kittay, *Love's Labor: Essays on Women, Equality, and Dependency* (New York and London: Routledge, 1999); Eva Feder Kittay, Bruce Jennings and Angela A. Wasunna, 'Dependency, Difference and Global Ethic of Longterm Care', *Journal of Political Philosophy* 13, no. 2 (2005): 443–469; Selma Sevenhuijsen, *Citizenship and the Ethic of Care: Feminist Considerations on Justice, Morality and Politics* (London and New York: Routledge, 1998); Joan C. Tronto, *Moral Boundaries: A Political Argument for an Ethic of Care* (New York and London: Routledge, 1993).

12 Thomas Burger, *Max Weber's Theory of Concept Formation: History, Laws and Ideal Types* (Durham, NC: Duke University Press, 1976); Simon Clarke, 'Ideal Type: Conceptions in the Social Sciences', in *International Encyclopedia of the Social and Behavioral Sciences*, ed. N. J Smelser and P. B. Baltes (Amsterdam and Oxford: Elsevier, 2001), 7139–7148.

13 Martin D. Stringer, 'The Sounds of Silence: Searching for the Religious in Everyday Discourse', in *Social Identities*, ed. Vincent Day and Christopher Cotter, 161–171.

14 Janet B. Eccles, 'Speaking Personally: Women Making Meaning through Subjectivised Belief', in *Religion and the Individual: Belief, Practice, Identity*, ed. Abby Day (Aldershot and Burlington, VT: Ashgate, 2008), 19–32.

15 Sariya Cheruvallil-Contractor *et al.*, 'Researching the Non-Religious: Methods and Methodological Issues, Challenges and Controversies', in *Social Identities between the Sacred and the Secular*, ed. Abby Day, Giselle Vincett and Christopher Cotter, 173–189. See also Siobhan Chandler, 'The Social Ethic of Religiously Unaffiliated Spirituality', *Religion Compass* 2, no. 2 (2008): 240–256.

16 Kristin Aune, 'Feminist Spirituality as Lived Religion: How UK Feminists Forge Religio-Spiritual Lives', *Gender and Society* 29, no. 1 (2015): 122–145; Chandler, 'The Social Ethic of Religiously Unaffiliated Spirituality'; Meredith B. McGuire, 'Embodied Practices: Negotiation and Resistance', in *Everyday Religion: Observing Modern Religious Lives*, ed. Nancy Ammerman (Oxford and New York: Oxford University Press, 2007), 187–200; Meredith B. McGuire, *Lived Religion: Faith and Practice in Everyday Life* (Oxford: Oxford University Press, 2008).

17 McGuire, *Lived Religion*: 28.

18 Aune, 'Feminist Spirituality', 122–145.

19 David Voas, 'The Rise and Fall of Fuzzy Fidelity in Europe', *European Sociological Review* 25, no. 2 (2009): 155–168. Ingrid Storm, 'Halfway to Heaven: Four Types of Fuzzy Fidelity in Europe', *Journal for the Scientific Study of Religion* 48, no. 4 (2009): 702–718.

20 See also Chandler, 'The Social Ethic of Religiously Unaffiliated Spirituality'.

21 Ibid., 243.

22 Bowman, 'Christianity, Plurality and Vernacular Religion', 304.

23 Ibid.

24 Shakman Hurd, 'Expert Religion', 7.

Part II
Gathering data

5 'Sometimes you need a question'

Structure and flexibility in feminist interviewing

Fran Porter

Introduction

Feminist research is an emancipatory endeavour. It seeks to liberate girls and women from the social-political, legal and religious constraints that keep them subordinated to men. Such constraints include ways of understanding as well as ways of organizing and infrastructure. The work of liberation involves seeing and deconstructing the mechanisms that oppress, and then reimagining and reconstructing ways of thinking and being that enable girls and women to embody their full and equal human personhood alongside boys and men. While the scope of what this means has enlarged and diversified as it has contextualized, feminist research has always been about more than simply a focus on the female. Rather, it has concerned itself with ending women's oppression, those 'dynamic forces, both personal and social, that diminish or deny the flourishing of women'[1] and girls.

It has been axiomatic in feminist research that the way the research is conducted is integral to fulfilling the goals of the research. So research that is intended to contribute to some aspect of girls' and women's flourishing should not be carried out in ways that diminish the personhood of either researchers or participants. Where there has been debate is about what this means in practice, particularly for female research participants who feminist researchers engage in their investigations. In this chapter I look at one aspect of that debate – the way research interviews are conducted. Consistent with the early claim that is it not a particular research method but rather the way various methods are employed that determines their suitability for feminist research work,[2] I outline my use of structured interview schedules (distinct from semi-structured, unstructured and narrative-pattern interviewing) in exploring the lives of women in two research projects. I introduce the projects, describe aspects of my schedule design, explaining how the interviews proceeded in practice, and I provide examples of the value of, and flexibility possible in, using a structured schedule. I begin with an outline of the broader context in which the choice of interview tool rests.

Feminist critique of androcentric research

Debates about feminist interviewing sit within a broader discussion about research methodology and methods that was prominent particularly in the 1980s and 1990s, namely how dominant, androcentric research paradigms and practices do not serve the interests of women and girls. Feminist researchers argued that, given the (usually unacknowledged) notion that the male is the human norm, research subjects frequently were male, and researchers similarly operated with the biases that go with the assumption of male normativity. So women were often left out of research in terms of focus or as participants. Even when they were included, the questions posed – whether through research hypotheses, questionnaire surveys or qualitative enquiry – reflected male experience and understanding, and this prevented women's realities being recognized or considered. Put another way, the positivist approach to scientific enquiry that initially underpinned (particularly quantitative) social science reflected how men had constructed the world, with patriarchal biases that meant the conception and focus of research questions inevitably obscured, and did nothing to challenge, women's inequality. The emphasis on women's experience that emerged as a theoretical, empirical and analytical category was to counteract the notion that women could simply be annexed to existing frameworks and practices – whether by adding women researchers to carry out research, or adding women as subjects of research.[3] Women's experience, while the focus of much debate and criticism within feminist theory, was – and is – concerned with women's lived realities from the standpoint of female subjectivity rather than male-constructed research enquiries.[4]

The feminist emphasis on ending the silence about women's lives – and ending the silencing of women about their lives[5] – led to feminist researchers making use of qualitative research methods because these allowed for the exploration of meaning-making from participants rather than testing particular researcher-determined hypotheses. In particular, listening to women through qualitative interviewing enabled previously unexplored areas of women's realities to come to the fore. Not only were female participants involved in shaping research outcomes, but also their own words were included in this process as researchers cited their women interviewees by way of providing vibrant and effective evidence of their research arguments.

Despite the value of qualitative interviewing for feminist purposes, this method was also subject to feminist criticism, which challenged the androcentric assumptions of much existing research interview theory and practice. Decades on from Ann Oakley's oft-cited critique, it is helpful to be reminded of how prevalent the rationale and mode of the dominant masculine interview paradigm was when feminist researchers began working in the social sciences. As she demonstrated, interviewing protocols that advocated researchers remain objective and maintain a distance between themselves and interviewees, and treat participants as passive objects of data collection, all in the interests of science, were the norm.[6] In contrast, the subjectivity and involvement of feminist research practice were considered the elements of poor interviewing, with the 'polarity of "proper" and "improper" interviewing . . . an almost classical representation of the widespread gender stereotyping' of modern industrial civilizations.[7] In engaging with their own modes of interviewing with female participants, feminist researchers reflected on their own practice, discussing and debating dynamics of power, reciprocity, responsibility, and vulnerability.

It is awareness of such matters that has meant semi-structured, unstructured and narrative interviewing patterns are often the preferred method for much feminist interview-based research. They are advocated particularly on the grounds of being a woman-centred and more equitable (in terms of power dynamics between researcher and respondent) method that allows for female patterns of conversation. The lack of imposition of a pre-designed order not only may facilitate women to tell their own stories in ways that are comfortable for them, but also prevents a researcher's predetermined agenda being imposed on women's accounts of their lives. While I affirm the value of these looser approaches to interviewing, I want to argue here that a structured interview used flexibly (by which I mean it serves the interview dynamic rather than the dynamic being coerced to fit the schedule) can help women articulate their thoughts and feelings because in order to do this, as one of my interviewees commented, 'sometimes you need a question'.

Using structured interview schedules

Structured interviews

Within the continuum of interview methods, Sharlene Hesse-Biber describes unstructured interviews as ones in which

> I have a basic interview plan in mind, but I have a *minimum of control* over how the participant would answer the question. I am often taking the lead from my participants – going where they want to go, but keeping an overall topic in mind.[8]

A semi-structured interview makes use of an interview guide in which there is a list of written questions to be covered, but the order in which this is done is not a particular concern. Rather they are questions 'I might try to interject during the interview'.[9] Hence, the interviewer has some control in terms of the sequence of questions and the specific content of each question, but 'I am still open to asking new questions, on-the-fly, throughout the interview. I have an agenda; but it is not tightly determined, and there is room left for spontaneity on the part of the researcher and interviewee'.[10] Structured interviewing is where the researcher has 'total control over the agenda of the interview . . . All participants are asked the same set of questions in a specific order'.[11] Epitomized in the survey, which often though not necessarily uses closed questions, this is the opposite end of the continuum to narrative interviewing, which 'goes further than any other interview method in avoiding pre-structuring the interview'.[12]

I describe below my use of structured interview schedules used flexibly, arguing that the flexibility is an essential part of a feminist use of the tool of structured questions. Hence, it may be asked, is this not rather a version towards one end of the semi-structured interview spectrum? After all, I will describe how I interjected supplementary questions, and how the question order came to be changed and even some of the questions obsolete, and in one case abandoned altogether, depending on the course of the particular interview. However, it is the following of a high structure versus low structure[13] that makes me continue to class it as structured. For, as far as made sense, it was a deliberate choice to ask the same questions to all participants, in a particular order, and not have the questions or the order evolve as the interviews progressed.

The research projects

I have used structured depth interview schedules in two research projects with women. The first of these projects was for my doctoral research, which was a feminist engagement with Christianity with particular reference to Northern Ireland.[14] I investigated the mechanisms involved in sustaining, and the resources available for challenging, women's secondary status within Christianity. I focused on four areas intrinsic to women's Christian faith experience: women's understanding of God; women's personal identity (their self-understanding); women's relationship to church institutions; and some of their life experiences. For this 'Faith and Feminism' research, I interviewed fifty-five women, ensuring a range of four criteria were represented: denomination (from Catholic and the range of Protestant churches); theological spectrum, which crosses denominations; age, from those in their twenties to seventies; and geographical location from throughout Northern Ireland. For each woman interviewed, I used the same structured interview schedule of thirty-two questions (some of which had follow-up questions depending on the answers received). For clarity in the purposes of this chapter, I will draw mainly on examples from this research. My experience of the value of this application of structured interviews encouraged me to use it again.

The second research project explored the church, community and political participation of evangelical Protestant women in Northern Ireland.[15] In Northern Ireland's evangelicalism, as elsewhere, the enormous social changes in the lives of women in the latter half of the twentieth century were often represented as threatening to norms of gender, family and society, this perspective being endorsed by forms of Christian theology and church practice. This 'Between Culture and Theology' project, which began late 1999, was carried out in the wake of the 1998 Belfast Agreement, intrinsic to which was, at the time, a UK-leading social agenda of equality,[16] and this sat alongside the political accommodations for which the Agreement is better known. While women's church and community activism was well established, the peace process of the 1990s had given greater visibility to women's political involvement. This project explored a variety of issues[17] faced by evangelical women in particular, as they were increasingly involved and visible in church, civic and public life.

For 'Between Culture and Theology' I interviewed seventy women and ten men from evangelical Protestantism. Each woman was initially identified because of her church, community or political participation, but many had diverse experience both within and across these boundaries, which I sought to capture through three separate but parallel interview schedules. These schedules had a total of twenty-eight potential questions, (some of which had follow-up questions depending on the answers received), that meant also that women's employment experience that was separate from her church, community or political involvement could be included if appropriate. The ten men interviewed were all church leaders for which interviews I designed a structured schedule of sixteen questions.[18]

The research questions

No research begins without context or questions to explore – whether these are clearly formulated hypotheses and objectives, enquiries into particular subject matters under scrutiny, or more akin to research hunches to be investigated. This is true whatever methods are employed to pursue the research in question. Even in narrative interviewing there is an *'initial central topic designed to trigger a self-sustainable narration'*.[19] For 'Faith and Feminism', I was investigating empirically the multiple and interconnected ways in which Christian women's inequality and subordination was perpetuated and the means whereby this might be challenged. I did so at a time when there was little published work of empirical engagement with a feminist critique of Christianity,[20] and none at all based in Northern Ireland in which the realities of its particular sectarian conflict further contextualized the experience of women there. And I chose to explore this feminist engagement by using a structured interview schedule based around the four areas (of God, self, church and life experience) I had identified.

In hindsight, I recognize that I had been influenced by a positivist approach in using the same questions with each interviewee. Having conducted a secondary analysis of quantitative data regarding Christian women in Northern Ireland for my master's research, I knew that a qualitative method would provide the 'greater depth rather than breadth'[21] that my current research question required. In wanting to cover specific areas and particular avenues of enquiry (see below), I would say I assumed that set questions were the appropriate method to choose in that they would give each woman the same invitation, as it were, to respond. But I was also very aware that I did not want to impose my own thinking on my interviewees, and this would be more of a motivation than the notion of objectivity or distance. While the choice of an unstructured interview means that 'the unfolding process of the interview itself, being amendable to shaping by the interviewee, could become a significant feature of analysis',[22] I contend that the same can be true for the way women respond to particular questions – and indeed, the comparison between the different types of response can also be revealing.

Whatever the method used, analysis involves interpretation by the researcher who is dealing not with a solo voice, but with a chorus – sometimes harmonious and sometimes discordant. 'Ultimately we have to take responsibility for the decisions we make, rather than trying to deny the power that we do have as researchers'.[23] I was very aware that each interview constituted an integrated whole; in some cases there was a gradual uncovering of Christian faith experience as additional questions produced responses that elucidated, clarified, provided context for or interpreted earlier ones. In my analysing therefore, while inevitably extracting various elements of each interview and choosing small sections of speech to include in my texts, I did so with the overall individual interview context very much in mind and in so doing sought to be faithful to the meaning of the story as it was given to me (even when my interpretation and explanation of it was different from the woman in question). In that sense I endeavoured to respect and not distort or misuse the thoughts and experiences of the women who so freely talked to me. The distinction always to be made, therefore, is that their stories are their own, while the analysis and use of them in my research is mine.

Faithful representation of women's individual and collective stories and of their complex realities is required by feminist research's aim to contribute to, and not to detract from, women's personhood. One reader (not an interviewee) of the published work of the 'Between Culture and Theology' project wrote to me appreciative of what she described as 'balanced' and 'authenticated' expression in the book that reflected much of her own experience and thinking. Balance has never been something I have strived for, but she was, I think, responding to the comprehensive and fair inclusion of views, opinions and experiences regarding women's participation in church, community and politics. While outside the scope of this chapter, if women can recognize themselves and their worlds in research findings, that can allow the research to make a constructive contribution to women's lives, which is one of the aims of feminist research. I mention it here because it illustrates that using a structured interview schedule can elicit voices and stories whereby not only interviewees but also readers of the research can recognize their realities.

Schedule design

Before describing my process, it is helpful to underscore that structured interview schedules do not in and of themselves make analysis of interview transcripts simpler or more straightforward. Even apart from the flexibility in practice that interrupts any neat schema of questions, there is no guaranteed correspondence between responses to a particular question and the presentation of findings. Women's lives are not neatly compartmentalized and neither are their responses and reflections. Nor do women respond alike depending on the style of interview chosen; even following a highly structured interview schedule, some women respond in more narrative style. Further, as I note below, sometimes it is the contrasting answers to related questions that inform analysis. While using a structured interview schedule did help in sorting thematically through transcript data, it does not shortcut the task of coding, comparing and analysis. The need for alertness, thoroughness and systematic handling of data is not diminished.

In constructing my interview schedules I began with general areas I wished to explore, from which I constructed my schedule of questions. For 'Faith and Feminism' I did one interview with a volunteer (with research experience) who then gave me feedback, after which I made substantial changes to my questions. I then carried out five pilot interviews with women representative of my selection criteria. In addition to the questions on my schedule, I asked these five women if there were any other questions they thought I should ask although none were offered. The only change I made to the interview schedule was to delete two words from a question for clarification purposes and I therefore was able to include the five pilot interviews in my main data. Particularly encouraging was one interviewee who in one section anticipated the next question in her current answer on five consecutive occasions indicating the development of theme that I had been aiming to capture in the question order. This anticipation from one question to the next occurred regularly throughout the interviews.

The interview schedule began with some general questions about the women themselves – their family and church backgrounds and current contexts, employment experiences, and 'Would you mind telling me your age?' As I had extended invitations to participate in my research through thirteen separate groups/organizations (in order to ensure participants representing the four criteria outlined above), I did not always know very much about the women before meeting them for the interview.[24] These initial enquiries also helped in settling into the interview, although some general conversation upon meeting and putting the kettle on had usually occurred. I then proceeded to explore the four areas on which I was concentrating: God, self, church institution and life experience, two of which I consider in more detail here (although I can give only the merest indicators of the wealth of data elicited). I generally began with invitations to descriptive responses before questions more directed at analytical reflections. Many of the questions were open to a variety of responses from the women and I tried to make them as broad as possible, not assuming the answer would be in a certain direction. I also had some specific questions because there were things I wanted to know.

I began with women's church involvement as I considered this to offer more concrete situations, which would be easier to talk about at the beginning of the interview. I asked five core questions with follow-ups/prompts when necessary:

C1. How are you involved in your church – what kinds of things do you do?

Does the church encourage you in this? Support you?

Would you like to do other things in the church?

C2. Would you generally like to see women involved in the church more?

(Doing what kinds of things?)

Why/why not?

C3. How free do you feel to express your own views and opinions in and about your church?

Why is this?

Do you do this often?

What kind of response do you get?

C4. Does your church use inclusive or exclusive language – by which I mean does it talk about man and men when it means all human beings and only use hymns and prayers with brother in it, etc.?

How do you feel about this – is it important to you?

C5. Are there any particular female figures from the Bible or Christian history that have strongly influenced your faith or life?

My first question focused on each woman's own involvement (C1), how she perceived it was viewed in the church, and whether there were other things she would like to do. Among other things, what responses to this question gave me was a long and varied list of what women did, underscoring their place as 'the backbone of the church . . . the bulk of the attenders and everything and the strength of the church'.[25] Attention to where the numbers of women were concentrated, however, confirmed there was a sexual division of labour within churches with the majority of women's lay involvement concerned with a variety of tasks generally assigned low status and that are more often considered women's domain. Much of this is the 'housework' role and responsibility for children that women typically occupy outside of the churches, much of it being unseen.

My second question broadened out to ask each woman whether she wanted to see more women involved in the church (C2). This allowed for a more gender-conscious response (which might be affirmation or resistance). It also endeavoured to uncouple preferences for women's involvement from each woman's sense of her own capacities or desires. My intention in these two broad questions about how the women might wish themselves or other women to be involved was to allow for each woman's own interpretation of how they saw women's contribution to their denominational life. I deliberately did not pose this in terms of her or other women's actual or potential leadership involvement or ask about particular roles that may be construed in those terms. The interviews took place during 1996–1997 against a background of a figure for Northern Ireland of 70 per cent active church membership in 1990,[26] yet, in 1999, no more than 9 per cent women among the ordained leaders in each of the three largest Protestant churches.[27] I wished neither to ignore the relevance of women in leadership roles, nor reduce the meaning of women's participation only to matters of access to leadership. Indeed, women's status within Christianity involves a more thoroughgoing analysis than whether women have formal access to leadership positions.[28]

While women themselves raised the question of leadership, this broad approach to women's church involvement also elicited responses about other areas of church life the interviewees thought currently excluded or needed women's gifts, presence or particular contribution. While some of these responses reflect the persistence of a sexual dualism that feminists have long argued is part of the controlling mechanism of patriarchy, they indicate that women from across the theological spectrum knew that women's contribution was about more than leadership and that the barriers prohibiting their wider participation were about more than the formal permissions. Underpinning many comments was the notion of church institutions insufficiently valuing women's contributions – of whatever sort. Women across the denominations and ages, including those who assigned overall leadership positions to men and did not support women's ordination, spoke with passion and in some depth about what they experienced and witnessed more generally about this sense of disvaluing. Further, around half of the interviewees specifically used some form of the term 'value' in their descriptions. In some interview processes, researchers will change the questions asked as interviews progress and they begin to see the important themes to be explored. Helen Thorne, for example, in her mixed-method study of the first women priests in the Church of England, pursued in a second set of interviews themes that had been introduced through comments on completed questionnaires, ensuring also that her interviewees included priests in contexts that had not been addressed yet in her research.[29] However, while my theme around value or, rather, lack of valuing became apparent early in the interview process, I did not introduce it into my interviews, keeping to my set questions, and still the theme kept emerging. While it could be argued that the questions implicitly invited comment on value, it is also true that the matter of value was never forced on any of the women, who were neither required to defend nor encouraged to complain about their particular churches. The unsolicited and unforced nature of this theme, I argue, underscores its merit as a finding. It also opens up the subject to show more about what is really going on with the way women are treated within church institutions, revealing the dominance of androcentric and patriarchal thinking and structures.

My third question (C3) invited women to reflect further on their relationship to their churches. Responses revealed a reticence among women to offend, and their various strategies for conflict avoidance. In analysing the data, there were clear links with responses to my questions on women's personal development and sense of self. My fourth question was specific about gendered language (C4); it was something I wanted to know so I asked a direct question, explaining what I meant as, at the time, I could not assume the phrase was well known. My final question in this section about female figures influencing the interviewees (C5) I now consider a bad question. In trying to get the balance between open and more particular questions, this question did not work well. It did not produce much data and many women clearly struggled to think of any particular influential female figures. A more useful question would have been to ask whether there were any significant people in the women's faith lives, which would have shown whether there were such figures, and whether males predominated for the women.

I used a similar pattern of questions for asking the women about God:

G1. How would you describe God?

G2. How do you feel about God at the present time?

G3. How do you think God would describe and feel about you?

G4. How well do you relate to the image of God as a father?

G5. Do you ever think of God in other ways? (Prompt if necessary: for example, the Bible uses images of God as creator, rock, spirit, mother).

If so are these helpful?

If not, do you think you would find it helpful to use such images?

G6. Statistics show that more women believe in God than men do. Why do you think this is?

G7. Do you think God is male?

G8. What do you think your understanding of God offers you as a woman?

My opening question asking for descriptions of God (G1) produced a variety of often very imaginative expressions, both personal and impersonal, relational as well as behavioural descriptions. While 'father' was the single image mentioned the most, only five women offered it as an exclusive term and most women offered a mix of images of God and God's activities. For my fourth question I asked how well the women related to the particular image of God as father (G4), which may have been prompted by the first question, but not inevitably. Another direct question was whether they thought God was male (G7). Twenty women thought God was male, sixteen thought that God was not, with some women expressing the view that God had no gender or was above gender. Despite this variety of understanding, however, all but four of the fifty-five women interviewed used 'he', 'his', or 'him' when referring to God, either frequently or at some point in the interview, indicating the prevalence of masculine terminology for God. Some women's articulation of how rooted is such language, sometimes despite what they believe, was as heartfelt as some women's resistance to any female metaphors for God.

Interview questions concerning women's sense of themselves then followed – I had deliberately not started with such potential introspection (my first question in this section was 'I would like to know how you understand yourself, how you see yourself?' with a potential prompt if required, 'Tell me how you'd like to be described/the ways you like to be known'). In introducing the fourth area of significant life events, in order to flesh out what could have been heard as a rather abstract idea, I gave each woman a list of the kind of life events/stages in which I was interested, stressing that it was not exhaustive, but that it gave them concrete examples of the kind of thing to which I was referring. A few women worked their way through this list, others read it and chose some topics, and others needed no prompting. The interview schedule concluded with an invitation for the women to say anything else that they wished. I also invited them to contact me after I had gone if with hindsight there was anything they wished to add to their story and this happened on one occasion.

I had designed some of the questions to cover similar aspects of my enquiry but from different entry points. In part this gave the women the opportunity to approach a subject in a variety of ways, different women responding to different types of questions, but it also had the potential to reveal inconsistencies within the thinking of one individual woman. Asking therefore about, for example, their description of God (G1), the image of God as father and other images of God (G4 & G5), the use of inclusive language in church (C5), and whether the women thought God was male (G7), did at times produce responses that conflicted with each other, and the explanatory reasons were an integral part of my analysis. The way the conversations occurred in fact lent towards exploring the various themes from a variety of questions, as there is much overlap and integration between the four areas of God, self, church institutions, and life experience. Similarly, in the 'Between Culture and Theology' research, the third question I asked each interviewee was, 'How have you been received as a woman doing what you do?' While women sometimes spoke at this point about not wanting to focus on gender and claiming that this made no difference, later on in the interview when talking about issues of authority, domestic responsibilities and leadership, other stories emerged that suggested gender was an issue, and some women acknowledged this themselves despite their earlier answer. Such question structure is not designed to catch women out. It is rather to help uncover the complexities of our lives, and in some instances, a specific question gives women permission to talk about certain things such as conflict in their working relationships (which was my fourth and a specific question). As with the 'Faith and Feminism' research, the 'Between Culture and Theology' interviews uncovered women avoiding conflict by their pre-emptive behaviour and attitudes, indicating that they carried, often unacknowledged, the responsibility for harmony in many situations.

Interview praxis

Despite the rigidity that may be summoned up by the idea of using a highly structured interview schedule, not least with what to those experienced in narrative interviewing may appear the daunting prospect of having around 30 questions to ask in a qualitative interview context, the dynamics of such interviews can have the feel and practice of informality. In the 'Faith and Feminism' research, the majority (forty-five) of the interviews lasted between one and a half and two and a half hours. All but three took place in the homes of the women and I was fortunate in that most of the interviews were conducted in relaxed settings with few time constraints. There were some exceptions: on one occasion an interview that lasted for three hours had twelve interruptions, including one for the interviewee to make refreshments for her ordained husband's visitors, and we also moved room. On another occasion I followed a woman around her kitchen with the tape recorder competing with the kitchen extractor fan while she made the family dinner. However, most interviews were relaxed and ran their course, easily coping with interruptions for children, the telephone, tea refills and toilet breaks! I met husbands, children and family pets (one interview was conducted with a cat ensconced on my knee).

The hospitality, interest and openness of the women was evident as I 'tea and caked' (and sometimes had meals) my way around Northern Ireland. I found as Janet Finch that the experience is one of 'being welcomed into the interviewee's home as a guest, not merely tolerated as an inquisitor';[30] in one case I was invited to sign the visitors' book. While the combined interview time for the 55 interviews was 86 hours, I actually spent a total of 135 hours of visiting time with the women. Indeed, it was sometimes in the time after the interview was officially concluded that a few women became more forthcoming about their thoughts, not I believe out of a distrust of the actual interview itself, but out of feeling more relaxed and at ease in social conversation than they were when focused so much on themselves. When these conversations yielded something a woman wanted included in her account, the information given was added to my interview notes.

In terms of the interviews themselves, while usually keeping to the interview schedule, I generally let the women take each question wherever they wished and in whatever manner. This was sometimes time-consuming – on one occasion a woman took a forty-five-minute detour in responding to a simple demographic question and, due to the way she narrated her stories, it was just not possible for me to interrupt her and redirect her thoughts at that point without, I felt, seeming rude or uninterested. I soon became so familiar with the question schedule that I could use it from memory and I am sure that helped the flow of the interviews. When an interviewee herself made a link to a subject covered by a later question in the schedule, I sometimes went there next, or when the question arose in order, would link back to the earlier comment to elicit further response. Such jumping across the schedule worked well.

For example, women may well have introduced the matter of inclusive language (C4) at an earlier stage in the interview, and this demonstrated how women linked their sense of participation and value with matters of linguistic visibility. At any stage, I would offer unscripted follow-up questions for clarification or to push further as appropriate depending on how the women responded. On one occasion I abandoned the schedule altogether as within the first few questions about her church involvement one woman spoke about how her life had been touched by significant family discord, physical attack, sectarian intimidation, mental illness and sexual abuse. After such disclosure, to continue with the schedule simply would have been absurd. As we talked through her life experiences and her thoughts and reflections all but two of the questions were in fact covered.

Flexibility is essential in using a structured interview schedule so that it serves the desired interview dynamic rather than the dynamic being coerced to fit the schedule. Hence, feminist commitment to an ethical approach to research participants in terms of the demeanour of the researcher and the rapport established with the interviewee can be exercised as much with a structured interview tool as with those of looser structure.

Conclusion

The potential of a structured interview wherein women not only have an opportunity to express themselves, but are facilitated in this in the very act of being asked, was summed up by one interviewee: 'Sometimes you need a question . . . And if we're not asked we can't begin to think of the answers so I actually think that this is good'.[31] Another woman spoke of the interview as 'a way of consolidating your faith' for 'it's been a learning experience for me to stop and to look back and to think about, you know, where I'm coming from, where am I going to and where I'd like [to be]'. For one woman, such benefit was anticipated:

> I was interested in doing the interview because even from the perspective of developing, or reviewing, you know, how my own perspective or attitude towards God or church had developed. Because it isn't a topic that I've ever specifically focused on.

Having multiple questions was not viewed as mechanistic or restrictive, rather the interview experience was spoken of as empowering and constructive:

> The thing about doing something like this is sometimes, sometimes I hear myself speak and that's good for me because it gives me clarity, it gives me direction and it gives me hope ... It's not only being heard by another person but hearing yourself ... It's in hearing myself, being heard, and then gaining understanding.

Self-expression, being heard, and understanding leading to clarity, direction and hope are all consistent with the purposes of feminist research, in this instance facilitated by a structured approach.

Notes

1 Serene Jones, *Feminist Theory and Christian Theology: Cartographies of Grace* (Minneapolis: Fortress Press, 2000), 71.
2 This claim particularly relates to the debate about the merits of qualitative rather than quantitative research, as discussed, for example, in Nicole Westmarland, 'The Quantitative/Qualitative Debate and Feminist Research: A Subjective View of Objectivity', *Forum Qualitative Sozialforschung/Forum: Qualitative Social Research* 2, no. 1, Art. 13 (2001), accessed 29 June 2016, www.qualitative-research.net/index.php/fqs/article/view/974.
3 Sandra Harding, 'Introduction: Is there a Feminist Methodology?' in *Feminism and Methodology*, ed. Sandra Harding (Milton Keynes: Open University Press, 1987), 1–14.
4 See the discussion in Joey Sprague, *Feminist Methodologies for Critical Researchers*, 2nd ed. (Lanham, MD: Rowman & Littlefield, 2016). Feminist theological contributions on women's experience include: Linda Hogan, *From Women's Experience to Feminist Theology* (Sheffield: Sheffield Academic Press, 1995) and Rebecca Chopp and Sheila Greeve Davaney, eds, *Horizons in Feminist Theology* (Minneapolis: Fortress Press, 1997).
5 Marjoire L. Devault, 'Talking and Listening from Women's Standpoint: Feminist Strategies for Interviewing and Analysis', *Social Problems* 37, no. 1 (1990): 96–116.
6 Ann Oakley, 'Interviewing Women: A Contradiction in Terms', in *Doing Feminist Research*, ed. H. Roberts (London: Routledge and Kegan Paul, 1981), 30–61.
7 Oakley, 'Interviewing Women', 38.
8 Sharlene Nagy Hesse-Biber, 'Feminist Approaches to In-Depth Interviewing', in *Feminist Research Practice: A Primer*, ed. Sharlene Nagy Hesse-Biber, (London: Sage, 2014), 186.
9 Ibid., 187.
10 Ibid.
11 Ibid.
12 Sandra Jovchelovitch and Martin W. Bauer, 'Narrative Interviewing', in *Qualitative Research with Text, Image and Sound: A Practical Handbook*, ed. Martin W. Bauer and George Gaskell (London: Sage, 2000), 62.
13 Hesse-Biber, 'Feminist Approaches', 188.
14 Fran Porter, 'Faith and Feminism: Women's Christian Faith Experience in Northern Ireland' (DPhil thesis, University of Ulster, 1999) published as Fran Porter, *It Will Not Be Taken Away from Her: A Feminist Engagement with Women's Christian Experience* (London: Darton Longman & Todd, 2004).
15 Fran Porter, *Changing Women, Changing Worlds: Evangelical Women in Church, Community and Politics* (Belfast: Blackstaff, 2002).
16 Section 75 of the 1998 Northern Ireland Act placed a statutory obligation on public authorities in Northern Ireland to have due regard to the need to promote equality of opportunity within nine categories, including that between women and men, and as such was the most extensive positive duty imposed in the UK.
17 Around the themes of participation, inclusion, difference, authority, domesticity and priority (that is, the relative importance of considering women's involvement).

18 All four interview schedules are available from Porter, *Changing Women*, 227–235.

19 Jovchelovitch and Bauer, 'Narrative Interviewing', 62.

20 The only British study I found was Alison R. Webster, *Found Wanting: Women, Christianity and Sexuality* (London: Cassell: 1995); the other seven journal and book texts were on studies based in the USA.

21 Janet Parr, 'Theoretical Voices and Women's Own Voices: The Stories of Mature Women Students', in *Feminist Dilemmas in Qualitative Research: Private Lives and Public Texts*, ed. Jane Ribbens and Rosalind Edwards (London: Sage, 1998): 89.

22 Nicola Slee, *Women's Faith Development: Patterns and Processes* (Aldershot: Ashgate, 2004), 54.

23 Jane Ribbens, 'Interviewing – an "Unnatural Situation"?' *Women's Studies International Forum* 12, no. 6 (1989): 590.

24 In all I circulated over 800 letters to the 13 groups via various gatekeepers. I received 76 responses, from which I interviewed 55.

25 Anglican woman interviewee.

26 Peter Brierley and David Longley, *UK Christian Handbook*, 1992/1993 ed. (London: Marc Europe, 1991).

27 These figures are for all of Ireland: Methodist Church in Ireland (MCI), 8 per cent; Presbyterian Church in Ireland (PCI), 5 per cent; Church of Ireland, 9 per cent (the figure for Northern Ireland was 6 per cent). Figures were supplied, respectively, by MCI Minutes of Conference 1998; Office of PCI; and General Synod Office. The Church of Ireland began ordaining women as priests in 1990, PCI first ordained women in 1976 and MCI in 1974.

28 I explore this in Fran Porter, *Women and Men after Christendom: The Dis-Ordering of Gender Relationships* (Milton Keynes: Paternoster, 2015).

29 In particular, those in chaplaincy roles and mothers. Helen Thorne, *Journey to Priesthood: An In-Depth Study of the First Women Priests in the Church of England* (Bristol: Centre for Comparative Studies in Religion and Gender, 2000): 51, 56.

30 Janet Finch, '"It's Great to Have Someone to Talk To": Ethics and Politics of Interviewing Women', in *Social Research: Philosophy, Politics and Practice*, ed. Martyn Hammersley (London: Sage, 1993), 167.

31 All the interviewee quotations in this section are from 'Faith and Feminism'.

6 Exploring young adults' faith lives through video diaries

Consent, voice and power

Sarah-Jane Page

Introduction

Utilising visual approaches in research has become ever more popular in recent years, especially within sociology.[1] Despite their muted presence within the sociology of religion[2] some are incorporating visual methods, especially projects involving young people.[3] Adopting apparatus such as cameras and video technology can enable research to become more participant-led, generating new perspectives from which to understand social life. Such collaborative endeavours complement feminist approaches to data collection where hierarchies between researcher and researched are challenged.[4] But critical reflection is necessary to interrogate how far this is achievable, or whether new vulnerabilities and hierarchies emerge. This chapter will critically assess these issues, using a feminist lens. First, I will consider the background literature in relation to feminist approaches to research and visual methods more generally. Then I will reflect on three issues: consent, voice and power/hierarchy. I conclude by reflecting on the implications of using this method when researching the faith lives of women and girls.

This chapter will utilize data compiled from the 'Religion, Youth and Sexuality: A Multi-Faith Exploration' project,[5] which used video diaries to capture 'lived religion'.[6] This method accompanied two others – questionnaires and in-depth interviews – and was used as a complementary tool to access a layered understanding of the everyday social worlds of young religious adults aged between 18 and 25 and living in the UK.

Feminist approaches to research

Feminist research approaches are concerned with examining the way social reality is gendered, and recognising how the very process of research has traditionally operated on privileged gender hierarchies.[7] Feminist projects are therefore highly reflexive, recognizing 'the fact that the researchers' choice of methods, of research topic and of study group population are always political acts'.[8] Despite this general commitment to examining the conditions upon which research is produced, and the critical awareness of the gendered implications of research processes, there is much diversity in how feminist projects are undertaken. Feminists use a plethora of methods available to them.[9] Therefore, while what unites feminist researchers is a commitment to a feminist methodology, how this is realized through the research design, methods used, analysis cultivated, and how findings are disseminated, will vary considerably.

There is a general perception that feminist approaches are highly compatible with qualitative methods, emphasized through much-used methods such as in-depth interviews, allowing participants to detail their experiences in their own words and in their own time. This is seen as undermining hierarchies between the researcher and 'the researched'.[10] Such methods are understood as being able to cultivate accounts from women who have traditionally been silenced in research.[11] Nevertheless, feminists have also cultivated a critical awareness that qualitative methods are not inherently participatory – as both Oakley and Letherby highlight, historically, the research interview was conceived in terms of detachment of the researcher, with the aim of creating 'objective' data.[12] The classical research interview was constructed in terms of an active researcher and a passive respondent.[13] But even feminist-inspired interviews can be critiqued for the extent to which a participatory and non-exploitative experience is being cultivated.[14] Finch's experience of interviewing clergy wives highlighted the hierarchies that emerged around developing rapport.[15] Her participants readily talked to her; Finch's disclosure that she was also a clergy wife consolidated trust. But Finch questions the rapport generated, arguing that rather than diminishing research hierarchies, it actually made her participants *over* trusting, generating potential for exploitation. In a similar vein, Stacey argues that there are implicit and hidden exploitative relationships in the interview method, meaning that they may be *more* exploitative than traditional positivist approaches.[16] The researcher and participant still exist in an unequal relationship but this inequality is masked when couched in terms of flattening hierarchies and creating rapport, so that the exploitative effects are hidden.

These examples emphasize some of the key dilemmas experienced in feminist research, namely, the power dynamics that emerge and the extent to which hierarchies can be diminished, as well as the extent to which participants themselves are allowed to give consent to their participation, and how their voice is recognized and understood. Feminist researchers manage these issues by critically interrogating the research process through on-going reflexivity,[17] at all stages of the research. This approach therefore does not contain ethical engagement to the start of the research journey when ethical clearance is being negotiated, but rather positions the researcher as actively reflecting on the research process as it unfolds.

Visual methods

There has been a proliferation in visual methods in the social sciences in recent years.[18] Despite this new-found visibility, visual methods have a long history in social science, dating back to the nineteenth century.[19] But visual methods became unpopular in the early twentieth century, deemed too 'unscientific' by emerging disciplines that wanted to 'prove' themselves conversant with the natural sciences.[20] The rekindled interest, occurring after the 1960s, was partly due to new theoretical insights that challenged the view that the social sciences should mirror the natural sciences, and partly due to advances in technology.[21] In the contemporary period, visual forms surround us, with the number of images we engage with on a day-to-day basis proliferating.[22] This is also connected to technological innovation, such as smart-phone technology enabling individuals to have the potential to take a photograph or video recording at a moment's notice.[23]

Researchers have started to realize the potential of these technologies, and the ability to create innovative approaches to research that can enable access to different forms of knowledge. A good example is using photo elicitation with children. Dunlop and Ward explored young Polish migrants' lifeworlds through photography.[24] Participants were given cameras and asked to take photographs of things that were significant to them. What such an approach enables is a different account of participants' lives, and a different means of accessing the social worlds of those who are traditionally more difficult to research. An understanding of the meanings attached to the photographs can later be generated through a photo elicitation interview, where participants explain the photographs and their significance. Such approaches are often seen as empowering vulnerable groups, as participants maintain control over the production of the visual output.[25]

This also highlights the ways in which visual methods are deemed to be participatory, with the potential for visual methods to minimize power imbalances. Taylor and Snowdon, who asked participants to draw mind maps in their research project with queer Christians, articulate that:

> (t)he distinction between researcher and researched can become destabilized through the use of visual approaches due to a greater transference of autonomy and authority over to the participant. This transferring of responsibility can create the potential for marginalized groups to 'show' and speak through their experiences with greater authorial confidence.[26]

Meanwhile in Dunlop and Ward's example of using cameras in research, participants are enabled to take the pictures they want, and are therefore making the decisions.[27] This offers a parallel to feminist approaches, but it also demonstrates some of the aforementioned pitfalls. For example, although participants may have a key part to play in the production of visual methods, they are not necessarily involved in the analysis and representation of data. Visual methods that are participant-led may also lead to greater burdens placed on participants. As Muir and Mason note, their video diary participants expressed ambivalence and irritation at being responsible for collecting data, some feeling that it interfered with their day, and others being uncomfortable in portraying themselves in visual terms.[28]

The 'Religion, Youth and Sexuality' project deployed video diaries, 'a method which captures not only the narratives of experience and lived cultural practices but also the visual nature of the construction and display of identities'.[29] This involved giving participants digital video cameras, enabling them to record their reflections over the course of about a week. Ammerman and Williams note that as researchers start to map lived religion, they become concerned with the everyday processes and practices of living out one's religion, rather than solely focusing on religious hierarchies and 'official' practices.[30] This creates the impetus for religion researchers to begin to explore different methods and different means through which they can understand the world. Ammerman and Williams emphasize not only that visual approaches can enhance our understanding of the everyday, but also that diaried approaches are well placed to capture 'the mundane happenings of everyday life',[31] which are harder to ascertain through other methods. Therefore the video diary is well placed not only to map the visual worlds of religious young adults, but also to elicit their narratives about their everyday worlds. As the diary is explicitly focused on the moment-by-moment and mundane routines of life, it does something different to a life history interview, which is more concerned with mapping the seismic shifts and major events that have happened in one's life.[32]

Focusing on the everyday narratives of individuals is situated in a broader context where '(s)tories have recently moved centre stage in social thought'.[33] Narratives are understood as being inextricably tied to conveying one's identity, and as identity comes to be something researchers are increasingly interested in, narratives become pivotal to this exploration.[34] But Plummer argues that this telling of one's narrative is socially constituted; some stories are 'allowed' to be told while others are silenced. This is because the individual story is positioned in broader social contexts – as Lawler argues, '(s)tories circulate culturally, providing a means of making sense of that world, and also providing the materials with which people construct personal narratives as a means of constructing personal identities'.[35] So a narrative does not occur out of nowhere, but is socially positioned and encoded. As Plummer argues, the story itself will be heard in a certain way; elements may be omitted or elaborated, depending on the audience. So a narrative is never a neutral account of one's life, but is co-produced in relation to wider contexts and the intended (imagined) audience.[36]

Narratives constitute a particular kind of self that is made manifest when video diaries are deployed. As Holliday articulates, the video diary offers a performative narrative, reminiscent of Foucault's confessional.[37] While the confessional has traditionally been understood as a religious practice where the Catholic believer confesses their sins to the priest, Foucault demonstrates the proliferation of a confessional culture in a more secular society, epitomized through the talk-show cultures of *Jerry Springer*.[38] This emphasizes not only storytelling as culturally encoded, thereby having an impact on how a video diary is produced and created, but also that this type of identity-narrativization cultivates a particular kind of self, embedded within Western norms. Brison highlights how Western philosophy promotes the idea that the self is made through the stories we tell.[39] Utilizing the philosophy of John Locke, Brison emphasizes how selfhood is determined by one's ability to tell a story, thereby demonstrating a self that is coherent and stable. The video diary itself becomes a product of this understanding of selfhood and identity. Holliday emphasizes that as a technique that is self-directed by participants, they come to imagine their audience in the telling of the video diary, and thereby construct their account on their own terms.[40] They reveal what they want to reveal. They focus on elements of their day that they can narrativize. Nevertheless, despite the rather mundane topics Holliday had asked her participants to reflect on, she observed the candour and honesty that participants conveyed, reminiscent of its links to a confessional format.

For the 'Religion, Youth and Sexuality' project, participants undertook a video diary once they had participated in both a questionnaire and an interview. The choice of a video diary was motivated by the youth demographic of our sample. Young people are embedded in technical social worlds – giving them a diary to write did not seem right given the youth cultures within which they were embedded.[41] Given that video diary formats are common within youth culture, evidenced through the proliferation of YouTube videos and the Diary Room on *Big Brother*, we used this method as a format that young adults would be culturally familiar with.[42] We were keen to allow participants the space to articulate their views in the absence of the researcher. Given that the topic of the research was extremely sensitive, yet also wanting to cultivate data on religion as lived, the video diary gave participants the option to disclose as little or as much as they wanted about their religious and sexual lives. While 693 people completed an on-line questionnaire for the research, 61 were interviewed, and 24 of these individuals participated in a video diary. Individuals were selected at each stage on the basis of diversity in terms of key factors such as religiosity, strength of religiosity, gender, sexual orientation, location and relationship status.

Research reflections

As articulated at the start of this chapter, feminists are concerned with cultivating reflexivity regarding the practices of research. This is to enable a more contextual understanding regarding how knowledge is being cultivated, as well as recognizing the costs and benefits embedded within the research process. This section is oriented around three key issues: consent, voice and power/hierarchy.

Consent

Consent formulates the bedrock of social science research. But consent is more than a participant ticking a box on a form to say that they permit the research to take place. Rather, consent comes to be something continually negotiated and crafted. Asking participants whether they would be interested in participating in a video diary occurred after they had engaged with an interview and a questionnaire.[43] Despite formulating a method we thought young people would want to engage with and be excited about, there was some resistance. For some, it was seen as too much to fit into their already-busy lives. Others resisted because of an immense dislike of the idea of videoing themselves and talking directly to the camera. Despite being perfectly will-ing during interviews to be audio recorded, there was reluctance from some participants to take on this 'confessional' diarist's role, despite assurances that the video diary would never be played publicly, if they did not want it to be. It therefore became quite challenging to encourage participants' participation, without being seen to be pressurising the participants. By this stage, partici-pants had already completed the questionnaire and in-depth interview. For those who agreed, there was also arguably a sense of obligation to participate. They had come to know us, after a series of e-mail communication and meet-ing face-to-face. Although it was stressed that participation was optional, we have to be mindful that young people may have participated in order to do us a 'good turn'. Indeed, even as participants created their video diaries, they could express their ambivalence on film, such as Akif, a Muslim, who said,

> I was just thinking when was the right time to start the video diary. I have been in two minds about it; I was just going to say sorry I can't do it because I was finding it hard to do it. And I was just sitting there with the prayer and thinking do you know what, maybe it is a good thing that I am doing this, maybe not. I will see at the end.

Akif had spent considerable time thinking through whether he wanted to par-ticipate in the diary, eventually turning to religious resources through prayer to help him decide. This indicates the obligations of time and energy engaged with by some participants, not in necessarily creating the diary, but in thinking through whether they should participate. One participant, Dev, a Hindu, ini-tially agreed to record a video diary, and tried to complete the task, but found it too hard, and returned the camera.

Other participants reflected that they had enjoyed the process. Kyle, a Christian, said 'I have actually enjoyed doing the video diary and it is quite unusual. I don't usually do any sort of diary'. Despite never having produced a diary before, Kyle's diary-keeping was engaging. He was a highly reflexive individual, taking everyday events, and then extrapolating ideas and thoughts about those events, and how they were situated more broadly. In one of his diary entries, Kyle recalls a presentation he had heard that day at his church, regarding Christians who were being persecuted in other countries. He linked this to a broader discussion occurring at the time regarding UK-based Christians who felt discriminated against if they were not allowed to visibly display a cross in their workplace. Kyle argued that in this broader context of persecution, such Christians complained too much. He was therefore able to take his expe-rience and link it to more encompassing national debates. This highlighted

Kyle's awareness of current affairs, enabling him to convey a detailed response to what he experienced. As Holliday argues, the greater levels of cultural and social capital, the better access one has to a broader range of discursive strategies and insights.[44] This also resonated with Amelia's thoughts on putting together a video diary, saying,

> I found this really, really interesting. I don't feel like I really had to force the issue at all; it has all just been around me and the books that I have already been reading and things that I have already been thinking.

Therefore Amelia, a Christian, was also able to present a compelling reflexive account with ease, but this ability seemingly 'naturally' to possess the required skills to navigate a video diary belies the privileged position she is in as a highly educated, articulate young woman.

Both Amelia and Kyle had been raised in middle-class environments; their parents had professional jobs. Both had experienced an upbringing that had cultivated certain types of capital. For instance, given the international focus to his parents' work, Kyle had lived in various countries around the world, and had undertaken a number of significant family moves during his lifetime. This meant he had not only experienced a wide range of cultures and environments, but had needed to develop certain resources of confidence in terms of fitting in with new contexts. Meanwhile, Amelia's father was a priest and her mother was a teacher. In the context of her family, education was of paramount importance; discussion and philosophical debate featured strongly. Amelia's choice to undertake an English Literature degree was welcomed and normalized. As a clergy daughter, Amelia had also developed a certain level of confidence and self-assuredness.[45] Both had taken up degree programmes at prestigious universities. Their backgrounds enabled them to feel like 'fish in water'[46] when narrativizing their experiences to camera. As Skeggs notes, the telling of the self, and the validation of experience, is heavily classed.[47] It is middle-class individuals who are routinely accorded the right to speak. As Skeggs articulates, 'It was only the bourgeoisie (usually male) who were considered to have depth of experience; it was their experiences that were classified as "real"'.[48] Therefore, given their more privileged classed backgrounds, Amelia and Kyle were already primed and positioned to excel at the video diary task. This classed privilege intersected with other privileged statuses, such as their ethnicity and normative Christian identity.[49] Their accumulated experiences, evidenced in a particular type of cultural capital that is esteemed and legitimized, enabled them to thrive at the task in hand. This was fostered through a taken-for-grantedness that their voices mattered and would be taken seriously.

The video diary method privileges certain ways of knowing, not only in terms of the aforementioned requirement to narrativize one's identity in order to secure one's sense of self,[50] but also because the visual is a primary means through which we understand the world.[51] Therefore, a video diary, combining the privileged elements of narrativization *and* the visual allows a powerful tool for those with the capacity to articulate their identities in a way supported by dominant Western norms, thereby securing and furthering their privilege. But this also has repercussions for those who participated with evident discomfort. This was specifically in evidence for disadvantaged and marginalized groups, particularly for Muslim participants, who had experienced widespread stigmatization and unjust treatment.[52] For example, Akif, mentioned earlier, was from a middle-class background, but expressed much unease about participating in the video diary. He had experienced overt discrimination as a Muslim; in one incident, he had had a glass bottle thrown at him. In this context, Akif's identity is constantly under threat; his right to speak and even his right to situate himself in Britain is continually questioned. In such contexts where regular attempts are made to silence an individual, this makes it more challenging to feel that one has the legitimacy to speak, especially if that voice challenges dominant norms and perceptions. A number of the Muslim participants (female and male) disliked looking directly at the camera, or would use notes as an aide, indicating a general unease with being asked to speak, to an unknown audience who may potentially hold negative and hostile views towards them. This is ameliorated in a face-to-face interview encounter, where the positive affirmation of the researcher encourages participation.

Although in some cases, one's marginalized status could contribute to this discomfort, in other cases, an individual's shyness could precipitate unease with the task. Some participants were unsure about what to talk about or how to present themselves. Although these participants consented to the data being used, their consent was not premised on enjoyment and perceived benefit, as was ascertained with other participants. Despite the proliferation of visual methods in youth culture more broadly, and the expectation that younger people would be more enthusiastic with this format, this is not necessarily the case, and cannot be automatically assumed.

We individually negotiated the visual consent participants were offering, and what would happen to the video diaries after their production. Participants could specify that videos were only viewed within the research team, and not to be publicly displayed. Others were happy for videos to be used for the purposes of conference presentations, but with a clear understanding that they would not be uploaded for public viewing. Consent issues were often complex, such as participants consenting to one part of a video being viewed publically, but not another part. Therefore consent had to be carefully negotiated at an individual level, with caveats attached.

Voice

The video diary method was premised on allowing participants to take control of the data process, producing a video on their own terms. But this sense of freedom was actually resisted by participants. We did not intend, in the first instance, to generate any guidelines, in order to encourage a free-flowing format. But most of the first wave of diary participants asked for specific instructions regarding what they should focus on. We therefore constructed a one-page guide, thereby keeping the guidance to a minimum. Despite this, Ricardo, a Buddhist, said in his video diary that he wanted further input, saying, '(i)t would be helpful to have questions, to reflect [on] them . . . I don't know what to say'.

Despite our efforts to create a method that put the participants in control, this occurred in a context where participants had experienced quite a bit of prescription. Given that the research was about *something*, this already put parameters around the research – it was clear that participants would not routinely be discussing their favourite football team or the last holiday they went on. The previous stages of research had been defined and led by the researchers. On the one hand, this enabled the participants to be familiar with the project, but on the other hand, could have discouraged them from raising issues they deemed irrelevant to the project. Their voice was mediated through particular structures. They had imagined an audience – the researchers – to whom they were speaking, and this cultivated a particular voice.

At the same time, participants were also engaged in determining what they would disclose on camera and what they chose not to reveal. How participants engaged with the video diaries varied considerably. As Amelia discusses:

> I have realized that I haven't spoken about my own sex life … I have alluded to it. I have had sex whilst doing this diary and didn't really know how to talk about it or what to say about it. It also felt like it was quite private and I guess as an open, liberal person, [I should] reflect about whether I am a bit more prudish than [I thought].

Women have traditionally been constructed as malleable research participants who will more readily reveal intimate details of their lives.[53] But here Amelia was acknowledging the parameters around which she was working, and the experiences she chose to disclose and those she chose not to. Some participants, such as Penny, chose not to talk about sex or sexuality at all. Meanwhile Tim, a Christian-Buddhist, went into further detail than he did in his interview about his sexual experiences, offering a compelling account of how he experienced orgasm as a religious encounter. Therefore, although participants were structured in the sense that they had participated in the project over a period of time and were well aware of its aims and researchers' interests, they were agentic in making decisions about what they felt comfortable disclosing.

Power and hierarchy

The video diaries enabled participants to have control of the data-collection process; they could conduct the diary at a time to suit them, could decide on what to talk about, and the researcher was not present to intervene. But as indicated above, some participants imagined that the researcher was there;[54] Kyle, for example, signed off his video diary with 'speak to you tomorrow', clearly invoking an audience in his response. Other participants doubted whether we as researchers would be interested in what they were saying. Without the verbal encouragement that can take place in interviews, the participant is actually engaging with an unresponsive piece of equipment. Hence at the end of her diary, Alyson, a Christian, quipped, 'I have rambled on enough; you will get more rambling tomorrow. How exciting, I am sure you are all thrilled'. The sarcasm Alyson conveys is tangible, and also highlights the disadvantages when a researcher is not present to offer support and encouragement. It also underscores a sense in which Alyson was doubtful of her contribution, and whether she was merely 'rambling'. Meanwhile Eliot, a Jew, also doubted his diary, but on different terms, saying 'I think that was a bit of a rant; I don't think it was logical. We will just have to see how the rest of these seven days go. I will see you sometime tomorrow'. For Eliot, it was not about the extent to which his video diary was of interest or not to the researchers; rather, he wanted to ensure that his presentation of self was clear, rational and logical. This also flags up some gendered patterns that could be observed, in that although some of the women were concerned that the researchers were getting what they needed, some of the men were more concerned that their own selfhood was projected in a manner with which they wanted themselves to be understood. As previously noted, Plummer argues that finding a voice to speak is not an automatic process; whether a topic has spoken currency is impacted on by various social processes. How a particular story is interpretively framed will differ cross-culturally and over time. Certain stories are simply impossible to be voiced in particular social contexts – and even if 'impossible' stories are voiced, Plummer's inference is that they will be ridiculed, minimized and dismissed if the social conditions are not ripe for the story to be heard. For example, Plummer notes how women's rape narratives are now far more likely to be given attention and taken seriously (to some extent) than fifty years ago.[55] There are therefore gendered consequences in narrative-making – as feminists have long-argued, women are not necessarily given the right to speak – but Plummer is arguing that the reason for this is that narratives depend on sympathetic audiences in order to validate and give meaning to the story. Plummer notes how stories and storytelling are increasingly central to the production of contemporary culture. Indeed, the video diary itself can be seen as an artefact of this, becoming understood as a means through which we can 'know', 'learn from' and 'understand' young people. Both Alyson and Eliot have absorbed the expectation to be able to tell a good story – so in Alyson's lifeworld, she is not stopped from telling her story due to her gender. But control and constraint are in evidence. Both are constrained by the conventions of storytelling – Eliot wants to be logical, Alyson wants to be interesting and relevant. They are expressing the pressure of needing to convey a compelling narrative – if narrative is so central to the contemporary endeavour, then as Brison contends, they are crucial in formulating a social identity.[56] Nevertheless, even though both have absorbed the narrative conventions and expectations, they are crafting *gendered* identities in the process, with both working within particular gendered social conventions. Alyson is thinking far more about her audience and whether she will bore them. She wants to please others – a long-standing feature of expected feminine behaviour. Meanwhile Eliot is more concerned about his own preservation of identity and that he conveys a rational and logical selfhood – with rationality long being understood as the hallmark of masculinity.[57]

Participants cultivated different relationships with the video camera equipment. For example, Karen, a Buddhist, positively responded to speaking to the camera, saying, 'It has been nice to have this little machine that I can talk to that doesn't ever interrupt', thereby treating the camera as a neutral object that affirmed her control of the situation. But John, a Buddhist, was more critical, and subverted the whole idea of speaking directly to the camera, saying, 'I've asked my girlfriend to ask me questions because it feels slightly less weird than having a deep and meaningful conversation with a camera'. He went on to reflect:

> I think I am probably not so comfortable talking to a camera about it. I think it is probably the least comfortable medium for me. I can write very clearly and expressively. I can even talk to a live person much more clearly, but I think to talk about these things to a camera where I don't know the people who are going to be watching it, it's just too awkward.

John deemed the interview experience a far more enriching one, and struggled with the video diary format, also hinting at the unknown elements regarding who viewed his 'performance'.[58] It was also telling that John – as a white, middle-class male – felt enabled to disrupt the video diary 'norms' more readily than other more marginalized participants who had also experienced discomfort with the process. John was seeking to control the terms of his engagement and felt enabled (and entitled) to do so.

Conclusion

Using a feminist criticality, this article has offered a reflective account of the use of video diaries within a mixed methods project. First, I highlighted the complexities around consent and how consent is continually negotiated. This is not just about mediating consent around visual data in which participants are easily identifiable – but also about the parameters of consent, and whether good will from participants who have developed rapport with researchers overly facilitates their participation in visual approaches, even when evident discomfort arises. Second, and related, is a critique of the types of voice that are enabled through this type of method. Different participants have varying levels of capital,[59] mediated through divisions such as gender, class, ethnicity and religious identity. We may be enabling those with the most resources to participate, and unwittingly disempowering those without access to similar resources. Third, I offered a reflection on the extent to which hierarchies and power dynamics diminish with this method. Despite being participant-led, in many instances, an audience (often the researcher) is being imagined in the minds of participants. Video diaries are embedded in power processes just like any other method of data collection; this is not an inherently participatory approach.

This is not to say that video diaries are inherently problematic, but as with any research method, critical reflection is required. Video diaries generate new research perspectives, allowing the relevance of the mundane and the everyday to be made tangible. There has not been the space to convey in detail the types of data we captured through the video diary data[60] but it was significant in portraying the everyday encounters between religion and sexuality, such as the conversations participants had with friends or parents, or how a film or book had inspired them to reflect on their values in relation to sexuality. This coheres with the idea that whereas interviews premised on capturing one's life history are concerned with the seismic moments of life, video diaries instead complement this through accessing the routine and ordinary components of the everyday.

In order for visual methods to be successfully adopted in the study of the faith lives of women and girls, careful critique is needed regarding any hierarchies that emerge (however unintentional). Do the research processes cultivate negative outcomes? Is the underpinning rationalization for the research method connected with privileged ways of knowing and seeing the world? How does the biography of the participant impact on this negotiation? It is clear from the data presented here that although gender has an impact on how participants navigate their visual methods participation, gender alone does not account for everything. Indeed, some women who were privileged in other ways (e.g. in terms of social class, ethnicity, type of religious belonging) were able to carve out accounts that enabled them to speak authoritatively about their experiences, and in ways that they found pleasurable and meaningful. This consolidated their existing advantage. Meanwhile those whose identities intersected with markers of disadvantage found the process to be more unnerving and uncomfortable. Rather than abandoning visual method techniques, which can be praised for the way they allow participants to speak on their own terms, we should instead seek ways to instil women and girls with confidence in their participation, emphasizing that their contribution is significant and important, and can be flexibly negotiated in order to account for their needs – which includes the confidence to critique their terms of engagement with the method. Finally this experience emphasizes that knowledge construction is contested and hierarchized. The accounts of those who seemingly express themselves with ease and confidence should not overshadow the accounts produced with discomfort and hesitation. Indeed, it is those accounts produced uneasily that can potentially disrupt normative accounts and terms of reference, thus allowing new meanings and knowledges to emerge.

110   *Sarah-Jane Page*

Notes

1 Marcus Banks, *Using Visual Data in Qualitative Research* (London: Sage, 2008); Caroline Knowles and Paul Sweetman, 'Introduction', in *Picturing the Social Landscape: Visual Methods and the Sociological Imagination*, ed. Caroline Knowles and Paul Sweetman (London: Routledge, 2004), 1–17; Sarah Pink, *Doing Visual Ethnography* (London: Sage, 2007); Jon Prosser and Andrew Loxley, *ESRC National Centre for Research Methods Review Paper: Introducing Visual Methods* (2008), accessed 1 April 2014, http://eprints.ncrm.ac.uk/420/1/MethodsReviewPaperNCRM-010.pdf.

2 Nancy T. Ammerman and Roman R. Williams, 'Speaking of Methods: Eliciting Religious Narratives through Interviews, Photos, and Oral Diaries', *Annual Review of the Sociology of Religion* 3 (2012): 117–134.

3 Lynn Schofield Clark and Jill Dierberg, 'Digital Storytelling and Collective Religious Identity in a Moderate to Progressive Youth Group', in *Digital Religion*, ed. Heidi A. Campbell (London: Routledge, 2012); 147–154; Sarah Dunlop and Philip Richter, 'Visual Methods', in *Religion and Youth*, ed. Sylvia Collins-Mayo and Pink Dandelion (Farnham: Ashgate, 2012); Sarah Dunlop and Peter Ward, 'Narrated Photography: Visual Representations of the Sacred among Young Polish Migrants in England', *Fieldwork in Religion* 9 (2014): 30–52; Yvette Taylor and Ria Snowdon, 'Mapping Queer, Mapping Me: Visualizing Queer Religious Identity', in *Globalized Religion and Sexual Identity*, ed. Heather Shipley (Leiden: Brill, 2014), 295–312.

4 Simel Esim, 'Can Feminist Methodology Reduce Power Hierarchies in Research Settings?', *Feminist Economics* 3 (1997): 137–139; Sharlene Hesse-Biber, 'The Practice of Feminist In-Depth Interviewing', in *Feminist Research Practice: A Primer*, ed. Sharlene N. Hesse-Biber and Patricia L. Leavy (London: Routledge, 2007), 111–148; Caroline Ramazanoglu, with Janet Holland, *Feminist Methodology: Challenges and Choices* (London: Sage, 2002), 38; Taylor and Snowdon, 'Mapping Queer'.

5 The research team would like to thank the AHRC/ESRC-funded Religion and Society Programme for funding this project (2010–2012; Award no. AH/G014051/1). We also wish to express our gratitude to the invaluable contribution from the participants, individuals and groups who helped with the recruitment of the sample, and the members of the advisory committee. The research team consisted of Andrew Kam-Tuck Yip, Michael Keenan and Sarah-Jane Page.

6 Nancy T. Ammerman, *Sacred Stories, Spiritual Tribes: Finding Religion in Everyday Life* (Oxford: Oxford University Press, 2014); Meredith McGuire, *Lived Religion: Faith and Practice in Everyday Life* (Oxford: Oxford University Press, 2008).

7 Gayle Letherby, *Feminist Research in Theory and Practice* (Buckingham: Open University Press, 2003), 6; Ramazanoglu, *Feminist Methodology*, 38; Shulamit Reinharz, *Feminist Methods in Social Research* (New York: Oxford University Press, 1992), 11.

8 Letherby, *Feminist Research*, 4.

9 Letherby, *Feminist Research*, 5; Reinharz, *Feminist Methods*, 4.

10 Hesse-Biber, 'Practice', 128; Ann Oakley, 'Interviewing Women: A Contradiction in Terms', in *Doing Feminist Research*, ed. Helen Roberts (London: Routledge, 1981), 30–61; Letherby, *Feminist Research*, 85; Reinharz, *Feminist Methods*, 19–21.

11 Letherby, *Feminist Research*, 89; Oakley, 'Interviewing'.

12 Oakley, 'Interviewing'; Letherby, *Feminist Research*, 85.

13 Letherby, *Feminist Research*, 82.

14 Hesse-Biber, 'Practice', 128.

15 Janet Finch, '"It's Great to Have Someone to Talk to": Ethics and Politics of Interviewing Women', in *Social Research: Philosophy, Politics and Practice*, ed. Martyn Hammersley (London: Sage, 1993), 166–180.

16 Judith Stacey, 'Can There Be a Feminist Ethnography?' *Women's Studies International Forum* 11 (1988): 21–27.
17 Hesse-Biber, 'Practice', 129–131; Ramazanoglu, *Feminist Methodology*, 118–119; Reinharz, *Feminist Methods*, 45.
18 Knowles and Sweetman, 'Introduction'; Pink, *Doing*.
19 Knowles and Sweetman, 'Introduction', 3.
20 Howard S. Becker, 'Afterword: Photography as Evidence, Photographs as Exposition', in *Picturing the Social Landscape*, ed. Knowles and Sweetman, 193–194; Michael Emmison, Philip Smith and Margery Mayall, *Researching the Visual*, 2nd ed. (London: Sage, 2012), 22–23; Pink, *Doing*, 9–12.
21 Becker, 'Afterword', 195; Pink, *Doing*, 12.
22 Pink, *Doing*, 21.
23 Stewart Muir and Jennifer Mason, 'Capturing Christmas: The Sensory Potential for Data from Participant Produced Video', *Sociological Research Online* 17 (2012), accessed 1 May 2016, www.socresonline.org.uk/17/1/5.html.
24 Dunlop and Ward, 'Narrated Photography'.
25 Charis Brown *et al.*, 'Capturing their Dream: Video Diaries and Minority Consumers', *Consumption Markets and Culture* 13 (2010): 419–436.
26 Taylor and Snowdon, 'Mapping Queer', 296.
27 Dunlop and Ward, 'Narrated Photography'.
28 Muir and Mason, 'Capturing Christmas'.
29 Ruth Holliday, 'Reflecting the Self', in *Picturing the Social Landscape*, ed. Knowles and Sweetman, 50.
30 Ammerman and Williams, 'Speaking', 117.
31 Ibid., 127.
32 Ammerman and Williams, 'Speaking'; Charlotte Bates, 'Video Diaries: Audio-Visual Research Methods and the Elusive Body', *Visual Studies* 28 (2013): 29–37; Jim Cherrington and Beccy Watson, 'Shooting a Diary, Not Just a Hoop: Using Video Diaries to Explore the Embodied Everyday Contexts of a University Basketball Team', *Qualitative Research in Sport and Exercise* 2 (2010): 267–281; Muir and Mason, 'Capturing Christmas'.
33 Ken Plummer, *Telling Sexual Stories: Power, Change and Social Worlds* (London: Routledge, 1995), 18.
34 Steph Lawler, 'Narrative in Social Research', in *Qualitative Research in Action* ed. Tim May (London: Sage, 2002), 242–258.
35 Lawler, 'Narrative', 242.
36 Plummer, *Telling*, 22, 120–121.
37 Holliday, 'Reflecting', 52–54. See also Michel Foucault, *The History of Sexuality*, Vol. 1 (London: Penguin, 1978).
38 Holliday, 'Reflecting', 52.
39 Susan J. Brison, 'Trauma Narratives and the Remaking of the Self', in *Acts of Memory: Cultural Recall in the Present*, ed. Mieke Bal, Jonathan Crewe and Leo Spitzer (Hanover: Dartmouth College, 1999), 41.
40 Holliday, 'Reflecting', 53; see also Gunilla Holm, 'Visual Research Methods: Where Are We and Where Are We Going?' in *Handbook of Emergent Methods* ed. Sharlene N. Hesse-Biber and Patricia Leavy (London: The Guilford Press, 2008).
41 Dunlop and Richter, 'Visual Methods', 209.
42 Elizabeth Chaplin, 'My Visual Diary', in *Picturing the Social Landscape*, ed. Knowles and Sweetman (London: Routledge, 2004), 35.
43 Michael Keenan, Andrew K. T. Yip and Sarah-Jane Page, 'Exploring Sexuality and Religion using an Online Questionnaire', in *Innovative Methods in the Study of Religion* ed. Linda Woodhead (Oxford: Oxford University Press, forthcoming).

44 Holliday, 'Reflecting', 56.

45 Sarah-Jane Page, 'Double Scrutiny at the Vicarage: Clergy Mothers, Expectations and the Public Gaze', in *Angels on Earth: Mothering, Religion and Spirituality*, ed. Vanessa Reimer (Bradford: Dementer Press, 2016), 23–24, 33–34.

46 Pierre Bourdieu and Loïc Wacquant, *An Invitation to Reflexive Sociology* (Cambridge: Polity Press, 1992), 127.

47 Beverley Skeggs, *Formations of Class and Gender* (London: Sage, 1997), 18–21.

48 Skeggs, *Formations*, 24.

49 Bob Pease, *Undoing Privilege: Unearned Advantage in a Divided World* (London: Zed Books, 2011), 18–22.

50 Brison, 'Trauma', 41.

51 Knowles and Sweetman, 'Introduction', 1.

52 Sarah-Jane Page and Andrew Kam-Tuck Yip, 'Gender Equality and Religion: A Multi-Faith Exploration of Young Adults' Narratives', *European Journal of Women's Studies*, advanced access, doi: 10.1177/1350506815625906.

53 Letherby, *Feminist Research*, 85.

54 Holm, 'Visual Research', 325–330.

55 Plummer, *Telling*, 22.

56 Brison, 'Trauma', 41.

57 Genevieve Lloyd, *The Man of Reason: 'Male' and 'Female' in Western Philosophy* (London: Routledge, 1993); Doreen Massey, 'Reflections on Gender and Geography', in *Social Change and the Middle Classes*, ed. Tim Butler and Mike Savage (London: UCL Press, 1995), 331–333.

58 Holliday, 'Reflecting', 52–53.

59 Pierre Bourdieu, *Distinction: A Social Critique of the Judgement of Taste*, trans. Richard Nice. (London: Routledge, 1984).

60 See Andrew K. T. Yip and Sarah-Jane Page, *Religious and Sexual Identities: A Multi-Faith Exploration of Young Adults* (Farnham: Ashgate, 2013).

7 Using social media for feminist qualitative research

A pilot study into women's experiences of Holy Communion

Kim Wasey

Background and context

The 'Women in Communion'[1] project developed from my doctoral research,[2] which used semi-structured interviews to gather qualitative data. Despite my efforts to mitigate power dynamics I was still aware of their potency and that my own and much similar work from fellow researchers[3] was heavily researcher reliant in terms of the outcomes and interpretation. Graham reflected this concern in her critique that 'little emerges of participants' voices independent of the principal, individual researcher'[4] in the various feminist qualitative research projects shared in *The Faith Lives of Women and Girls*.[5] Without the possibility of return interviews or focus groups to reflect mutually on findings or to generate creative interpretations in collaborative ways, the development of new insights and frameworks for understanding the results lay with me as researcher. While this is not to invalidate the creative skill and insight of the individual researcher, I was left questioning how more collaborative approaches might be facilitated within the constraints of the realities of women's lives while they are conducting research and what a more contemporary methodology might look like particularly among young participants.

My response to this question was to trial the use of social media to invite women to share and discuss their experiences of Holy Communion, enabling a comparison of the two different methodologies of data gathering (qualitative interviewing and using social media) and an evaluation of the differing results. The approach of using social media arose partly from my context working as chaplain at the University of Salford, named as one of the UK's top ten most influential higher education institutions on social media in 2015.[6] I was aware of the extent to which the higher education learning environment was changing rapidly to embrace virtual and online learning methodologies, and that this cannot help but shape the research environment too. However, social media is underexplored within the context of research in faith and feminism, least of all from a qualitative perspective, as much existing work has focused on methodologies for researching social media posts that are already extant as a data field, rather than utilizing the tools of social media as a means of generating new data. This difference in approach to data gathering is a key distinction within current approaches towards social media research, and for me as feminist qualitative researcher it was 'essential to ethical conduct that the use of social media is integrated into the research process rather than just a novel way to access data for analysis'.[7] In my research the use of social media was a means of involved and engaged research both *for and with* those in the field of research, rather than regarding social media content as a data gathering field where there could be no mutuality or consent. This collaborative model of working through social media is helpfully discussed, though not from a research context, by Coleman and Augustine's writing about blogging as 'Ministry To, Through, With and From'.[8] My commitment to researching in a transparent way via social media, so that participants retained choice and control, arose from my conviction that a feminist research methodology prioritizes transformation and justice-seeking.

These same priorities of justice and transformation mean that feminist research has recognized and sought to reveal the dispersed and therefore often isolated nature of minority voices that are silenced by the dominant discourse. Researchers such as Dunne[9] have, as Mann points out, seized on 'the anonymity of the technology to access the voices of socially marginalized communities such as gay fathers',[10] and Dunne reflects on the benefits of this access in the endnotes to her paper. It can be hard for women, particularly young women within the church, to find mutual support or work together for their voices to be heard and, as Messina-Dysert argues, young women 'look to online blogs and forums to find feminism, and the result can be life-saving connectivity'.[11] In 'Women and Children Last: The Discursive Construction of Weblogs',[12] Herring and her co-authors provide evidence that women rather than men are the dominant bloggers among the teenage (under 20) and emerging adult (20–25) age groups. Statistics cited by Messina-Dysert in '#FemReligionFuture' bear this out,[13] and the same gendered bias has been found in the use of social networking sites by Brandes and Levin who explore some of the reasons for this, particularly among teenage girls.[14]

One of the few early examples of feminist faith-based research in social media is Piela's *Muslim Women Online: Faith and Identity in Virtual Space*. She reflects how users of online Islamic discussion groups 'are interested in the transformation of the religious status quo, as they are often underprivileged in the current power dynamics'.[15] From this Piela talks about how online groups provide a locus where positions and identities can be explored and formed with transformational potential for participants, who can then 'apply their own interpretations of this knowledge to their own actions' and so 'construct their identities', which can then be lived out in the offline world.[16] This potential for exploration and effecting change is echoed by Thornton in her work on attitudes about menstruation on Twitter. Despite finding that 'with all the expressiveness in the uncensored environment of Twitter, the license to communicate freely was not used to advocate, enlighten or redress misconceptions', she nonetheless concludes that 'vigorous discourse about menstruating women . . . on Twitter . . . employs powerful tools of influence'[17] and therefore 'ready access to multiple realities in a transparent media environment might influence or alter how menstruation is positioned within various communities of knowledge'.[18] Korn and Kneese also point to the 'activism' that they argue is 'inherent within . . . feminist approaches to social media research', through 'public forums where feminists may collectively create discourses apart from the dominant narrative' described as 'counter-publics'.[19] Coleman and Augustine also view blogging as 'religious activism', arguing that blogs provide a platform for three feminist elements of 'breaking silence and raising consciousness', 'cultivating a hermeneutic of suspicion' and 'creating community', and that 'as an offering of self and voice, blogs are poised to reflect the values of religious feminism'.[20] Messina-Dysert goes further to contend that social media is actually 'feminist in nature'.[21] I would argue that this focus on self and voice, coupled with Reuther's observations that social media's 'reliance on personal experience allows women to speak from their own story and history, without being intimidated' and so 'dismantles hierarchies based on gender, education and social status',[22] affirms the appropriateness of trying to utilize the tools social media offers for the conduct of *feminist qualitative research* with its concomitant concerns for both voice and personal experience as well as justice-seeking.

Recognizing the paucity of feminist research methodology in social media and its potential as a methodological tool going forwards, I reasoned that there was a need for further practical exploration. As the authors of the National Centre for Research Methods Methodological Review paper concluded in 2013:

> We are still at the start of our journey into the methodology of social media research … yet to agree a coherent set of epistemological or ethical frameworks … some … argue this is a positive, allowing researchers fluidity and freedom in the methods and approaches they adopt.[23]

Research design

My research design consisted of a dual platform of blog and Twitter, interrelated by embedding the Twitter feed in the blog site, and supported by the use of Facebook to recruit participants. I hoped this would enable people to contribute and engage in differing ways. The Twitter feed would provide open and uncensored access but would be limited by the maximum 144 characters per tweet. In contrast the blog would provide a more controlled environment with the potential for more extensive contributions from participants, but would also provide me, as researcher, both a platform to address difficulties that may arise through the Twitter feed and the ability to moderate the comments posted to the blog. While there are conflicts about participant power by adopting the role of blog moderator, this is mitigated to some extent by the uncensored Twitter feed and seemed a measured response to the need for open access, balanced against the need to create safe space, which I will touch on later.[24]

This chapter focuses on the initial two-week period from start-up, providing rich insights into the process, patterns and results from developing such research from the earliest stages. Over the first 14 days, the project received 513 views from 240 visitors; an average of about 17 visitors a day. From these visits six women contributed directly to the blog and a further three contacted me to say they were intending to contribute but busy, so over a longer period of time those women could be engaged further. While these are small numbers, the level of engagement achieved over just fourteen days via social media outreach compared favourably with the total of ten women who agreed to be interviewed by me over a period of some years while working on my doctorate.

Insights arising from the pilot study

The statistical and tracking information afforded to me as researcher through the use of online technologies offered significant insights into how the process of connecting with viewer and participants snowballed over this initial period. The blog insights provided me not only with numbers of visitors and page views, but the popularity of different pages, and which sites or social networks viewers were being referred from and where visitors were located in the world, as well as the most popular days and times for participant engagement. My invitations to engage were retweeted and passed on through Facebook by both women and men, which I was aware of through seeing Twitter notifications and Facebook timelines. However, the blog statistics suggested that the research invitation was being passed on far more widely than I could see within my own networks and connections. I had referrals to my site listed not only from Facebook and Twitter but also many social media sites, some of which I did not recognize, and both viewers and participants were shown to come from across the world. This provides evidence of the way that online engagement facilitated access to research participants, but also the differing types of contact made by the women participants and the interweave of private and public engagement. I was struck by the way several of the women who posted online then contacted me privately, and others contacted me several times privately without then posting. There was an interweaving that reflects Benite-Montagut's findings, in her ethnographic study of technology in social interactions and relationships, which Kara draws on in *Creative Research Methods*. Kara suggests that Benite-Montagut has demonstrated how 'interpersonal communication is the same online as offline, and that online social interactions are often inextricably linked with offline social interactions'.[25]

There was also a significant difference in the nature and quality of the data that was generated by this social media method in comparison with data generated through face-to-face interview and transcription.

The extracts in Table 7.1 show on the left the data in the form it is generated as comments on the blog, alongside an example of a page of transcription from an interview in my previous research on the right. All research data is affected by the method of data gathering and by the variety of the individuals who participate and their preferences, for example, some will

Table 7.1

The experience of celebrating the Eucharist together feels most authentic to me when every person in the gathered circle both receives and offers the elements, so that we are truly being fed by/feeding one another. Such a circle, for me, truly becomes the Body of Christ – we become what we have received, in order to go out in the world and give our very selves away to others.

Demi

I have mixed feelings about queuing for Communion. We sat in a square for the morning meeting at the Gospel Hall when we celebrated community passing the bread and one to each other. We sit in a circle at Othona, the community I attend on the south coast. I prefer the sense of community the circle engenders to the individualistic edging forward of the queue yet I appreciate that a circle is also exclusive, and is hard to break into. The circle may be a symbol of eternity but it is finite.

Sandra

I usually sit at the back of a church if I know there is a queue for Communion as then I don't have to negotiate the queue as I know I'll be near the end. The part that annoys me is if the queue leads to receiving Communion standing up where is never enough time to pause and contemplate receiving from God. The part I am very aware of as a priest is observing who is together in the queue as they come forward so I wait for them to kneel together to receive Communion together.

Becky

Is there anything else that you would like to say to me about your experience of Communion in the church as a young woman?

(Long, long pause)

I'd like the church to think about

(Sigh)

(Long, long, long pause)

(Sigh)

What it thinks people are hearing when they do Communion,

when they take part in Communion.

Why Communion has to be, em, using a particular liturgy,

Uhum

With a male God.

How Communion affects eh people who are suffering, whether it encourages suffering and sacrifice amongst people who are already victims, of whatever form of abuse.

(Sigh)

(Very heavy feeling emotionally – emotion so great by this point that I felt it almost eliciting tears in me)

That'll probably do *(very low, almost dejected voice)*

Ok?

Umm.

Thank you

speak more easily than they write and vice versa, some will rely heavily on gesture and facial expression while others will not. Just five days of activity on the blog generated approximately eight hundred words of comment and I want to suggest that this data has a 'different quality'[26] to the interview transcript data. The process of an individual formulating and typing a tweet, comment or post has led to more concise and formed data, in comparison to the interview context where the participant is required to think as she speaks. For this reason, a smaller quantity of data may be just as helpful and insightful for the researcher in terms of the quality of condensed reflection it provides. In addition the data generated from the blog reduces or removes many of the practical and ethical struggles a researcher faces in questions about how to transcribe through its potential to eliminate aspects of 'transcription bias' because a 'digitally generated script . . . is complete and immediately available for analysis. Nothing is left out'.[27]

There are legitimate concerns that feminist researchers may face in online qualitative research. From a feminist perspective, personal relationship and listening to the whole person is a priority. Conducting research via social media, where communication is confined by the limitations of the written word, might be considered depersonalized and disembodied, leading to a lack of nuance and the possibility of misunderstandings of individuals' perspectives. These dangers exist in the conduct of all research that relies on human interaction, but social media lacks the benefits of body language, facial expression, tone of voice and the myriad other indicators that researchers may be attuned to in face-to-face qualitative research. But this concern needs to be balanced with the realization that these methods of communication and relationship are already normative for a majority of young people. New means of communicating feelings and the ability to understand one another within this arena are developing at an equally rapid pace. Mann and Stewart in *Internet Communication and Qualitative Research* consider how individuals now relate to computers and cite a 'student from the Graduates of the Millennium study' who says, 'in a way, although it's a computer screen, it brings out a lot more than speaking to someone does'.[28]

Also significant, particularly from an ethical perspective, is the difficulty in verifying either the identity or the intent of participants. In terms of defining the field, for example, by gender, age, or background of participants, it is extremely difficult to verify the identity of contributors, particularly if the research allows participants to be anonymous in public postings in order to protect privacy and enable otherwise silenced voices to be heard. This potential difficulty affects not only the ability to define the field, but also the possibility of creating 'safe space'. The history of feminist research has demonstrated how important this has been to enable the development of new impulses where nascent or controversial ideas can be safely explored and nurtured, while, in contrast, online-based interactions can run the danger of 'trolling'[29] and the effects of this can be highly destructive, as explored by Beeching in *Trolling and Feminism*.[30] Being alert to these areas of concern will help feminist researchers shape research designs that can both seek to mitigate and be transparent about these concerns in an effort to empower beneficial and informed engagement.

Identifying potential benefits

Alongside the concerns acknowledged above are many potential benefits of the use of social media, and the pilot project highlighted five benefits that relate directly to a feminist approach to qualitative research. First, the method allowed one line of enquiry to arise organically from the previous and to bring differing voices into conversation with one another openly and transparently within the research process as it engaged with participants. This is demonstrated by the following extract from my research blog:

> As I write this, all three of the women who have contributed thoughts to this blog have reflected on the significance of sharing Communion in a circle – both positively and negatively ...
>
> Circles often came up in my research interviews too. Often the circle seemed to reflect something of the 'horizontal orientation in women's spirituality'[31] ...
>
> Demi has posted here about how the sharing of Communion in a circle can reflect the theological significance of what it's all about 'every person in the gathered circle both receives and offers the elements, so that we are truly being fed by/feeding one another', and Sandra and Ferial have both acknowledged the potential for circles to be exclusive, as well as embracing.[32]

In addition, the process felt more democratic through being open to all and enabling wider participation among people who could see what was taking place and how the research was developing. Hence, they could choose their engagement in a much more informed way than when entering into an interview uncertain of what questions they might face or what topics and issues within the general subject area might be the focus. Even over a short period, the process of researching utilizing social media felt less static and more integrated in engaging the different steps of data collection and analysis with each other, than in my previous research process.

This leads to the second finding from the pilot study, which was the effect upon the researcher's own role within a qualitative method due to the way that reflection could be more fully integrated into the data-gathering stage. I had planned to blog using sections from my original findings, and began doing this, trying to do justice to nuance and breadth, but that quickly felt too long and formal. Myers, talking about blogging as theological discourse, points to the lightness of blogging, describing it as 'an extraordinarily *playful* activity',[33] and I found by being immersed in something alive that I found my voice very quickly, and was able to write blogs easily – more short, succinct, focused and with a touch of lightness:

> Fliss' comment about receiving Communion, her description of 'my time' (posted on 'Circle of Communion') reminded me of how much the women I interviewed spoke about peace and Communion as a point where they could pause in life.
>
> 'I think it always brings me to a stop' – the word 'stop' was surprisingly common ...

The peace experienced in that moment of 'my time' had the potential both *to transform how the rest of life was experienced* as the peace flowed onwards from that moment, and also *to be transformational for the women's sense of self*, 'it's like an inner response ... feeling transformed ... that I'm ok and that I'm accepted'.

... *What is significant for you about receiving Communion, about that 'moment in time'?*[34]

Instead of asking a set of questions, and then analysing later, I was able to bring my thinking as a researcher into the data generation process with more reflection space than in a spoken conversation, while still addressing key questions directly to blog readers to encourage response, as at the end of the blog quotation above.

Third, the organic nature of the research process afforded transparency to both researcher and participants. The process became one characterized by a sense of dialogue and collaboration, enabling a fluidity of exchanges, and refinement of ideas with a degree of mutuality. This could be reflective of the way women often shape ideas collaboratively, 'in conversation', rather than through abstract or isolated theorizing, and in this way social media platforms provided a collaborative space not possible in a sequence of one to one interviews. As researcher, I appreciated the ability to bring differing voices into conversation with one another transparently for those involved, again demonstrated by the first blog extract above. This also enabled people to come back and agree or clarify things, creating an internal verification process, as seen in the comment:

Hi Kim, What you've written sums it up nicely and is encouragingly affirming. Thank you!

Alison[35]

However, I also recognized in this pilot study that the dialogue *between* voices was largely facilitated by me as blogger/researcher. This may reflect Lövheim's observations in 'Young Women's Blogs as Ethical Spaces' where she identifies three different strategies used by bloggers to elicit responses. She concludes that the 'strategy of invitations', which is the one closest to my own approach, 'seems to generate many individual responses in which readers express their opinions and experiences but, generally, less discussion among readers', and this is an area worthy of further exploration as the project develops.[36]

Fourth, I found that raising research questions online enabled women to notice their current experiences, for example, while participating in Communion at their church, and then feed this directly into the research. This living engagement of participants in the research and reflection process contrasts with the reliance on recall and reflected memory required by interview-based methods:

I was thinking about this this morning, standing behind a mother who was holding the hands of two small children. She knelt at the rail, one child standing on her left and one on her right, and the three of them received the Eucharist/blessing together. It was endearing, and I found myself quite moved, suddenly remembering seeing my mother at the same rail.

Ferial[37]

This evidence also helps demonstrate the potential of social media to generate 'live' data very swiftly. The ability to reflect and report on events, feelings and reflections 'in the moment' has exciting potential for research when compared with the much slower processes of traditional qualitative research, which often relies on long data-gathering and analysis timeframes and can cause final outcomes to be reliant on data that may by then be several years old.

Finally, a number of practical advantages for both researcher and participants were identified in using social media methods. Many methodologies have acknowledged the impact of the realities of women's lives upon the research process: from the number of participants accessed; to the ability to find language to discuss the issues under consideration; to the disruptions of women's lives, often including caring responsibilities of many kinds. Using a medium that is reliant on brief posts, 144 character tweets, and 'conversation' that doesn't have to happen in 'real time', may be well suited to, and more reflective of, women's experience of relating through brief encounters. This style of communication and relationships (for example, outside school gates, in the loos, snatched and partial sentences amid the interruptions of child care), and women's ability to pick up strands and continue conversations later on is potentially mirrored in the brief exchanges and connections made by Twitter users or Facebook posters, which are broken up over time by many other activities rather than one consistent period of engagement. Undertaking qualitative interviews required my participants to commit to time and place, and although I always assured participants that they were not obliged to answer every question and could choose to end the interview at any point, in reality once begun it would have been challenging to withdraw. In contrast, engaging remotely through social media enabled power and control to lie far more with the participant than the researcher, and participants can both self-select whether, when and how to engage, as well as control the ongoing level of their personal engagement. The process also worked for me as a researcher. Not only did I not feel I was putting anyone under pressure for timings of interviews, but my own input could also be responsive to other aspects of life. I could tweet when it was convenient, around the other demands of my life. In lots of ways this form of data generation was a living, holistic process, rather than what can become a compartmentalized one.

Conclusion

While being aware of the potential difficulties or concerns about methodologies using social media for feminist qualitative research, this study identified many benefits and the significant potential of these methods for engaging with marginalized, dispersed and isolated groups in a reflective, transparent, practical and collaborative research process. One of the criticisms often levelled at feminist qualitative research in theology is the specificity of the research contexts, which may often be 'at the small-scale and specific level of the case-study'.[38] There are positive responses to be made to that point of view about the value of insights arising from such specificity; however, this study demonstrated how research utilizing social media tools has the capacity to provide a platform for much broader engagement, beyond the confines of immediately available contacts, and the ability to engage in research with far more diverse participation, potentially drawn from many parts of the world.

There will also be implications for models of supervision or accountability (for example, to research steering groups) in the arena of academic research. The development I experienced within the short time period of this study demonstrated how swift and immediate is the responsiveness necessary for research within this medium: this may not fit easily with the traditional pattern of working alone for a period, before meeting with a supervisor or co-researchers, and then deciding on new angles or approaches, needing instead a more fluid and consistent means of guidance or reflection.

The lack of existing resources to underpin or guide social media research in this type of qualitative research means that there is an urgency to developing and sharing good practice, particularly regarding ethics. The constant alertness to motivation demanded by social media engagement is challenging. In tweeting, for example, I didn't want to be exploitative, using people's voices and stories for my own ends, and yet my role was to generate engagements and of course there is inevitably an element of such tension within all such research.

It is my hope that as researchers continue to explore and publish in this area a stronger foundation in practical and ethical qualitative methodologies will emerge, which, given the evidence of gendered online practices and previous research around young women online outlined in this chapter, will be of particular benefit to women and girls in both participating in and initiating research to empower them in the challenge and transformation of unjust contexts and the renewal and encouragement of their lives of faith.

Notes

1 *Women in Communion Blog*, https://womenincommunion.wordpress.com.
2 Kim Wasey, 'Being in Communion: A Qualitative Study of Young Lay Women's Experiences of the Eucharist' (ThD thesis, University of Birmingham, 2013), accessed 30 April 2016, http://etheses.bham.ac.uk/3980/.
3 Personal experience of sharing research journeys and process of producing findings with other feminist researchers through membership of the Manchester Women's

Research Group and the Symposium on the Faith Lives of Women and Girls, based at the Queen's Foundation, Birmingham.

4 Elaine Graham, review of *The Faith Lives of Women and Girls*, ed. Nicola Slee, Fran Porter and Anne Phillips, *Journal of Beliefs & Values*, 35, no. 3 (2014): 384, accessed 2 August 2016, doi: 10.1080/13617672.2014.980076.

5 Nicola Slee, Fran Porter and Anne Phillips, ed., *The Faith Lives of Women and Girls* (Farnham: Ashgate, 2013).

6 'Top 100 UK Universities on Social Media', *Rise*, accessed 30 April 2016, www.rise.global/top-uk-universities/r/2435899.

7 Belinda Lunnay *et al.*, 'Ethical Use of Social Media to Facilitate Qualitative Research', *Qualitative Health Research*, 25, no. 1 (2015): 107, accessed 1 March 2016, doi: 10.1177/1049732314549031.

8 Monica A. Coleman with C. Yvonne Augustine, 'Blogging as Religious Feminist Activism: Ministry To, Through, With, and From', in *Feminism and Religion in the 21st Century: Technology, Dialogue, and Expanding Borders*, ed. Gina Messina-Dysert and Rosemary Radford Ruether (New York and Abingdon: Routledge, 2015), 30.

9 Gillian A. Dunne *The Different Dimensions of Gay Fatherhood: Exploding the Myths*, accessed 30 April 2016, www.lse.ac.uk/genderinstitute/pdf/gayfatherhood.pdf.

10 Chris Mann and Fiona Stewart, *Internet Communication and Qualitative Research* (London: Sage, 2000), 5.

11 Gina Messina-Dysert '#FemReligionFuture: The New Feminist Revolution in Religion', in *Feminism and Religion* ed. Messina-Dysert and Ruether (New York and Abingdon: Routledge, 2015), 11.

12 Susan C. Herring *et al.*, 'Women and Children Last: The Discursive Construction of Weblogs', *Into the Blogosphere* Online edited collection (University of Minnesota, 2004), accessed 30 October 2015, http://hdl.handle.net/11299/172825.

13 Messina-Dysert, '#FemReligionFuture', 9.

14 Sigal Barak Brandes and David Levin, '"Like My Status" Israeli Teenage Girls Constructing their Social Connections on the Facebook Social Network', *Feminist Media Studies* 14, no. 5 (2014): 743–758, accessed 1 March 2016, doi: 10.1080/14680777.2013.833533.

15 Anna Piela, *Muslim Women Online: Faith and Identity in Virtual Space* (Oxon: Routledge, 2012), 2.

16 Ibid., 4.

17 Leslie-Jean Thornton, '"Time of the Month" on Twitter: Taboo, Stereotype and Bonding in a No-Holds-Barred Public Arena', *Sex Roles* 68 (2013): 50–51, accessed 30 April 2016, doi: 10.1007/s11199-011-0041-2.

18 Ibid., 41.

19 Jenny Ungbha Korn and Tamara Kneese, 'Guest Editors' Introduction: Feminist Approaches to Social Media Research: History, Activism, and Values', *Feminist Media Studies* 15, no. 4 (2015): 707–708, accessed 1 March 2016, doi:10.1080/14680777.2015.1053713.

20 Coleman with Augustine, 'Blogging as Religious Feminist Activism', 22.

21 Messina-Dysert, '#FemReligionFuture', 9.

22 Rosemary Radford Ruether, Introduction to *Feminism and Religion in the 21st Century: Technology, Dialogue, and Expanding Borders*, ed. Gina Messina-Dysert and Rosemary Radford Ruether (New York and Abingdon: Routledge, 2015), 1.

23 Kandy Woodfield *et al.*, 'Blurring the Boundaries? New Social Media, New Social Research: Developing a Network to Explore the Issues Faced by Researchers Negotiating the New Research Landscape of Online Social Media Platforms', National Centre for Research Methods Methodological Review paper (2013), accessed 30 October 2015, http://eprints.ncrm.ac.uk/3168/1/blurring_boundaries.pdf.

24 For a fuller discussion of the use of Facebook to facilitate research with young women, and the issues of managing open access and responsible levels of privacy and confidentiality, see Belinda Lunnay *et al.*'s use of Facebook in their 'photo elicitation research with underage women drinkers', which provides a thorough review of the ethical challenges, practical responses to these and the overall benefits of using Facebook, though their research related to a project conducted both on and offline. Lunnay *et al.*, 'Ethical Use of Social Media', 99–109.

25 Helen Kara, *Creative Research Methods in the Social Sciences: A Practical Guide* (Bristol: Policy Press, 2015), 86.

26 See Mann and Stewart, *Internet Communication*, 94.

27 Mann and Stewart, *Internet Communication*, 22.

28 Ibid., 94.

29 'Trolling' is defined as: '[To] make a deliberately offensive or provocative online post with the aim of upsetting someone or eliciting an angry response from them', accessed 30 April 2016, www.oxforddictionaries.com/definition/english/troll.

30 Vicky Beeching, 'Trolling & Feminism' in *FaithinFeminism.com: Conversations on Religion and Gender Equality*, accessed 30 April 2016, http://faithinfeminism.com/online-trolling-and-feminism.

31 Jan Berry, *Ritual Making Women: Shaping Rites for Changing Lives* (London: Equinox, 2009), 109.

32 Kim Wasey, 'Circles of Communion', *Women in Communion Blog*, 5 October 2015, accessed 30 April 2016, https://womenincommunion.wordpress.com/2015/10/05/circles-of-communion.

33 Benjamin Myers, 'Theology 2.0: Blogging as Theological Discourse', *Cultural Encounters* 6, no. 1 (2010): 59, accessed 18 July 2016, www.academia.edu/5793572/Theology_2.0_Blogging_as_Theological_Discourse.

34 Kim Wasey, 'Communion: A Time to Stop', *Women in Communion Blog*, 7 October 2015, accessed 30 April 2016, http://womenincommunion.wordpress.com/2015/10/07/communion-a-time-to-stop.

35 Alison, 8 October 2015 (9:01 a.m.), comment on Kim Wasey, 'Standing Together: Loving the Communion queue!', *Women in Communion Blog*, 2 October 2015, accessed 30 April 2016, https://womenincommunion.wordpress.com/2015/10/02/standing-together-loving-the-communion-queue.

36 Mia Lövheim, 'Young Women's Blogs as Ethical Spaces', *Information, Communication & Society* 14, no. 3 (2011): 338–354, accessed 26 October 2015, doi:10.1080/1369118X.2010.542822.

37 Ferial, 4 October 2015 (6:06 p.m.), comment on Kim Wasey, 'Standing Together: Loving the Communion queue!', *Women in Communion Blog*, 2 October 2015, accessed 30 April 2016, https://womenincommunion.wordpress.com/2015/10/02/standing-together-loving-the-communion-queue.

38 Graham, Review of *The Faith Lives of Women and Girls*, 384.

Part III

Analysing data

Part III

Analysing data

8   Choosing the right key

Glaserian grounded theory, NVivo and
analysing interviews with survivors

Susan Shooter

Introduction: hearing voices

> I never spoke up to you because I could never get a word in.[1]

Laura Hoff, aka Little Voice, yells these words at her mother, Mari, who is
unaware that her shy daughter has an amazing gift. Little Voice can mimic
superbly every female diva from Marlene Dietrich to Judy Garland, yet has
spent her adolescence cooped up in her room, protecting herself from the
verbal abuse her vicious mother dishes out. The trigger that releases her tirade
against Mari is the loss of her most precious possession, the record collection
with which she has identified her own voice, burnt in the house fire caused by
her mother's negligence. Having finally made Mari listen to her, she reclaims
her real name, Laura, and discovers the confidence to fly the nest.

Getting a word in edgeways is very difficult for the quietly spoken, since it
is invariably the loudest voice that commands the floor. It is even more difficult for those who have been crushed and excluded by the dominant and the
powerful. The voice heard in Christian theology has been resoundingly that of
the powerful male, to the exclusion of all others. Our tradition has had a way of
demanding that all theologizing should fit into pre-ordained categories, mostly
decided upon in the fourth and fifth centuries by a group of dominant men.
Anything outside of these boundaries has been regarded as heresy. In research
with survivors of abuse, however, I wanted to find a way of hearing my participants clearly, without forcing onto them a framework of a priori theological
concepts which would filter their meaning. They have been subject to enough
force. So how could I expose Christian theology to what survivors know, how
could I allow the 'little voices' to sing in their different key?

In this chapter I offer Barney Glaser's approach to grounded theory as a
suitable social scientific method that permits research participants to get their
word in first. His methodology allows concepts to 'emerge' from data, that is,
directly from within the interviews given by respondents, without 'forcing'
their words into pre-selected categories. This freer type of analysis, demanding rigorous attention to all the words of all participants, inevitably leads to
exponential growth in data that requires good systematic handling. I propose

NVivo software[2] as a suitable aid for the analysis of these masses of data. Glaserian grounded theory, with the aid of NVivo, helped me produce an integrated study that addressed the real issues of survivors, not concerns that are merely academic or imposed.

Starting out: feminist themes

Shortly after I completed my research, the revelations about Jimmy Saville in 2012 opened the door to hearing survivors' voices in the mainstream media. However, programmes focusing on survivors' words alone, and the enormous problems they face, are still scarce. Most reporting is obsessed with the scandal of celebrity abusers, and how the authorities are dealing with their crimes.[3] Survivors, already victims of power abuse, continue to be the marginal voice excluded from the dominant narratives that tell their story.

The aim of my study was to embody, in a qualitative research design, feminist methodological principles that seek to give precedence to marginal voices that are as yet unheard. These principles include two important aspects: the levelling out of inequitable power in the production of knowledge by connecting with the 'grass roots' of lived experience, and requiring the role of the researcher to be listening, interactive and non-directive. Consequently I drew on oral life history ethnography[4] to inform the interview process, and I used grounded theory, an inductive mode of analysis.[5]

Two hallmarks of feminist research methodology I took into account were 'reflexivity', which requires the researcher to locate her own voice in the project, and owning up when mistakes have been made in carrying out the research. In regard to the latter, a problem arose as a consequence of the first stage of my analysis, but this 'mistake' actually proved fortuitous. I had to return to the theoretical literature on method where I found a divergence in the approaches of the two co-founders of grounded theory, Barney Glaser and Anselm Strauss. As I outline each stage of my research with reference to methodological issues, I will show the effect of this divergence of opinion, and why Glaser's freer approach proved the more appropriate for my study with the vulnerable.

Tuning in: grounded theory, the method

Creating theology from the 'grass roots' was fundamental to my aim of finding out how Christian survivors relate to God, and how they have retained their faith despite abusive experience. In order to lay the foundations for developing their theology, I first needed to settle on the definition of 'abuse' for the study.

As it is 'the concern of the people in the substantive area' of research that is important in grounded theory,[6] I wanted to keep the research question quite loose. I did not want to 'close down' the field, since it is only what the subjects are saying that should open up the avenues of analysing the data. Assumptions from the researcher's experience and knowledge can prevent theory from being truly grounded.[7] Therefore I allowed 'abuse' a relatively broad meaning, including spiritual, physical, emotional or sexual abuse. I stated this clearly in my advertisements for participants, and on the information sheet containing interview details that I sent to respondents to aid them in making a decision about participation. I also gave assurances of anonymity.

Sixteen women and one man responded to the advertisements. After considering the information sheet, the eleven who agreed to the interview were all women. It was not my intention to draw lines on the variable of gender, rather an approach that allowed 'the marginalized' a voice. However, the feminist methodological underpinning of the study may have created an inherent gender bias, striking a note that did not resonate with male survivors. Perhaps a different key has to be found to unlock their voices.

The volunteers, who self-selected as 'survivors of abuse', brought with them a wide range of experiences of abuse. Some experiences were individual instances, for example, a rape or an assault. Some were experiences of long-term exposure to abusive environments, for example, domestic violence or systematic physical abuse in an institution. Some participants had suffered a combination of abuses.[8]

I used a non-directive, open-ended style of interview,[9] beginning each time with a cue similar to: 'What I'd like you to do is to tell me about your journey of faith'. This allowed the participant freedom to take the 'telling' in any direction she wished, interview length depending entirely on her.[10] Two women related their whole story from start to finish, so time ran well over the suggested hour. Both women gladly agreed to give a second interview to complete their contribution. Most of the women were happy talking about their story and faith without any contribution from me. One participant commented on this and thanked me for not butting in; she said no-one had ever listened to her story before without interrupting and asking 'silly' questions.

A common remark made by participants was that it had been a very valuable experience, because it was a rare opportunity for them to talk about this important issue, specifically in relation to their faith. The women invariably reported that their motivation for giving the interview was to aid research, and more specifically to help other victims. I answered any questions the interviewees asked of me,[11] which were usually about what had motivated me to study this subject.

In all, seventeen hours of material were recorded, the shortest interview lasting forty-three minutes. The longest comprised two recordings which ran over five hours. The median was seventy-five minutes. I used a Samson C01U USB 2.0 microphone so that all the interviews were recorded as .wav files. This eased transcription into MS Word documents: I could type freely, stop the recording at a click of the mouse, and quickly move forwards or backwards to any point in the recording.[12] Although one interviewee declined to give a recorded interview, I carried out and transcribed ten interviews and sent them to participants for their comments and/or correction.[13] I offered them a final opportunity to withdraw their contribution from the project before I began analysis. Nine responded with full permission to use their interviews. I then imported their transcripts into NVivo 8 software to begin analysis.

Fine tuning: data analysis

> The research problem is as much discovered as the process that continues to resolve it and indeed resolving process usually indicates the problem. They are integrated.[14]

This evaluation of grounded theory by one of its founders, Barney Glaser, was well illustrated in the use of this social scientific research method in my study. The meaning of Glaser's monograph, subtitled *Emergence vs Forcing*, will become clear in this section, since scrutiny of the controversy between the co-founders of grounded theory helped me ensure that my interview data was as free from pre-conceptual control as it is possible to be. In explanation, I first give an overview of the method. I then offer a more detailed account of the process of data analysis, highlighting the discrepancy between Glaser and Anselm Strauss. My rationale for choosing the Glaserian approach as the most appropriate for my study will emerge.

Integration is the byword of grounded theory in which constant comparison of data for differences and similarities helps to create an overarching theory. Constant comparison reduces researcher bias when conceptualizing raw data because it prevents the analyst from following only one track exclusively; that is to say, *all* the data has to be taken into account.[15]

Data analysis proceeds by assigning conceptual 'codes' to units of interview text. A unit of text can be a word, a phrase or a whole paragraph, provided it represents a stand-alone incident that encapsulates the meaning of the concept. Connections begin to emerge between the different coded meanings, building up further creative conceptualization. This is aided by the writing of 'theoretical memos' to chart the thinking behind the developing theory, i.e. to 'show the workings' of the analyst. As the relationships between codes develop, ever higher-level concepts become indicative of a 'core category'. This 'core category' is an explanation that accounts for what is central in the data;[16] it is a succinct term that should explain what is really going on for the participants.

Thus the foundations of a grounded theory lie always in effective coding throughout, which ensures that concepts fit well with the recorded incidents they represent. This produces research that has relevance to the real concerns of participants. Glaser calls this relevance 'grab', and maintains that results are not of academic interest only, because although social processes are being conceptualized, there are practical implications. A truly grounded theory explains how problems are processed with wide variation. It therefore meets 'the two prime criteria of good scientific inductive theory: parsimony and scope'.[17] Moreover, it is modifiable, because it can be adjusted when new, relevant data are compared with existing data.

There is some encouragement in the methodological literature to begin transcribing and analysing data while fieldwork is still progressing, allowing researchers to check the 'fit' of emergent concepts in the field with new participants.[18] However, I had carried out all my interviews before starting the processes of transcribing and coding. This was due to time pressures, as well as the emotionally taxing nature of the material, which required that I waited until I had sufficient time and space away from full-time ministry. However, following Strauss and Corbin's advice, I began reading material for the theological literature review, which would be the 'analytic tool' that 'fosters conceptualization'.[19] This was the mistake I made and I return to this point below in the course of describing the coding process.

Coding in grounded theory has three distinct stages. The first stage is called 'open' coding. Open codes are the foundational building blocks of the theory, involving close scrutiny of the data, breaking it 'open' line-by-line to discover abstract concepts that connect together the incidents related by the respondents. Table 8.1 illustrates how four 'incidents' gave rise to an early open code in my analysis, which I named *difficulty in forgiving*.

During this stage many more concepts emerged from the data than were suggested by the review of theological literature. Therefore by the second stage of analysis, named 'axial coding' by Strauss and Corbin,[21] I was faced with two sets of codes: one set commensurate with the literature, and one 'emerging' set. I felt stuck, as there seemed to be a choice of which set I should

Table 8.1 Examples from early coding of incidents into open code *difficulty in forgiving*[20]

Incident 1	I've had to forgive my husband much more than that, and forgiveness is not the sort of thing you do, a one-off thing. It's something you have to work at all the time. On a nice day forgiveness is easy. It comes with the sun. But on a nasty [day] all your things come out of the woodwork and you have to do your forgiveness all over again. *Esther*
Incident 2	I can make a decision to forgive those people and let them go away from me for God to redeem them, but that doesn't mean that I'll forget what they've done, and it doesn't open up the way for me to have a relationship again, unless they can honestly say what they've done to me, and I accept what they've done and believe in what they're saying. So that's really helpful to me, because you feel guilty that you're not forgiving, but you can't pretend to forgive. *Miriam*
Incident 3	That's where it gets difficult because I know in my heart that Jesus died for me, and I know that he's taken all my sin, forgiven me every last bit of it, and yet I am holding on to this sin of my Grandfather's. *Priscilla*
Incident 4	I think it's quite difficult really because during most things in my life, if something happens, whatever it be, I'm fairly willing to forgive and move on, but I think it's when it comes down to that, it's just that one issue, one event, two people, I have the issue with forgiving. *Tamar*

conceptualize further. How could I discern which were the most important codes? It was when I returned to assess the literature on grounded theory to address this query that the subtle, but major differences between Strauss and Glaser's methodology became clear. Glaser argues there are significant divergences in Strauss and Corbin's book *Basics of Qualitative Research*[22] from the method he and Strauss developed, and originally published together in 1967. Two of these differences are pertinent here.

First, the early reviewing of literature in Strauss and Corbin's approach advocates the 'verification of categories' that have been found in early coding. This then leads to subsequent directive questioning of respondents in the field, encouraging a 'forcing' of concepts rather than allowing their natural emergence. Carrying out 'verification' did not affect my data collection since, as mentioned earlier I did not hold any further interviews after I'd begun coding. However, the lack of 'fit' between my two sets of codes was explained: one set of codes were 'forced' from concepts in the theological literature I had read, and one set were 'emerging' from the interviews. I'd identified in grounded theory methodology the very problem I'd been trying to avoid at the outset.

Second, while Strauss and Corbin's next phase of coding, called 'axial coding', appears identical in meaning to Glaser's term 'theoretical coding', there is in reality a discrepancy between the two.[23] In this second stage of coding, the analyst examines relationships between the abstract concepts that have been formed in the first stage of 'open coding'. However, in 'axial coding' Strauss and Corbin prescribe the use of only *one* pre-selected set of six relationships between codes and concepts. Glaser, on the other hand, identifies *eighteen* sets of relationship types, each with six variants,[24] and argues that these relationships should not be pre-determined in the second stage of coding: otherwise the theory is 'forced' too narrowly into specific criteria, rather than being allowed to emerge. This breadth of coding becomes crucial when determining the 'core category', which is not explicit in the data: it is only through the painstaking constant comparative method, noticing and following up numerous connections, testing out all the variables, that a grounded theory is created from implicit themes.

Significantly Strauss wrote that, 'in the analysis, it is the phenomenon focused upon [by the analyst] that is the researcher's core category'.[25] On the contrary, Glaser argues that for the grounded theorist the exact opposite is true: the researcher's core category is 'that which emergence from data forces upon *him*'.[26] This is a humbling task because it requires that the data, i.e. the participants' words, must be in control of the process, not the analyst. Although I had not begun coding with Strauss and Corbin's single set of six relational types,[27] my attention had been drawn to a pivotal issue: that is, I'd moved away from the principle of allowing the respondents' words to determine the coding, which led to premature conceptualizing because I had begun to use themes from the literature, and I was about to limit the scope of relationships between codes.[28] The Glaserian principle of 'What concerns them?' (i.e. the participants) underscored my main aim of allowing the survivors to be heard, not theologians and pastors, even the feminist ones and those few writing about abuse. I decided now to give priority to the emerging codes: I followed Glaser more closely and proceeded with free 'theoretical coding', which further conceptualized the data to a 'higher level of abstraction'[29] by forming a wide variety of unspecified relationships between codes.

When a 'core category' began to emerge, I then delimited systematic coding to relating only concepts I had already discovered to that core idea, thereby strengthening it. In other words, 'open coding' ceased in this next phase, which is known as 'selective coding':[30] all the interview data was still being worked through, but it was coded in relation to the core category only, without creating any new open codes. It is important in this third stage that the analyst checks continually for alternative explanations of relationships by going back to the raw data, and crucially, by not speculating. This validates the core category, which might be modified in order to harmonize all the incidents and concepts where there is discord. The result is that the grounded theory becomes integrated by elaborating the 'core category' as far as possible, in terms of all its properties.

After this final stage of coding, 'theoretical sampling' usually follows. This further 'saturates' the developing grounded theory, by carrying out more field work to fill out the aspects where it is less dense. The aim is to achieve theoretical 'saturation', that is, no further data produce any modifications to the theory: the grounded theory is conceptually complete.[31] Another way of saturating the theory, which Glaser and Strauss encouraged in their earlier partnership, is to 'use any material bearing in the area' at this stage, including writings of other authors.[32] Neither pioneer changed his mind about this.[33]

One final aspect of grounded theory method is the writing of 'theoretical memos', which continues apace throughout all stages of the research. These are ideas about the emerging theory that occur to the analyst at any point during the process and that are immediately written down. Glaser calls these memos 'the frontier of the analyst's thinking'.[34] At the end of data analysis, these stored ideas are sorted and ordered, a process that helps construct the full theory.

In sum, I have presented grounded theory according to Glaser as an appropriate method for a study such as mine. I have argued that it is designed to create theory from a new field of research, putting the respondents' concerns at the centre. Rather than beginning with a hypothesis and then verifying or disproving it, the analysis produces a relevant theory grounded faithfully in the interviews. Specifically it resists the use of pre-conceived concepts from 'experts' in the field, and so provides the key that will unlock a new set of voices. This helps us to truly listen, so that we can discover what 'processes the main problem that makes life viable for' the participants.[35] For survivors of abuse with faith this turned out to be a spiritual process: *knowing God's timeless presence transforms*. This process had complex nuances, which would need teasing out.[36]

Working with a reliable instrument: NVivo 8

In addition to the interview transcripts, the meticulous process of analysis as described above produces an enormous amount of new data. When working with completely unstructured data, codes multiply exponentially. So how does the analyst see the wood for the trees when numerous and complex new relationships are noted between codes and higher concepts, not to mention dozens of memos? This is where I found NVivo 8[37] indispensable.

The first, most obvious point to make about working with NVivo, is the enormous amount of data that can be stored in one place. This software enables text documents, as well as photos, audio and video files, to be imported and analysed with a variety of tools. The second point, which takes up the remainder of this chapter, is to explain how grounded theory analysis translates into use of the software.

In NVivo, the foundational building blocks of conceptual codes are called 'nodes'. Selections of incidents that illustrate these concepts are easily made by highlighting the text with the mouse and dropping it into the labelled node. These developing nodes can then be set into hierarchies called 'tree nodes', with the higher codes being called 'parent nodes'. 'Memos' can also be typed and stored, and linked to any of the appropriate nodes throughout. When the intricate analysis in the second and final stages of coding requires the creation of ever more complex relationships between nodes, tree nodes and memos, these relationships can be given a name to denote the type of relationship and are stored elsewhere in the programme.

Add to this the facility of moving data around, creating searches, and producing tables and diagrams when reporting to show how concepts and categories build, this makes for a powerful tool. While the intricacy of the software is daunting, the support package is excellent, in that there is a full programme of tutorials provided online.[38]

The following explanation uses diagrams created by the NVivo programme in order to demonstrate how concepts building up into a core category can be reported.

Table 8.2 gives examples of 'incidents' chosen from many examples in my data that contributed to 'open codes' concerning change. Figure 8.1 shows how these seven particular codes were later grouped in an NVivo hierarchical tree node, to form a higher code called *Transformation*. The arrow in the diagram denotes upward direction from the open codes toward the 'parent node'. This higher code/parent node therefore encompassed all these incidents in Table 8.2, as well as any attributed to the original open codes concerning change and transformation throughout the data.

It has to be said at this point, that titles for codes, open or otherwise, are personal to each analyst. In retrospect, I believe some of my own naming of codes could have been sharper. Working as an individual, this posed no problems. However, when a team of analysts is working from the same data set, to avoid misinterpretation, labels with clear and agreed definitions would need to be chosen.

Table 8.2 Examples of open codes later grouped into higher category *Transformation*

Open code	Example of incident from raw data
Change in view about abuse etc.	I've found that if you think about things, you always look and think, that was horrendous, but it's not until you've started writing things down that you begin to see there's some really lovely things, in horrible situations . . . and once I started remembering things, I actually started remembering far more lovely things about the camps than the horrendous things . . . You know, life is not made just out of horrible things. *Esther*
External change in life	Oh it's completely changed now. My whole lifestyle is completely different. And when I was first left on my own, because he did walk out on me, after that time when he beat me so badly, when I came home from the hospital, he'd gone, packed his bags and gone, and I suddenly realized that was it, and that was my escape route. So I went straight to the solicitor's and filed for a divorce. Looking back now I don't know how I had the guts to do it but I did. And of course it's then my relationship has changed so completely. Because all I had then was God. *Esther*
Transformation of self, behaviour	He's worked with me all this time and helped me, like he's been nurturing me. And for so many years I've felt like a child and wouldn't have been able to do this interview because I just would have sat here crying and crying. *Joanna*
Change for worse, going away from God	I suppose for some people, they either fall off the edge, don't they? and they feel so let down that they don't turn back to God again. *Lydia*
Interpretation	Part of the healing of abuse came when I was made to understand: children are good observers but poor interpreters. *Lydia*
Spiritual awakening, conversion	I can't ever turn back, and I don't have any plans at all because – you know that song, 'All I once held dear, built my life upon'? It says to know you in your suffering . . . ? I think at some level, that I have experienced that and I suppose in a way then it's a privilege. So my relationship with God then . . . I'm in a completely different place. *Lydia*
Transforming evil/pain into good	Through all of it I realize that humanity has choices and people make choices and God uses what you're in for good to come out of it. And I don't know but if it hadn't been for all of that I wouldn't know in my – I mean we know things with our heads, but it's a difference when we feel them, when it moves from here to here. *Priscilla*

Figure 8.2 reflects the growing complexity of the analysis. In Table 8.1 above, we saw that the open code *difficulty in forgiving* was created from four incidents within the data. Open codes *forgiven by God* and *forgiving self* were likewise created from a number of incidents in the raw data. Later in my analysis,

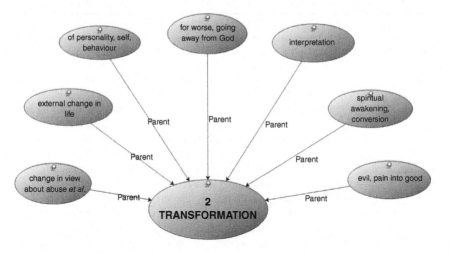

Figure 8.1 NVivo model of advanced coding relationships in a 'tree node'

I set all three of these early open codes into a 'tree node' under the 'parent node' *forgiveness*.[39]

Forgiveness, which now encompassed all the incidents in the 'open/child nodes', in turn contributed at a later stage to an even higher concept,

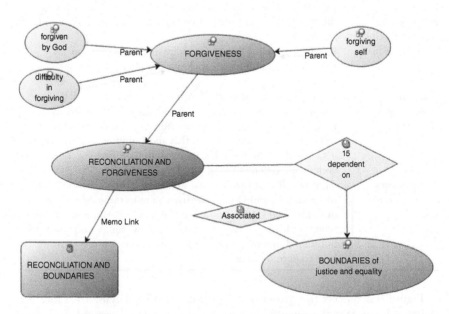

Figure 8.2 NVivo model of advanced coding relationships. Shapes and colours help differentiate codes, relationships and memos when producing diagrams in NVivo

Table 8.3 Example of a memo recorded in NVivo

Memo: reconciliation and boundaries
There are difficulties reconciling with perpetrators because barriers have to come down in order to be on a level again Boundaries that are trampled over are like scars How do boundaries relate to forgiveness?

Reconciliation and Forgiveness. Many of the participants grappled with the issue of reconciliation with an abuser. While I was working on this data, a thought about 'reconciliation and boundaries' occurred to me. I recorded it in a memo (see Table 8.3). Early on I had attributed some text to an open code '*difficulty in forgiving*' (see Incident 2 in Table 8.1 above), which I now saw was just as clearly about difficulty in reconciling.

Later, a relationship developed in the data between the two higher concepts *reconciliation and forgiveness* and *boundaries of justice and equality*. This relationship appeared to have the quality of 'dependency', which is indicated in the diamond shape connecting the two concepts. I could refer back to the memo in Table 8.3 and link it into this higher concept now that it had emerged. It had been implicit in the data, and therefore in what the participants were saying: namely, that reconciliation and forgiveness were dependent on boundaries of justice and equality. This concern checked out with the participants and with the literature when I returned to it.

There is one final point to make. The thinking and hard work of immersing oneself in the data cannot be done for the analyst by software. NVivo is a tool, not the finished product and is therefore only as good as the craftsman or woman. The analyst still has to understand the methodological underpinning of grounded theory, and make the decision whether to enforce her own categories, hierarchies and narrow the variety of relationships, or let them emerge word by word, phrase by phrase. NVivo can only aid the process.

Conclusion: a resonant composition

Coaxing out a tiny voice, a vulnerable voice, which has not been heard before, needs extra special attention from researchers. Grounded theory, according to Glaser, allows the researcher to keep power firmly with the participants. While the analyst is creating the overarching theory, it must be based in the living words of people so that we can hear their voices clearly. NVivo is a tool to aid our discovery.

Allocating accurate conceptual codes at the beginning of analysis, right the way through to discovering a 'core category', is painstaking, but crucial. It is like finding the right riffs or themes for a grand composition; the memos are sketches, and the grounded theory is the final orchestrated symphony that includes all the variations on each theme. We need to be silent and receptive, a good audience, so that we can distinguish all the soft tones in which 'little voices' speak, particularly those who are vulnerable to the dominant narratives that have excluded, ignored or even damaged them. It is time for survivors of abuse to be heard.

Notes

1 From *Little Voice*, directed by Mark Herman (Miramax Films and Scala Productions, 1998).
2 Other software for data analysis is on the market, e.g. Atlas.ti and HyperRESEARCH, but I used NVivo 8 software, developed and marketed by QSR International.
3 An exception was BBC, *Abuse: The Untold Story* 12 April 2016.
4 See S. B. Gluck and S. Armitage, 'Reflections on Women's Oral History: An Exchange', *Frontiers: A Journal of Women Studies* 19, no. 3 (1998): 1–11; S. B. Gluck and D. Patai, *Women's Words: The Feminist Practice of Oral History* (New York: Routledge, 1991); E. Lawless, 'Women's Life Stories and Reciprocal Ethnography as Feminist and Emergent', *Journal of Folklore Research* 28, no. 1 (1991): 35–60.
5 See Susan Shooter, *How Survivors of Abuse Relate to God: The Authentic Spirituality of the Annihilated Soul* (Farnham: Ashgate, 2012), 42–47 on the development of feminist research methodology.
6 B. G. Glaser, *Basics of Grounded Theory Analysis: Emergence vs Forcing* (Mill Valley, CA: Sociology Press, 1992), 4.
7 Glaser, *Basics*, 50; D. Douglas, 'Inductive Theory Generation: A Grounded Approach to Business Inquiry', *Electronic Journal of Business Research Methods* 2, no. 1 (2003): 48.
8 See Shooter, *Survivors of Abuse*, 52, for table 3.1 'Range of different abuses experienced by nine interviewees'.
9 Nicola Slee, *Women's Faith Development: Patterns and Processes* (Aldershot: Ashgate, 2004), 54; Lawless, 'Women's Life Stories', 39–40; K. F. Punch, *Introduction to Social Research: Quantitative and Qualitative Approaches* (London: Sage, 2005), 172.
10 Lawless, 'Women's Life Stories', 40.
11 A. Oakley, 'Interviewing Women: A Contradiction in Terms', in *Doing Feminist Research*, ed. H. Roberts (London: Routledge, 1981), 35–37; K. Minister, 'A Feminist Frame for the Oral History Interview', in *Women's Words: The Feminist Practice of Oral History* ed. S. B. Gluck, and D. Patai (New York: Routledge, 1991), 36; M. L. DeVault, 'Talking and Listening from Women's Standpoint: Feminist Strategies for Interviewing and Analysis', in *Qualitative Research*, Vol. 4, ed. A. Bryman, and R. G. Burgess (London: Sage, 1999), 93.
12 I used the Creative Media Source Software, manufactured by Creative Technology Limited.
13 Lawless, 'Women's Life Stories'; Slee, *Women's Faith Development*, 54.
14 Glaser, *Basics*, 21.
15 Glaser, *Basics*, 14.
16 Punch, *Introduction to Social Research*, 205. Regarding terminology: there is interchangeability in the literature between 'category' and 'variable', the latter originating in quantitative methods. There is also correlation between 'properties' and 'incidents'.
17 Glaser, *Basics*, 18.
18 M. B. Miles and A. M. Huberman, *Qualitative Data Analysis: An Expanded Sourcebook*, 2nd ed. (London: Sage, 1994); Punch, *Introduction to Social Research*; A. L. Strauss and J. M. Corbin, *Basics of Qualitative Research: Techniques and Procedures for Developing Grounded Theory*, 2nd ed. (London: Sage, 1998).
19 Strauss and Corbin, *Basics of Qualitative Research*, 53.

20 I gave participants biblical pseudonyms to preserve their anonymity.

21 Strauss and Corbin, *Basics of Qualitative Research*, 123–142.

22 Strauss and Corbin, *Basics of Qualitative Research* (1988 edition).

23 Glaser, *Basics*, 29; Punch, *Introduction to Social Research*, 210.

24 B. G. Glaser, *Theoretical Sensitivity: Advances in the Methodology of Grounded Theory* (Mill Valley, CA: Sociology Press, 1978), 74–82.

25 Strauss and Corbin (1988 edition), quoted in Glaser, *Basics*, 82.

26 Glaser, *Basics*, 82, emphasis added.

27 Strauss and Corbin's set is called the 6 Cs by Glaser in *Theoretical Sensitivity*, 74: Causes, Context, Contingencies, Consequences, Co-variances and Conditions.

28 See also J. Kendall, 'Axial Coding and the Grounded Theory Controversy', *Western Journal of Nursing Research* 21, no. 6 (1999): 743–757. Strauss and Corbin's 'axial coding' had changed the focus of Kendall's study from the concern of her respondents, which was 'doing well with ADHD children', to the code 'disruption'. This provided her with vast descriptive detail about how disruptive ADHD is for families, but did not answer her research question about how they coped; this confirms Glaser's view that description of a problem is not the aim of GT: its aim is to conceptualize social processes. Kendall concluded that both Glaser and Strauss's methods are viable, the goal of the study must determine which to use. See also G. Allan, 'A Critique of Using Grounded Theory as a Research Method', *Electronic Journal of Business Research Methods* 2, no. 1 (2003): 1–10 for analysis problems resolved by the Glaserian method.

29 Punch, *Introduction to Social Research*, 205.

30 Glaser, *Basics*, 75.

31 Punch, *Introduction to Social Research*, 214–15.

32 B. G. Glaser, and A. L. Strauss, *The Discovery of Grounded Theory*, 4th ed. (New Brunswick, NJ: Aldine Transaction, 2009), 169.

33 In my study there were no further field samples, but I carried out this wider comparison of the theory by relating the core category to the book of Job, and to Marguerite Porete's *Mirror of Simple Souls*. See Shooter, *Survivors of Abuse*, chapters 5 and 6.

34 Glaser, *Theoretical Sensitivity*, 83.

35 Ibid., 51.

36 Before writing up the results for the original thesis, I sent a copy of all the quotes I planned to use to the interviewees, with an explanation of the emergent theory, for their permission and comments. All nine responses were positive about the core category of my grounded theory.

37 The software moves on quickly and the up-to-date version in 2016 is NVivo 11. See www.qsrinternational.com/product/nvivo11-for-windows.

38 I was fortunate in that Kings College London provided IT training for its postgraduate students.

39 There were more than three, but I've shown only three here for purposes of clarity.

9 Listening for the 'I'

Adapting a voice-centred, relational method of data analysis in a group interview to examine women's faith lives

Kate Massey

Introduction

The tensions facing women who attempt to combine mothering with work outside the home have been well documented, but less attention has been given to the impact of faith upon those tensions and the resultant decisions women made. 'The intersection between spirituality, motherhood and vocation is largely unexplored in contemporary writing and research' argued one article that examined the faith lives of North American women who were both mothers and academics.[1] The article went on to question whether such women were simply too busy to contribute to the discussion! This chapter concerns the method I adapted to explore the faith lives of women called to both motherhood and career.

My interest in this subject began in my own experience. When I started my research,[2] I was a mother to three small children, and spent much of my time in the toddler groups, play dates and school playgrounds that constituted the middle-class stay-at-home-mother social scene. While immersed in this world, I was introduced to the work of American sociologist, Sharon Hays. In her book *Cultural Contradictions of Motherhood*, Hays asserts that the prevalent parenting model in Western society is that of 'intensive mothering' where mothers are expected to expend great emotional, financial and temporal resources nurturing 'the sacred child'.[3] This correlated so perfectly with my own local observations on contemporary child-rearing that I was encouraged to research the topic of motherhood, and in particular the experiences of mothers who could not embrace unquestioningly the intensive mothering ideology. I found that my own call to vocational work provided a counter-narrative to expectations around intensive mothering, and so I wanted to hear the stories of Christian mothers, who through being called to something as well as motherhood had to make decisions regarding the place and priorities of child-rearing. In particular, I wanted to explore how their faith influenced the decisions they made, and to investigate that neglected intersection of spirituality, motherhood and vocation.

In doing this, I was researching an area in which I had significant personal investment. By the time I conducted the extended group interview with my four participants, I had recently returned to full-time work, while continuing to care for my three children who were then aged between three and seven years of age. I was engaged in similar struggles to those experienced by my research participants, and my experience felt very present and raw. Listening to the recording of the interview and reading the transcript, I was aware of the emotional impact that the subjects' stories and observations had on me. I was completely enmeshed with my field of research. Also, I was faced with a complex collection of data: four interwoven individual stories, which became the story of the group, overlaid with my own story in this emotive area. As a feminist researcher, committed to the voices of my participants being heard, how was I to handle the data entrusted to me, responsibly and reflexively?

In all other areas of my methodology, I had created a transparent and well-considered process, which had been scrutinized by others and gave me a framework in which to contain and name any bias. I had intended to adopt a simple thematic analysis of the transcripts as my means of data analysis, but it became clear to me that this process was not robust enough given my own emotional connection to the subject matter. It was essential that I had a clearly articulated method of data analysis that allowed me to pay attention to each voice, including my own, and enabled me to approach the data from varying perspectives, freeing me as much as possible from the tunnel vision of my own particular point of view.

In this chapter, I discuss my experience of using a voice-centred relational method of data analysis in a group interview. From this experience, I high-light three key themes. The first is the value of using this method in feminist research which was committed to paying close attention to the voice of the subject, to recognizing the personal involvement of the researcher in the sub-ject matter and to creating appropriate processes to aid reflexivity. The second is identifying the benefits and limitations of using this method in a group interview setting, and to describe the reading for emotional language that I built into my process. The final theme is a reflection on the use of indirect speech among the women who participated in this group interview. These themes overlap as I describe the research process; however, I begin with a discussion of Natasha Mauthner and Andrea Doucet's voice-centred relational method,[4] in which I found an answer to my problems of transparency and reflexivity in data analysis.

Voice-centred relational method of data analysis

During their doctoral research, Mauthner and Doucet had identified a paucity of practical guidance on how to conduct qualitative data analysis. They agreed with the importance feminist scholars placed on understanding women's experience 'in and on their own terms', but found no method that allowed this: in the most commonly used qualitative data analysis methods either the researcher or a computer program imposed categories upon the subject's experience. However, they had the opportunity to work with Carol Gilligan who, with Lyn Brown and other colleagues at the Harvard Project on Women's Psychology and Girls' Development, had developed a voice-centred relational method of qualitative data analysis. Mauthner and Doucet took this process and adapted it for their own research.

Brown and Gilligan's approach recognized the located nature of the voices of the young women they interviewed. This was not geographical location, but rather that these voices were located in female bodies, in young women who existed within a web of relationships and within a societal and cultural framework.[5] They also acknowledged that if a voice was speaking, then someone was listening, and the girls' stories were told not into a vacuum but to the researchers in a very specific relationship. Therefore, their method tried to 'speak about human experience in a manner that re-sounds its relational nature and carries the polyphony of voice'.[6] Finally, their method focused on the participants' voices rather than their 'selves', recognizing that the inner self can be divided, and we may speak with different voices in relation to different things.[7]

This method consisted of at least four 'listenings', which was how they spoke of either listening to recordings or reading a transcript, with each listening following a different 'voice' through the interview. The first listening focused on the story the girl told and the researcher's response to it; the second listened for the 'I' and what the girl said about herself. Both these listenings were relational and responsive – eliciting the otherness of the subject and the relationship that had developed with the researcher. In the third and fourth listenings, the researcher moved to a position of 'resisting' listening, where they listened to the voices speaking of relationships and the girls' experience of their societal landscape. As feminist researchers, Brown and Gilligan were acutely aware of the patriarchal norms that influenced the girls' environment and, in these resisting listenings, they looked for the things that enlivened and diminished the speaker.[8]

Mauthner and Doucet took these principles and adapted them to suit their own research topic, disciplines and personalities. They described two core readings, which were similar to the first two listenings described by Brown and Gilligan above. However, in the first reading, they emphasized the value of the researcher recording not simply their emotional response to the participant's story, but their intellectual response, for example, to identify the theoretical framework they use to interpret the narrative.[9] In the second reading, they listened for the I-language of the participant, physically marking each place where the speaker uses personal pronouns when talking of themselves. They described this technique as 'increasing the volume' of the participant's voice, and felt that was useful for shedding light on the internal conflicts and quandaries that precede decision. They felt this was particularly important in feminist research which recognizes that the participants may not always have the freedom and agency to choose the option they prefer.[10] Mauthner and Doucet described these two readings as 'staples' of this method to which a further number of readings could be added depending on the discipline and topic being researched. They both chose to adopt readings similar to Brown and Gilligan's third and fourth listenings: reading for relationships and wider social and cultural context.[11]

Using Mauthner and Doucet's voice-centred relational method

Mauthner and Doucet's voice-centred relational method of data analysis was a valuable resource for my research in that it provided a robust, explicit process, which enabled me to disentangle my own story from the stories of the participants and pay close attention to the voices of the respondents from different perspectives. It also enabled me to use my own responses as further data and was flexible enough to allow me to build in further readings should my analysis identify new areas of interest.

First reading

Using the first reading, which focuses on the narrative content and reader's response, I found that my use of the method was complicated by the fact that I had undertaken a group interview.[12] Therefore, the narrative of the interview was the narrative directed by the group rather than a single individual and told more about the collective dynamic than the specific experience of each respondent. However, it remained a valid and helpful stage in analysis. The way in which ideas were recognized, affirmed and elaborated upon among the women, with story and anecdote building on the ones that had gone before, provided helpful data for my research. One of the features we listen for in the first reading is the characters that populate the participants' worlds, and it was fascinating to observe the group create a character that they nicknamed the Alpha Mummy. One woman introduced her:

> [O]ne of the benefits [of working] for me is that I am not in any danger of turning into one of those Alpha Mummies at the school gate.

Then later, when discussing another topic, she revisited it:

> Or I could give up work ... But then I'd go mad (group laughter) and become an Alpha Mummy.

When I asked for clarification, others in the group contributed – it was clearly an image they could understand:

> Oh they're terrifying! Surely they have them at every school ...

> They run everything. They're chairperson on everything. They know everything. They're friends with everyone, but they've got a finger in everything, an opinion on everything.

[T]hat's sort of it. There are the ones that run everything and are a bit cliquey, but then there's some aren't there who are just always there and that's their world – yeah?

[T]hey just hang around together all of the time. They're at the school gate, and then they go to the coffee shop and then they go to the toddler group and then they go here and then they go there and they sort of … It's a bit kind of like a swarm.

Even allowing for humour and caricature, the language is strong. The Alpha Mummy – like some sort of grown-up bogey(wo)man – is terrifying, dangerous and could drive one from one's senses. This grotesque, comedic character, generated within the group narrative, was a powerful indicator of some of the fears and conflicts the group participants shared.

The reader-response element of the first reading remained highly useful as a means of transparently identifying and recording my emotional and ideological reactions to aspects of the conversation. For example, one participant discussed how she had a separate bank account to her partner, but due to differences in earning, they had quite complex arrangements to meet the family expenses. It also left her very careful not to spend money on herself that she hadn't earned. My jottings in the margin addressed my emotional and personal response to this:

My partner and I combine all our money, so emotionally I find this 'His and Hers' cash concept weird (while understanding the need to earn my keep).

I then go on to analyse my own ideological position, which means that I am content to spend my partner's money:

I think the way my partner and I share our financial resources … takes account of my years of maternal labour.

It felt healthier, somehow, to externalize these responses and document them, so later I could look at them critically as data in their own right.

Second reading

The most fruitful and creative reading was the second reading in which I listened for the I-language of the participants. In the transcript, I physically highlighted every phrase which included a first-person personal pronoun. My first observation was how little I-language there was in total, as the women chose to speak instead of daughters, husbands, mothers and churchmen to make their point. The I-language decreased further when I made the decision to remove the phrase 'I think' from my analysis of this reading. Mauthner and Doucet believed that an important aspect of identifying the I-language – and particularly phrases like 'I think' – was that these phrases could highlight times when the respondent is struggling to articulate something.[13] I felt that, in the different relational context of a *group* interview, this phrase was used as a verbal filler. It was something that held the speaker's place in a lively conversation while they pulled a response together. It was also a relational buffer in a group of women meeting for the first time – prefacing a statement with 'I think' made it provisional and less likely to cause offence. My observation was that the phrase 'I think' was rarely followed by a statement that related to the woman herself directly, and as I wanted this reading to show me the individuals and their perceptions of themselves more clearly, I chose to ignore this phrase in this reading. These 'I think' phrases – in association with the lack of direct I-language overall – were not without significance in another sense, which I shall discuss below.

Ignoring those that began with 'I think', I then listed the highlighted phrases for each participant. In some ways, this constructed a little narrative of what each participant chose to say directly about herself during the course of the group interview. It helped me to focus on each participant as a unique individual within the noise of the group – amplifying her voice as Mauthner and Doucet would say. I found reading the direct statements each woman made about herself rather poignant – hidden among all the humour and anecdote was a portrait of each woman as she experienced herself. There were strong statements:

> I work at the university ... I am a careers advisor ... I am interested in the theory of career ... I chose to be a parent ... I think of [my work] as pleasing to God.

Along with statements that exuded vulnerability:

> My career has flattened off ... I earn less than [my husband] ... If I was a better mother [my son] would behave ... I sometimes feel a bit judged by the other mums.

This listing of I-language is similar to the I-Poems that Gilligan *et al.* described in a later adaptation of their method called the Listening Guide. In the second reading in the Listening Guide, they suggest listing in order every personal pronoun with its verb and any other important associated words to make a 'poem'.[14] Gilligan describes these poems as a 'sonograph of the psyche' picking up conflicts and associations that the person speaking may not fully recognize themselves.[15]

This close reading of what the women chose to say about themselves also highlighted for me the amount of emotional language used by my respondents, and this observation was to be crucial to later readings.

Third and fourth readings

I found reading for relationships and context quite challenging. In the example given in Brown and Gilligan's early method, they draw out relational and conceptual voices from a rich and lengthy anecdote involving relationships with peers and authority figures.[16] In an individual interview, a skilled researcher may use silence to create space for extended, reflective anecdotes. A group interview is a different milieu with little silence and space. My participants shared stories of partners, children and faith leaders, but mainly in ambiguous snippets, and therefore it was difficult to draw confident conclusions from these slight tales in themselves.

I had chosen group interview as a method because of evidence that in bringing together people with shared experiences, groups have the potential to create a safe space where stories may be heard by others who understand 'intellectually, emotionally and viscerally',[17] and the similarity of the shared stories can validate the individual's testimony, which dominant discourses had led them to believe were 'idiosyncratic, selfish or even evil'.[18] Motherhood is a role where failure to meet cultural expectations can leave mothers feeling odd, selfish or unworthy so a group process felt appropriate for such exploration.[19] However, group interviews have limitations, and from the specific perspective of using this data analysis method, one such limitation was that, compared to individual interviews, there is less time to explore an individual's story in detail.[20] In examining relationships and context, I was working with fragments of voice, and therefore I struggled to draw conclusions confidently from them in isolation. I needed a process that could weave these fragments together to identify the voice of the group, while still staying close to the voices of my participants.

Mauthner and Doucet had chosen to adapt the third and fourth readings to fit their specific area of research, and so rather than letting the concepts emerge freely from the anecdotes, they went looking for evidence relating to a pre-determined research question in and among the anecdotes. In particular, Doucet had chosen to focus on the ideological context of motherhood by identifying the places where women used 'moral' language like 'should', 'ought', 'good', 'bad', 'right' and 'wrong'. My interest in the participants' lived experience of their dual calling to motherhood and work, combined with my observation during the second reading that there was a lot of emotional language, meant that I decided to pay attention to this emotional language and see where it was directed. Therefore, I decided to approach my reading of resistance from the perspective of emotion – trying to identify what enlivened and what diminished my participants.

Reading for emotion

In reading for emotion I began very simply by identifying and listing every phrase that indicated some inner experience alongside a brief indicator of the external experience that precipitated it. This exercise produced a long list of phrases that described an emotional experience combined with the external trigger. From this reading, I then began to try and loosely group these triggers together. This was not a particularly tidy process. Not every trigger fell within any grouping, and several of the groupings had significant overlap, but as I did not want to impose upon the data any more than was necessary, I was careful not to shoehorn any data into groupings where it did not truly fit. From this untidy process, I found that the most frequent triggers fell in areas like mothering, work, domestic responsibilities, childcare, God, expectations, balancing or integrating roles and finding creative ways to fulfil both callings. Having identified these key groupings, I returned to the original list of emotions and triggers to try and identify whether these groups of trigger experiences were associated predominantly with positive or negative emotions.

Identifying emotions as positive or negative is itself problematic – many emotions can be both positive and negative, and much depends on the context. However, by staying close to the text, I tried to identify whether these experiences were enlivening or diminishing to the lives of my participants. In the main, experiences of joy, freedom, excitement and encouragement would be grouped as positive, while experiences of sadness, guilt, judgement, exasperation or limitation would be grouped as negative. I felt this honoured Brown and Gilligan's original vision that such readings should identify relationships (and situations) that were narrowed and distorted versus empowering and healthy.[21]

This third reading for the emotional, internal voices of the women – how things made them feel – illuminated some of those snippets bringing them together into a more cohesive whole. The main sources of positive emotions were the fulfilment the participants found in both work and mothering, the satisfaction they experienced in finding new models in the domestic sphere, and the security they had in their relationship with God which seemed to make all else possible. The main sources of negative emotions were the pressure of external expectations, the disabling guilt they experienced about imperfect motherhood, their domestic 'failings' and being absent from their children, the limiting confinement they felt in the domestic sphere, and the difficulty of integrating working and mothering roles and balancing the demands of work/motherhood. While their relationship with God seemed to make their demanding lives possible, traditions within the church contributed to the pressure, guilt, limitation and challenge, whether that was conservative teaching on gender roles, stereotypes around traditional festivals like Mothering Sunday, or patterns of church worship and fellowship that either excluded or overburdened women with work and family responsibilities.

This simple analysis allowed me to return to the transcript for my fourth reading, which examines the social context, with fresh eyes and spot new connections between anecdotes and remarks. Through the medium of paying attention to the women's emotional language, I found that not only did I address the political aspects of their relationships and contexts, as suggested in Mauthner and Doucet's original schema, but also the theological aspects too. Attending to the participants' emotional experience directed my gaze to the highly dualistic and gendered landscape in which my participants negotiated their lives and to the role of their faith in sustaining them in the face of their challenges. It is possible that I may have identified some of these themes myself eventually, but the close attention to the I-language, and following that the emotional language of the participants, both highlighted the communal voices in the group interview and provided a clear process through which these voices were identified.

Indirect language in women's conversation

Paying attention to the emotional language of the women who participated in this interview both united fragments of voice into a coherent whole and made explicit some of the things the women were saying more obliquely through the stories of the 'daughters, husbands, mothers and churchmen' they shared. It struck me how my participants used indirect means to express their experience – illustrative, tentative, provisional language, rather than more propositional speech. Working from a transcript, it became very difficult to evidence in actual spoken words the impressions I had more clearly *felt* during the interview. Due to my proximity to the subject matter, my feelings, while not without epistemological value, could not be entirely relied upon to guide my analysis. Examining the emotional language, as described above, created a process to bring to the fore what the participants were saying about certain experiences. However, it left me asking questions about the preponderance of indirect language. Did my participants, as women, use more emotional and indirect language than men would have done, and if so, should this be considered when analysing transcripts of women's conversation?

I discovered that answering this question was not a simple process. Describing differences in speech between genders has long been controversial. Robin Lakoff was the first to try and describe women's language in her book *Language and Woman's Place* in 1975.[22] She described features of women's communication, for example, hedges, tag questions or excessive use of adjectives, and argued that these features made women's speech tentative, powerless and trivial. Hedges are linguistic forms including 'I think' or 'sort of', which make a phrase less certain, and the name comes from the idiom 'to hedge your bets'.[23] Tag questions are phrases like 'isn't it?' tagged on to the end of a statement, which Lakoff argued reduced the statement's strength.[24] To Lakoff, these differences were a deficit – a problem – resulting from differing socialization of young girls, and left them oppressed and unable to engage in the language of power and authority.[25] Her assertions both about the features of women's speech and the reasons behind them provoked a flurry of research and criticism, and the debate about whether and why women speak differently has continued ever since.

Studies that try and quantify these differences have been critiqued for an over-simplistic approach to gender, which ignores the way in which gender intersects with race, class, education and sexuality and pays rather too much attention to the experiences of white middle-class Western women.[26] Many such studies have tended to look at linguistic features, such as tag questions, hedges or interruptions, assuming them to be indicative of powerlessness/dominance without careful consideration of what is actually being communicated within that interaction.[27] Furthermore, after decades of work and multiple studies, meta-analyses show very small differences indeed between women and men in the language styles they use – what is more significant is the great similarity and flexibility in language use.[28] Both women and men adapt their language style depending on the context, their degree of expertise and the person to whom they are speaking.[29] However, the small differences that do exist tend to support my own observations. They find that women's language is more communal and tends more to mitigation, i.e. indirect or deferential speech.[30] Is such indirect speech a problem, or is it a strategy?

Jennifer Coates conducted ethnographic research in a white British context where she recorded multiple conversations in all-women groups of friends. Like Lakoff, she noted that the women she studied used a number of linguistic features like story-telling, hedges and tag questions; however her interpretation of the meaning and function of those features was very different. In the conversations Coates analysed, hedges and tag questions were not signs of uncertainty, but rather sophisticated techniques used to fulfil a number of different functions. A hedge feature might indicate genuine doubt or buy time to find the right word, but it may also be used out of sensitivity to others' feelings, to soften a controversial or difficult statement. This was certainly my impression when I removed the phrase 'I think' from the second stage of my data analysis, believing that this was a relational buffer rather than a statement relating to the speaker's own self. A hedge may also be used to avoid playing the expert, the 'uncertainty' it generates creating space for communal learning and discovery.[31]

Questions, including tag questions, were likewise a strategy to facilitate the conversation, rather than a sign of ignorance. They could be used to check for potential conflict and to invite others into the conversation. They can be a means of expressing solidarity, or a way of expressing a different view without causing a rupture in the relationship. Again, they are a means of avoiding the expert role and sharing the task of discovery.[32]

Both of these linguistic features were widely used by the participants in my group interview. In the excerpt above where the group creates the outrageous Alpha Mummy caricature, the participants use both these techniques (examples underlined):

> [T]hat's <u>sort of</u> it. There are the ones that run everything and are a bit cliquey, but then there's some aren't there who are just always there and that's their world <u>– yeah?</u>

> [T]hey just hang around together all of the time. They're at the school gate, and then they go to the coffee shop and then they go to the toddler group and then they go here and then they go there and they sort of … It's <u>a bit kind of like</u> a swarm.

The hedges 'sort of' and 'a bit kind of like' make provisional some quite critical assertions, while the tag question 'yeah?' checks that this idea is acceptable and the underlying principle recognized by the others in the conversation.

Questions can be used to stimulate stories, too. In her research, Coates observed how women told mirroring stories, which built on the stories that had gone before, introducing or developing topics in the group discussion. While my participants spoke little of their own lives in a direct sense, the stories they told of their daughters, husbands, mothers and churchmen built up layers of experience and knowledge within the group. Coates argues that story-telling is an important tool in tackling sensitive issues, and self-disclosure a key aspect of building relationship.[33]

Ultimately, Coates argues that all these linguistic forms are used by the women she studied to create an intentionally provisional and tentative space where the speakers share in the construction of talk. For the women, the *group voice* that expresses their shared experience and communal discovery was key and not individual self-expression.[34] She calls this phenomenon 'the collaborative floor', where participants interweave and interject and improvise the conversation and generate wisdom.[35]

As a researcher working in a similar white British context to mine and analysing a conversation among an all-women group, Coates' observations were incredibly helpful. They helped me recognize that the indirect speech that so challenged the latter stages of my analysis was part of a sophisticated communication style on the part of the participants, which enabled them to discuss some extremely sensitive and painful topics and build a communal wisdom around them. Together they generated a group voice in the midst of their individual voices, and through paying attention to the emotional language of the participants, I was able to hear what that group voice was trying to say.

To return to my discussion of a voice-centred relational method and its usefulness for the analysis of group interview, my observations combined with Coates' theory highlight the need to be aware of the particular nature of a group interview and the impact of the group relationships not just on what is disclosed but *how* it is communicated. The indirect and provisional modes of speech employed by the group I studied made the third and fourth readings more challenging. However, the first two close and careful readings, which are the staples of this method, usefully highlighted features of the conversation (in my case the large volume of emotional language) that, upon exploration, revealed the group voice. Therefore, the process needed to be adapted for best use within a group interview, while the process itself helped identify and direct that adaptation.

Conclusion

The experience of motherhood can be a site of profound theological reflection with wisdom to benefit communities beyond the women themselves. Bonnie Miller McLemore's attempts to combine her mothering with her own academic work led her to critique the church's traditional treatment of labour and consider the types of generativity necessary for fulfilled personhood.[36] Emma Percy's thesis on mothering as a model of priestly ministry has offered fresh and life-giving insights that benefit women and men, those who have caring roles and those who do not.[37] I believe that women who live their lives negotiating the competing narratives of the perfect mother and a market capitalism economy will have wisdom and theological insights that may benefit all who straddle fault-lines in our divided society. The challenge is to hear them.

Finding women who have the time to participate in research is the first challenge. I found the group interview to be an efficient way – for both participant and researcher – of gathering wide and deep data, as four women's stories created a group story that I received in the context of my own. However, analysing this data offered many challenges, and as I have described above, the voice-centred relational method was both robust enough and flexible enough to allow a transparent, reflexive and responsive method of data analysis. Ultimately, it enabled me to hear not just the individual contributions but also to hear the agreed voice and wisdom of the group – they had built Coates' 'collaborative floor'.

What was that wisdom? For the women in my group, attempting to live in a gendered and dualistic world – caught between the public and private spheres, between work and non-work, between absence and presence – their faith offered the possibility of integration. It is not possible to elaborate here on the complex and nuanced understandings the women conveyed, but what emerged in individual and shared voice was the hope of a God who was wholly for them. In different ways, they described God as someone who knew their hearts, who shared their burdens, who partnered with them in this business of living fully and who delighted in their efforts to use the gifts they had been given. To God, they were not a good or bad mother, a good or bad worker or any other label their social, political or theological context might impose upon them – they were themselves.

Notes

1 T. S. Sellers *et al.*, 'Women Called: A Qualitative Study of Christian Women Dually Called to Motherhood and Career', *Journal of Psychology and Theology* 33, no. 3 (2005): 199.

2 Kate Massey, 'How Does the Experience of South Warwickshire Churchgoing Women, Who Feel Dually Called to Both Motherhood and Career, Help Us to Understand the Ideals of Motherhood as Expressed in their Church and Community? To What Extent Does their Faith Help them in Balancing Dual Callings?' (MA diss., University of Birmingham, 2013).

3 Sharon Hays, *The Cultural Contradictions of Motherhood* (London: Yale University Press, 1996), 8.

4 Natasha S. Mauthner and Andrea Doucet, 'Reflections on a Voice-Centred Relational Method: Analysing Maternal and Domestic Voices', in *Feminist Dilemmas in Qualitative Research: Public Knowledge and Private Lives*, ed. J. Ribbens and R. Edwards (London: Sage, 1998), 119–146.

5 Lyn M. Brown and Carol Gilligan, *Meeting at the Crossroads: Women's Psychology and Girls' Development* (New York: Ballantine Books, 1992), 21.

6 Ibid., 23.

7 Mechthild Kiegelmann, 'Making Oneself Vulnerable to Discovery: Carol Gilligan in Conversation with Mechthild Kiegelmann', *Forum Qualitative Sozialforschung/ Forum: Qualitative Social Research* 10, no. 2 (2009), accessed 3 August 2016, www. qualitative-research.net/index.php/fqs/article/view/1178/2718#g5.

8 Brown and Gilligan, *Meeting at the Crossroads*, 26–29.

9 Mauthner and Doucet, *Reflections*, 127.

10 Ibid., 130.

11 Ibid., 131–132.

12 While there are limited examples of use of this data analysis method – or related methods – for group interview, it is more usual to use it to analyse individual interviews. An example of the use of the Listening Guide for focus group data analysis can be found in Xochital Alvizo, 'The Listening Guide: A Practical Tool for Listening Deeply to the Body of Christ', *Perspectivas* 13 (Spring 2016): 99–106, accessed 4 August 2016, http://perspectivasonline.com/downloads/the-listening-guide-a-practical-tool-for-listening-deeply-to-the-body-of-christ-5/#_ftn21.

13 Mauthner and Doucet, *Reflections*, 128.

14 Carol Gilligan *et al.*, 'On the *Listening Guide:* A Voice-Centred Relational Method', in *Qualitative Research in Psychology: Expanding Perspectives in Methodology and Design* ed. Paul M. Camic, Jean E. Rhodes and Lucy Yardley (Washington, DC: American Psychological Association, 2003), 157–172.

15 Kiegelmann, 'Making Oneself Vulnerable to Discovery', para. 39.

16 Brown and Gilligan, *Meeting at the Crossroads*, 36–37.

17 George Kamberelis and Greg Dimitriadis, 'Focus Groups: Strategy, Articulations of Pedagogy, Politics and Inquiry', in *Collecting and Interpreting Qualitative Materials* ed. Norman K. Denzin and Yvonna S. Lincoln (London: Sage, 2008), 388.

18 Ibid., 389.

19 Ann Willard, 'Cultural Scripts For Mothering', in *Mapping the Moral Domain* ed. Carol Gilligan, Janie Victoria Ward and Jill MacLean Taylor (Cambridge MA: Harvard University Press, 1988), 225–243. Willard describes how women receive 'cultural scripts' as 'messages from the culture about the "right way" to be a mother'. She posits that cultural scripts are helpful until they do not match the lived experience of the mothers, at which point the women experience conflict or crisis. Willard identifies one cultural script in American culture as the 'selfless wife and mother'.

20 David L. Morgan, *Focus Groups as Qualitative Research* (London: Sage, 1997), 10.

21 Brown and Gilligan, *Meeting at the Crossroads*, 29.

22 R. T. Lakoff, *Language and Woman's Place* (New York: Harper & Row, 1975).

23 Jennifer Coates, *Women Talk: Conversation Between Friends* (Oxford: Blackwell, 1996), 152.

24 Jennifer Coates, *Women, Men and Language: A Sociolinguistic Account of Gender Differences in Language*, 3rd ed. (Abingdon: Routledge, 2016), 90.

25 Penelope Eckert and Sally McConnell-Ginet, *Language and Gender*, 2nd ed. (Cambridge: Cambridge University Press, 2013), 38.

26 Lia Litosseliti, *Gender and Language: Theory and Practice* (Abingdon: Routledge, 2013), 40.

27 Ibid., 40.

28 Linda Carli, 'Gendered Communication and Social Influence', in *The Sage Handbook of Gender and Psychology* ed. Michelle K. Ryan and Nyla R. Branscombe (London: Sage, 2013), 210.

29 Ibid., 203–206.

30 Ibid., 200–203.

31 Coates, *Women Talk*, 154–162.

32 Jennifer Coates, 'Women's Friendships, Women's Talk', in *Gender and Discourse* ed. Ruth Wodak (London: Sage, 1997), 251–252; Coates, *Women, Men and Language*, 130.

33 Coates, *Women's Friendships*, 248–249.

34 Coates, *Women Talk*, 67.

35 Coates, *Women, Men and Language*, 131.

36 Bonnie Miller McLemore, *Also a Mother: Work and Family as a Theological Dilemma* (Nashville: Abingdon Press, 1994).

37 Emma Percy, 'Reverend Mother: How Insights from Mothering can Inform the Practice of Leadership in the Church (Part 1)', *Modern Believing* 44 no. 2 (2003): 33–44; Emma Percy, 'Reverend Mother: How Insights from Mothering can Inform the Practice of Leadership in the Church (Part 2)', *Modern Believing* 44 no. 3 (2003): 24–36; Emma Percy, *What Clergy Do Especially When It Looks Like Nothing* (London: SPCK, 2014).

10 Wholly sound

A Feminist reframing of the 'problem' of interview silence as a methodology for discovering new knowledge

Alison Woolley

Introduction

In this chapter I consider periods of silence in interviews with research participants. I propose that, far from being a 'problem' inhibiting effective data collection,[1] when researchers allow space for silence in the interaction between themselves and participants these silences can facilitate the emergence of valuable new knowledge for the researcher and greater self-knowledge for participants. I also explore how paying attention to interview silences through-out all stages of the research process, from transcribing to re-presentation of data, can further enhance understanding of the subject being investigated. I illustrate the potential of interview silence by drawing on my own qualitative research exploring spiritual disciplines of silence among Christian women.

The relational importance of silence

Since the earliest Christian writings, theologians have advocated that silence is indispensable in humanity's relationship with God and with one another.[2] Hannah Ward and Jennifer Wild present silence as an 'irreplaceable element', where we venture at 'the thresholds of faith and meaning'. Here, 'knowledge can grow and flourish' as we express what we know, 'and explore beyond that frontier'.[3] Maggie Ross proposes that silence is necessary if humans are to recognize their responsibility towards others. Having forgotten our responsibility to maintain an appropriate balance between silence and speech, reflection and action, attention and distraction, Ross depicts humanity as no longer able to thrive.[4] Beverly Lanzetta proposes that silence's wisdom can awaken us from the 'linguistic slumber' that modulates the world's cries of pain and steals away our humanity.[5] Ross and Lanzetta portray silence as essential at a time when the survival or extinction of all creation hangs in the balance. Rowan Williams suggests treasuring silence as it offers a means of restoring our interactions by freeing language from the evasions and control that form most of our speech.[6] For Rachel Muers, silence that reflects God's 'divine hearing' must be understood as fundamental to all communication if the oppressive silencing of others is to end. Listening to others with 'God's responsible silence' – as we are ourselves heard by God – shapes not only who we are, but who we are in relation to God and to one another.[7]

For each of these theologians, transformation in all our relationships is intimately intertwined with our appropriate engagement in silence. Yet, as Ward and Wild identify, this is 'not to be entered into lightly': letting go into silence can be challenging as well as creative.[8] It is the very presence of another, not their words, that commands our attention, tells us we are responsible and calls for our appropriate response.[9]

Feminist theologians have emphasized women's need to find authentic self-expression as a transformational response to the damage caused by their imposed silencing. Seeking to broaden the feminist portrayal of silence in women's faith lives, my qualitative, interview-based research investigated the role and value of chosen practices of silence in the faith lives of contemporary Christian women, and brought these findings into dialogue with areas of discourse in feminist theology.

Attending to process and silence in research interviews

Svend Brinkman proposed that learning to conduct qualitative research interviews well rests upon the researcher's familiarity with what is expected as 'the end product of the research process' – books, chapters and papers – for 'one should know what to aim for'.[10] This focus on attending to the pre-existing, expected output of academic inquiry gestures towards two implicit assumptions: that today's researchers have no reason to aspire towards generating literature differing from that published in the past, nor to conduct research using methods that attend to formerly overlooked aspects within the research framework, which may uncover previously unenvisaged knowledge. However, Christine Valtners Paintner suggests that it is by focusing attention on aspects of *process*, rather than any end point, that engagement with the subject matter becomes a true journey of discovery. By relinquishing 'our own plans and expectations' the researcher's attention shifts 'to what is actually unfolding'. This heightens the researcher's awareness of God's activity within people's lives, and their consideration of how it is most appropriate to proceed and respond to what emerges.[11] Painter's proposal invites qualitative researchers to let go of expectations about the end point of investigations shaping the methods they use, and to foster fresh and more appropriate methods that emerge within their unfolding research process.

Despite qualitative research interviews being described as 'a construction site of knowledge',[12] researchers have largely neglected periods of interview silence as potential sites of new understanding. Muriel Saville-Troike reports that the 'minimal amounts of data' collected about silence indicate that its importance within the framework of communication 'has been largely overlooked'.[13] Her observation is pertinent in reflecting on considerations of silence within the research process. Although some interview accounts acknowledge silences within the flow of questions and responses, these are rarely annotated and less frequently considered as an area for particular attention. As Blake Poland and Ann Pederson state, '[t]he degree to which the field is silent on the issue of silence is surprising'.[14]

Within the limited discussions of silence in interviews there is a spectrum of attitudes towards such silences among qualitative researchers. These range from dismissive perceptions of silence as a 'problem' indicating either 'failure on the part of the interviewer' or a 'troublesome' participant,[15] to the reverence shown by Eileen Campbell-Reed and Christian Scharen, for whom silences during small group interviews were 'moments of standing on "holy ground"'.[16] However, such respectful endorsement is found infrequently within feminist research, where Karen Nairn, Jenny Munro and Anne Smith assert silence is all too often interpreted 'solely as an indication of powerlessness'.[17] Within feminist methodological literature references to silence most often relate to the silencing of certain aspects of the stories of women's lives, or to the privileging of the narratives of others as presenting a normative position. Some feminist researchers intentionally distinguish between the societal silencing of women's experiences and the 'silent subtexts'[18] in interviews with women: such silence in interviews results from 'what is not spoken, not discussed, not answered',[19] recognizing that 'what participants do not' say 'may be as telling as what they do'.[20] Others identify the silences of what women cannot say – 'the story that is not there'[21] – termed 'unstory' by Riet Bons-Storm.[22]

Feminist qualitative research methodologies emphasize listening to, and for, the particularity of each woman's narrative and forms of self-expression as both a key principle underlining research design and as valuable sources of new knowledge. However, feminist literature has paid little attention to silence as periods of time without speech and differing degrees of other sounds – either in women's experiences, or within qualitative research interviews. Similarly, feminist theologians have focused on identifying the silencing of women's faith lives by the dominant discourses of patriarchy. Some researchers in the discipline have attended to the narrative silences during interviews with women, recognizing them as sources of 'very fat and rich information',[23] which are 'pregnant with subjective meaning'[24] that is 'yet to be known and understood'.[25] However, addressing the value of chosen practices of silence within women's spiritual journeys has largely fallen outside their areas of concern. In part, this may be due to the enormity of the ongoing work involved in 're-membering' women's role in the story of Christianity, and the relentless struggle for the voices and concerns of women to be heard within the persistently patriarchal structures of contemporary faith communities. As a result of the feminist methodological emphasis on the particularity of women's narratives, and in response to the silencing of women's voices, feminist theologians using qualitative research methods have understandably focused on what is verbally articulated by research participants. Yet despite acknowledging the presence of periods of silence during interviews, their methods, analysis and findings have not addressed the particularity of periods of silences within interviews – the 'apparent' opposite of speech[26] – and what new knowledge these may reveal. While feminist theology has heeded Nelle Morton's renowned call to hear women into speech, its methodological emphases and the issues addressed by its discourse have left little space for wider acknowledgement of her fundamental observation that being heard 'all the way' emerges from within a 'powerful silence'.[27]

Poland and Pederson identify that the potential significance of periods of silence emerging between participant and interviewer fare no better in the broader arena of the qualitative research process: it is rarely interpreted positively or creatively during interviews, infrequently annotated when constructing transcripts, barely considered while analysing data, and rarely discussed affirmatively in reflections on what interviewees say.[28]

A method emerging from silence

Although I read widely about in-depth interviewing, this offered limited insights into the significance that periods of silence might play in interviews with my twenty individual participants or, as the research process progressed, into the later stages of transcription, analysis and reporting on findings. This contrasted with my professional experiences as a music therapist and spiritual accompanist,[29] which contributed substantially more to my being comfortable with and well prepared for silences that emerged between participants and myself.[30] Kathleen Gerson and Ruth Horowitz identify that the in-depth interviews of qualitative research 'closely resemble the therapeutic interview of clinical practice'. These settings share a coming together of 'two engaged people, both of whom are searching to unravel the mysteries and meanings of a life'.[31] In each context both parties are present in different capacities, with attention focused towards one particular individual. Such opportunities for telling one's story to an attentive listener – whether researcher, therapist or 'soul friend' – are often experienced as a relief in today's Western culture that 'waits for nothing'.[32] As Raymond Lee and Claire Renzetti propose, what many interviewees 'desire' and appreciate about participating in research is 'catharsis'.[33]

When beginning interviews in my research exploring women's chosen practices of silence, I asked participants about their understanding of the word silence, and whether these perceptions changed in the context of their spiritual practice. Their responses revealed a clear shift between the two, from focusing on 'absence' of this or that to heightened awareness of 'presence' – their own, God's, and that of others. Following these initial inquiries, interviews were unstructured. I asked prepared questions only at moments when these related to a comment in a participant's unfolding narrative, or late in an interview if intended areas of exploration had not emerged spontaneously within a woman's account. Steiner Kvale advises interviewers of the requirement for detailed knowledge of a phenomenon in order to pose significant questions.[34] However, Mary Clark Moschella describes the need for the 'care-full' researcher to 'give up the role of expert, and become a learner again', proposing that in doing so researchers 'start really being there'.[35] I found that by trusting the women's contributions without the interruption of a question, I was more able to be fully attentive to what they expressed. It also allowed space for them to lead me into areas of their experience that I had not considered exploring. Asking less enabled me to discover more.

With the first participant my use of silence was not planned. By being fully present and listening intently I was instinctively mirroring my therapeutic practice of using few words to demonstrate interest in and acceptance of another. In creating a transcript of this interview I recognized my instinctive use of silence and realized that it helped this woman to talk about her experiences. Having noticed this, I more consciously utilized silence as a method when interviewing others. During the interviewing and transcribing process my understanding of silence grew as I allowed it to be present, and attended to it (or its absence) and within it more intently. As my curiosity about the functions and value of interview silences developed, I learned to pose questions only when really necessary, reflecting Melanie Mauthner's report of developing an interview style that asked 'fewer questions' over time.[36]

I also learned that minimizing interjections of any kind was valuable. From the initial interviews my use of 'mmm' responses was relatively infrequent. Nevertheless, in listening back to recordings I felt aware of how much each 'mmm' interrupted, particularly when a woman's narrative seemed hesitant, precarious, or a struggle to articulate. They seemed to impede self-revelation and sounded unsupportive, though often presented as encouraging in literature discussing interview techniques. Instead, careful attention to the interplay between the first two interviewees' tentative comments and my interjections or silences showed that receiving their explorations in reverential silence facilitated their nascent and fragile self-expression. My response – to consciously eliminate 'mmm'-ing – became increasingly natural. Instead, when a woman's words faltered, or ceased, I waited in silence: if she appeared stuck, I indicated my willingness to hold open the space of silence with a gentle head nod or by facial expression.

The additional silences generated in my developing method enabled me to be present more fully to the women in ways that facilitated the emergence of insights that would have been unlikely to surface had I employed a more traditional interview style. As Michalinos Zembylas and Pavlos Michaelides state, allowing space for, and attending to silence, particularly when exploring what is difficult to express, 'is an important step in reaching towards the Other'.[37] This will be discussed in more detail as the chapter continues.

Generating interview transcripts is a creative act. As their form and content significantly impact on analysis, 'transcription quality should not be neglected'.[38] Transcripts cannot be exact representations of interviews: like topographical maps, they are abstractions to be re-interpreted later, emphasizing some features and omitting others, depending on their intended usage.[39] As chosen periods of silence were the subject of my inquiry, it intuitively felt important to 'see' each period of silence that occurred during interviews. To do so, I adapted Nicola Slee's use of 'speech spurts'.[40] In my transcripts, line breaks indicate periods of silence, with the length of those beyond two seconds annotated in brackets and in red font.[41] Visually, the resulting text resembled sparse poetry. Also noting false starts, repeats, para-linguistic features – sighs, laughter, tears – and speech fillers such as 'y'know', my transcripts reflected Carol Grbich's proposal that retaining participants' rhythm, tone, pauses and repetitions is essential in preserving the 'proper flavour' of interviews.[42]

When re-presenting interview extracts in my thesis I ensured that readers were alerted to every silence. Longer quotes retained the visual structure of speech spurts. In shorter excerpts the line return was replaced with a solidus (/). Both retained the numeric lengths of silences and paralinguistic features. Examples will be found in the remainder of this chapter.[43] Readers are encouraged to pause appropriately, representing the period of silence indicated within the woman's narrative, particularly in the extended extracts.

Creating transcripts that visually identified every silence proved valuable as the interviewing phase of research continued, and later when analysing the interview material. Re-reading transcripts as each was finished,[44] multiple areas of interest emerged. Given the scope of this chapter, two of these cannot be discussed in detail here, but are important to acknowledge. First, I realized the difficulties in ascribing any 'ownership' of longer silences without the accompanying nuances of body language, eye gaze and facial expression present during interviews. It was unclear which of the following was happening in any silence: was it actively being held by a participant; being extended by me to allow them to reflect further; re-claimed from my holding by a participant to consider what more she might say; a reflective or companionable shared silence; or a shifting combination of these silences flowing between us? Second, just as norms of quantities of silence and speech are culturally and socially prescribed,[45] each woman's style of speaking included an individually normative length of silence as a pause between her spoken phrases, which also had a typical, personal length. As a result, I found it necessary to keep in mind the particular 'norms' for each participant when attending to their silences and considering what these might indicate.

There were also several recurring ways in which fostering periods of silence within interviews was beneficial within the overall process of my research. In addition, interview silences also reflected a key theme that emerged unexpectedly from the women's narratives. It is to these significant areas I now turn.

From the first interview I unexpectedly began to find that my instinctive interview style exemplified what almost every participant stated to be an aspect of the subject of the research: they repeatedly named 'listening' to others as an aspect of their practice of silence. The women's descriptions of their fully attentive presence to another person, at the same time as also being attentive to God's presence and activity within and between them, indicates their intentional 'listening' extends well beyond the usual understanding of this word. Reflecting the quality of attention they bring to silence in relationship with God, their listening to others has become an integrated part of this spiritual discipline. Although I identified such listening as integral to my own practice of silence, I had not expected this to be explicitly named by the women as belonging to their discipline.[46] To my surprise, as a researcher I was unknowingly enacting a key practice of silence that the interviews were unearthing. The emergence of these unexpected findings created a coalescence of research subject and process that, I suggest, bestows additional legitimacy on my intuitive method of attending to silence across all the stages of research.

My method contrasted with that of many feminist researchers for whom interviewing has been necessarily conversational since Ann Oakley's assertion that, as there can be 'no intimacy without reciprocity', interviewing women is a contradiction in terms.[47] Consequently, they have sought rapport with participants by evolving interview styles that are intentionally 'mutual and reciprocal'.[48] Yet Jan Berry proposes that rapport is primarily established by researchers conveying their genuine interest and desire to understand an interviewee's experiences, rather than the use of any particular interview technique.[49] During interviews, my professional familiarity with therapeutic practices facilitated the development of rapport within an instinctive 'holding' of silence, in which I intentionally spoke little and consciously avoided interjections. This minimalist style generated particularly rich descriptions from participants. Additionally, many made appreciative comments about how I had conducted the interviews. Alison's remarks were typical:[50]

> I've really appreciated
> the way
> you've asked
> the questions and
> and just
> just
> the quietness in between and
> just the sense that we [*hand gesture moving forwards and backwards between us*]
> yeah
> not erm
> not like
> a lot of research [*laughs*]

Both rich descriptions and appreciative comments from participants occurred despite the absence of a reciprocally revelatory or conversational interview style, and were seemingly enhanced by consciously not interrupting each woman's narrative. Alongside Jack Douglas' advice that a researcher's interviewing experience should take precedence over the methods advocated by others,[51] these and similar comments reinforced my perception that a method that attends to silence in the research process is equally as effective as well-used methods advocated by other feminist qualitative researchers.

A pattern I noticed in completing the first five or six interviews and their transcripts recurred in the remaining interviews. Over the course of each, silence lengths increased considerably during the latter half to third of the interview. Where longer pauses had been 7–10 seconds, these stretched on to 20–30 seconds. This shift later in the interviews seemed to indicate the women's gradual realization that I was unlikely to foreclose their need for valuable space to reflect by interjecting. Echoing Moschella's proposal that listening within research is about striving to 'create a safe space for honest reflection in which new connections can be forged',[52] such periods of silence were almost always followed by articulation of fresh understanding about their engagement with silence and additional insights into their practices. In a tone that expressed sadness and frustration, Julay commented that she didn't 'understand/what it is/that/makes me/avoid/silence sometimes'. It was not about being 'afraid to go into it' or trying to 'resist' or 'block things out'. In halting phrases, scattered with repetitions that suggest uncertainty at the newness of her thoughts, Julay reflected further:

Julay: let me have a think (7)
what comes to mind is
it feels like hard work
actually
it's it's easier
to
turn on the radio
or (4)
something like that y'know
it's just easier (7)
Alison: What is it that's hard? (16)[53]
Julay: It's not
the silence itself
it's the stopping
it it's
yeah it's the it's the it's the moment
of stopping
and erm (4.5)
of moving
from
y'know
from
from one
moving into it
moving from
ordinary kind of
noise
into the si [*incomplete*]
into the silence

An initial, requested gestational silence, 'let me have a think', enabled naming the 'hard work' involved as what is 'unbearable'. My silence invited further exploration, but Julay seemed to need the encouragement of a verbal invitation 'What is it that's hard?' intentionally containing a repetition of the beginnings of her new understanding that something is 'hard work'. A significantly long transitional silence, '(16)', enabled her to identify what is hard. Having acknowledged the difficulty not understood minutes earlier, Julay went on to affirm for herself that she never regrets choosing silence, and, as if making a mental note for future occasions, that it is only 'the moment/of stopping' to move into silence that feels hard. This post-reflection explanation was significant for Julay – and within the wider context of the research. Her unique articulation of this transitional moment offered valuable insight into this issue identified by many other participants, but who could not pinpoint its cause. Re-reading their comments in the light of Julay's reflection illuminated an area of difficulty about silence that had remained somewhat veiled in mystery in other interviews. It also raises significant queries, beyond the scope of this discussion, about whether researchers experience a similar, unacknowledged difficulty in stopping their flow of questions to allow time for silence within interviews, and the reasons why this might seem a hard decision to make.

From the first interview, longer silences felt as if they took on different qualities from shorter silences, particularly in the latter half of interviews. They seemed to resonate with a sense of intimacy, depth and connection with every participant at a level I had not anticipated experiencing with more than a few. Reviewing transcripts confirmed my interview perceptions that the longest periods of silence were frequently followed by particularly noteworthy descriptions of the participant's engagement in silence.

By refraining from unnecessary interjections that would have fragmented the women's attempts to articulate their experiences, I fostered a safe enough space for the women to be able to temporarily dip back into silence and re-connect with their past experiences in a sensorial and embodied way in those moments. My research journal linked these observations:

> they *are* able to be incredibly articulate about silence, particularly when given the space to re-engage with it in the interview… the women don't have as much difficulty articulating their experiences of silence as I expected, particularly when given opportunity to do so in a way that allowed this re-engagement. Maybe that is the success of the method?[54]

Returning to dwell in silence enabled the women to express perceptions of silence that they had struggled to communicate to their satisfaction earlier in their interview. Ali's comments towards the end of our time together typify those also expressed by other women.[55] She recalled 'starting off in one place' in describing silence, yet, when doing this also noticed 'I could actually hear myself thinking "nah/that's not/that's not all there is"': she identified finding a 'turning point' during more extensive periods of silence later in the interview, which enabled her to convey better her 'deep and profound experiences' of silence.

Space to re-engage briefly with silence during interviews created opportunities for the women 'to find a voice and a language to name [their] experience in terms which are authentic and empowering'[56]: they frequently employed the rich and evocative language of metaphor to convey new thought. Metaphor's important role in women's faith development is well documented by Slee,[57] and its place in bringing clarity to participants' meanings during the process of qualitative data analysis is highlighted by Grbich.[58] Multiple, sustained silences within interviews enabled participants to re-encounter silence. This allowed the women to mine their experience more deeply with each subsequent silence until their exploration yielded verbal expression that, containing fresh insights into their experiences, was the most authentic description they could articulate of this world-beneath-language. With closed eyes, Claire began describing silence as 'something that's spreading'. Nine seconds later she added 'and it's mobile/it's definitely got/a sort of fluidity to it'. After a 34-second silence Claire described trying not to 'think' of a metaphor but of the importance of space for it 'to emerge because it's/something that's describing (4)/the nothing there/but the utter certainty that everything's there'. This was immediately followed by three long silences totalling 52 seconds, separated only by 'mmm', twice, from Claire. Claire then offered 'there's some sort of/of dance/emerging/out of the movement but I/I can't erm (4)' – she needed a further 10 seconds re-entering silence before saying the dance-type movement is 'totally unpredictable/it's not got steps/it's more like a flowing'. After 6 seconds silence, her metaphor for contemplative silence emerges with an embodied acting out of her experience:

Claire: what one does the other
will just react to [*here, dancing her two hands with palms facing each other at neck level, moving together in an opposite mirroring*]
a bit like –
ah!
you know when the flocks of birds behave such that they develop these sort of amazing patterns?
Alison: Mmm
Claire: There's something of that quality to it …
the encounter has that
that sense about it of that movement of
of
of birds
that you sometimes see
in a flock [*this reflected her hands' movement*]

Claire's journey to uncover this metaphor took 210 seconds (within which I uttered only the 'mmm' noted above) and contained 123 seconds of longer silences.[59]

This was made up of silences of 34, 21 and 20 seconds, three silences around 10 seconds, four of 4 to 6 seconds, with multiple pauses of 2 seconds or less. It was through acknowledging such silences by recording them in transcripts and attending to their presence during data analysis that a more detailed, nuanced and richer engagement with data was possible.

Researchers are appropriately cautioned that their silence may be interpreted as indicating dissatisfaction with or challenge to what participants have expressed. Feminist researchers also highlight that interviewee silence can be used, or perceived by participants, as part of an authoritative, 'power-over' dynamic. While acknowledging both of these difficulties is essential, the risk of either occurring can be minimized by a combination of the rapport established with participants and the non-verbal expressions accompanying the silence of a researcher aware of these concerns. Participant remarks following longer silences also indicate that, conversely, such silences offered the women more control and choice within interviews. Silence was a form of non-directive inquiry offering them freedom to choose *not* to say more because I did not directly request this. Silence also gave participants space to develop their train of thought, to make tangential detours, or to initiate different areas of discussion rather than follow a path I indicated. In the wider context of qualitative interviewing, employing a methodology of silence with these intentions can subvert the dominance of a discourse that has historically privileged questioning and probing by researchers.[60] As Poland and Pederson suggest, there is much to be said for 'giving people time to reflect, ponder, and engage with you and the subject matter at their own pace'. In the training of researchers, 'perhaps too much emphasis is placed on asking questions, when the real skill may be listening' in attentive silence.[61] Through such listening, silences in research interviews can become a 'true site of possibility',[62] responsibly communicating respect for alterity in the experience of others, and where all that is exchanged between researcher and participant may be received as valuable gift by both.

Interview silence and new participant self-knowledge

It is widely acknowledged that although interviews are conducted to generate new data of interest to the researcher, participants also derive benefits from engaging in research. Above, I outlined how attending to silence throughout the research process was significant to my research. However, silence also contributed to many women stating that their participation was a valuable experience: periods of silence within the interviews had enabled their discovery, acknowledgement and articulation of new self-knowledge.

The easy flow of the women's initial, comparatively simple responses to my planned, opening interview questions suggested they were voicing familiar perceptions, in thought if not in verbal expression. Silence in interviews created time for reflection on what had already been expressed, allowed the women moments of sensorial re-engagement with silence, and space to express additional thoughts that emerged from these moments. Further periods of silence were often followed by comments whose faltering, hesitant articulation and frequent repetition of single words or phrases indicated that these thoughts were unfamiliar. This repeating pattern of speech and silence allowed participants to explore deeply within themselves, enabling newly discovered, or previously unvoiced ideas to be articulated for the first time. Silence, rather than the 'dialogue' suggested by Brita Gill-Austern, seemed to help their tentative, 'half-baked ideas and perceptions develop . . . to fuller maturity'.[63] It created opportunity to move gradually down through the more openly acknowledged layers of 'public' and 'private' voice, identified by Tina Miller, into the rarely revealed perceptions of their most 'personal' self. In silence, this personal voice – constructed around emotions, intimacy and the body, seldom matching, but often contradicting the accounts offered by public or private voices – found a more secure space to risk its self-expression.[64]

Dawn's comments, when asked if engagement in silence was changing her, were a striking example of transformation in self-knowledge. During almost eight minutes in which Dawn explored this question, her responses transition through the five epistemological stages identified by Mary Belenky and colleagues in *Women's Ways of Knowing*.[65] Starting from the position of Belenky's 'silent women',[66] Dawn replied, 'I wouldn't know'. She then proposed relying on the external opinions of 'received knowledge'[67]: 'I think somebody has to tell me that'. Next, brief, hesitant moments of the conditional assertions of 'subjective knowledge' emerged[68] – Dawn can 'imagine' silence 'might' change someone – but still remained unable to name this as her own experience of self: 'that is something I should ask somebody about/whether I have changed'. My emphatic reply, giving Dawn opportunity to claim this for herself, 'Are *you* aware of any ways that it's changed you?' initially received a positive response: 'probably it makes me/calmer'. This was instantly questioned – 'but then again/I just want to be open minded' – and then retracted as, reflecting 'procedural knowledge',[69] it might be due to something else entirely. I remained silent, not questioning further as Dawn explored again, eventually stating 'so/I would say it's the silence', but then instantly negated this possibility: 'I don't know/I cannot say to you it is the silence . . . I really/really/can't/tell you'. Dawn then stated that she *has* changed but remained unsure whether she can 'attribute it to . . . observing/more time in silence or/some other reason'. Following further reflection and exploration: 'if I'm just to look at it [silence]/specifically/I would imagine it would change me'. Here, she reflected that as silence is a place of encounter with God 'that should change you', concluding 'so I think yes/I would imagine it's changed me': Dawn is still imagining, not certain. She then acknowledged her circuitous exploration:

I've gone round and round but I think I've
I said I wouldn't
I wouldn't know how to answer but I think y'know I would say it's changed
    me
yeah

Dawn's 'I think' suggests remaining hesitation. She returned to considering silence and her relationship with God. When intentionally considering these two elements together Dawn said with now unambiguous 'subjective knowledge', 'yes/definitely/yes' silence has changed her. Finally, after further silence, Dawn eventually spoke authoritative, new self-knowledge from reflecting on her experiences, relational contexts, the subjective comments of others and a stated desire to make fair-minded, balanced judgements, concluding that:

> something you are doing over a period of time
> you know
> day in day out
> is going to change you
> I have the time now [to engage in silence] [*laughs*]
> so
> I can do it
> and it can change me
> you see

Belenky *et al.* describe the movement towards and presence of this authoritative, interior voice of 'constructed knowledge'[70] as 'the hallmark of women's emergent sense of self and sense of agency and control'.[71] I suggest that this demonstrable process within Dawn's narrative was, at least in part, enabled by the sparsity of my questions and by lengthy silences during which I listened attentively to her self-exploration and growing, confident articulation of developing self-knowledge. Within my research, this interview was far from unique as a space where, in my offered silence, a woman's initially tentative voice gained strength and confidence, contributing to her emerging and expanded awareness of self and agency by the time the interview finished.

Conclusion

In this chapter I have demonstrated a method of research that, by embracing periods of silence within interviews and attending to silence throughout the research process, has generative potential for uncovering new knowledge, valuable both to the researcher and to interview participants. A particular strength is how this method enables participants to identify and articulate new insights into experiences which are generally considered difficult to express. It also creates space where their self-understanding and authenticity of self-expression can develop, increasing their sense of agency. It acknowledges that by attending to silences within research interviews, these can contribute to a more nuanced understanding of what participants communicate verbally, or in other ways. In addition, by visually identifying all periods of silence in interview transcripts – however brief these may be – and retaining these indications throughout the research process, researchers and those reading research reports are reminded to consider what was occurring or being conveyed beyond the immediacy of words on the page. Finally, this method communicates the researcher's willingness and ability to bear with participants as they move beyond their familiar 'public' and 'private' voices and begin uttering the perceptions of an infrequently articulated, deeply 'personal' voice.

Inevitably, silence in interviews will function differently depending on the context and the subject being investigated. Not all interviewees will necessarily respond positively to silence, nor find it comfortable or affirming, especially if silence has been a negative experience for them. Researchers, too, may find the attentive listening involved in intentionally attending to interview silence challenging. However, my own research suggests that qualitative researchers should reconsider perceptions of interview silence as merely a problem to be solved. Given its potential for enriching the material yielded by qualitative inquiry, for further facilitating increasingly responsible relationality between researchers and participants, and for augmenting the presentation, reception and deliberation of research findings, this method merits further investigation, particularly by feminist qualitative researchers with whose methodological principles it readily coheres. Were this to be pursued, attending to silence in qualitative research may shift from its current, largely overlooked position to being acknowledged as a wholly sound and even irreplaceable element of the research process.

Notes

1 Blake Poland and Ann Pederson, 'Reading Between the Lines: Interpreting Silences in Qualitative Research', *Qualitative Inquiry* 4, no. 2 (1998): 295.
2 Nicholas Lash, *Holiness, Speech and Silence* (Aldershot: Ashgate, 2004), 91.
3 Hannah Ward and Jennifer Wild, *Guard the Chaos: Finding Meaning in Change* (London: Darton, Longman & Todd, 1995), 122.
4 Maggie Ross, *Silence: A User's Guide* (London: Darton, Longman & Todd, 2014), 11.
5 Beverly J. Lanzetta, *Radical Wisdom: A Feminist Mystical Theology* (Minneapolis: Fortress Press, 2005), 211.
6 Rowan Williams, *Silence and Honey Cakes* (Oxford: Lion Books, 2003), 45, 69.
7 Rachel Muers, *Keeping God's Silence: Towards a Theological Ethics of Communication* (Oxford: Blackwell, 2004), 18–20.
8 Ward and Wild, *Guard the Chaos*, 122.
9 Terry Veling, *Practical Theology: 'On Earth as It Is in Heaven'* (Maryknoll, NY: Orbis Books, 2005), 124.
10 Svend Brinkmann, *Qualitative Interviewing: Understanding Qualitative Research* (New York: Oxford University Press, 2013), vii.
11 Christine Valtners Paintner, *Eyes of the Heart: Photography as Christian Contemplative Practice* (Notre Dame, IN: Sorin Books, 2013), 3.
12 Steinar Kvale, *InterViews: An Introduction to Qualitative Research Interviews* (Thousand Oaks, CA: Sage, 1996), 42. Kvale describes five features of the postmodern construction of knowledge: conversational, narrative, linguistic, contextual, interrelational.
13 Muriel Saville-Troike, 'The Place of Silence in an Integrated Theory of Communication', in *Perspectives on Silence*, ed. Deborah Tannen and Muriel Saville-Troike (Norwood, NJ: Ablex, 1985), 4, 11–12.
14 Poland and Pederson, 'Reading Between the Lines', 293.

15 See the discussion in Poland and Pederson, 'Reading Between the Lines', 295.

16 Eileen R. Campbell-Reed and Christian Scharen, 'Ethnography on Holy Ground: How Qualitative Interviewing is Practical Theological Work', *International Journal of Practical Theology* 7, no. 2 (2013): 244.

17 Karen Nairn, Jenny Munro and Anne B. Smith, 'A Counter-Narrative of a "Failed" Interview', *Qualitative Research* 5, no. 2 (2005): 231.

18 Lisa Mazzei, 'Inhabited Silences: In Pursuit of a Muffled Subtext', *Qualitative Inquiry* 9, no. 3 (2003): 356.

19 Ibid., 358.

20 Kathy Charmaz, 'Stories and Silences: Disclosures and Self in Chronic Illness', *Qualitative Inquiry* 8, no. 3 (2002): 304.

21 Joan Laird, 'Women and Stories: Restorying Women's Self-Constructions', in *Women in Families: A Framework for Family Therapy*, ed. Monica McGoldrick, Carol M. Anderson and Froma Walsh (New York: Norton, 1991), 437.

22 Riet Bons-Storm, *The Incredible Woman: Listening to Women's Silences in Pastoral Care and Counselling* (Nashville: Abingdon Press, 1996), 57.

23 Mazzei, 'Inhabited Silences', 358.

24 Charmaz, 'Stories and Silences', 304.

25 Mazzei, 'Inhabited Silences', 358.

26 Poland and Pederson, 'Reading Between the Lines', 293.

27 Nelle Morton, *The Journey Is Home* (Boston: Beacon Press, 1985), 205, 210.

28 Poland and Pederson, 'Reading Between the Lines', 308.

29 Also referred to as a spiritual director or 'soul friend'.

30 My work as a music therapist is mostly with people with profound, or severe and multiple learning difficulties. Their lack of speech, limited vocalization, often severely limited physical movements and slow response time results in more silence than sound in many sessions.

31 Kathleen Gerson and Ruth Horowitz, 'Observation and Interviewing: Options and Choices in Qualitative Methods', in *Qualitative Research in Action*, ed. Tim May (London: Sage, 2002), 210.

32 Poland and Pederson, 'Reading Between the Lines', 296.

33 Raymond M. Lee and Claire M. Renzetti, 'The Problems of Researching Sensitive Topics', in *Researching Sensitive Topics*, ed. Claire M. Renzetti and Raymond M. Lee (London: Sage, 1993), 6.

34 Kvale, *InterViews*, 96.

35 Mary Clark Moschella, *Ethnography as a Pastoral Practice* (Cleveland, OH: The Pilgrim Press, 2008), 142–3.

36 Melanie Mauthner, 'Bringing Silent Voices into a Public Discourse: Researching Accounts of Sister Relationships', in *Feminist Dilemmas in Qualitative Research*, ed. Jane Ribbens and Rosalind Edwards (London: Sage, 1998), 49.

37 Michalinos Zembylas and Pavlos Michaelides, 'The Sound of Silence in Pedagogy', *Educational Theory* 54, no. 2 (2004): 207.

38 David Silverman, *Doing Qualitative Research: A Practical Handbook* (London: Sage, 2010), 200.

39 Kvale, *InterViews*, 165.

40 Nicola Slee, *Women's Faith Development: Patterns and Processes* (Aldershot: Ashgate, 2004), 57.

41 Although discourse analysts often record pauses of fractions of a second, I identified silences from two seconds in length as it is proposed that interactional momentum is lost after this time. See Daniel Stern, *The Present Moment in Psychotherapy and Everyday Life* (New York: W. W. Norton, 2004), 46.

42 Carol Grbich, *Qualitative Data Analysis: An Introduction* (Thousand Oaks, CA: Sage, 2007), 318.

43 In this chapter, numeric indications of silences appear in black font.

44 All but two transcripts were completed before subsequent interviews.

45 Saville-Troike, 'The Place of Silence', 4 and 11–12.

46 For a more detailed discussion, see Alison Woolley, 'Women Choosing Silence: Transformational Practices and Relational Perspectives' (PhD diss., University of Birmingham, 2015), 322–328.

47 Ann Oakley, 'Interviewing Women: A Contradiction in Terms', in *Doing Feminist Research*, ed. Helen Roberts (London: Routledge, 1981), 49.

48 John Swinton and Harriet Mowat, *Practical Theology and Qualitative Research* (London: SCM Press, 2006), 26.

49 Jan Berry, *Ritual Making Women: Shaping Rites for Changing Lives* (London: Equinox, 2009), 37.

50 Participants chose whether to be identified by name or a pseudonym. Within this chapter some are the former and some the latter.

51 Jack D. Douglas, *Creative Interviewing* (Beverley Hills, CA: Sage, 1985), 38. Douglas borrows from Polonius' last words of advice to his son: 'to thine own self be true', in Shakespeare's *Hamlet*, Act I, iii, 78.

52 Moschella, *Ethnography*, 145.

53 All occurrences of 'Alison' in extracts from interview transcripts refer to me, not the participant also identified as 'Alison'.

54 Emphasis in original.

55 'Ali' and 'Alison' are different participants.

56 Slee, *Women's Faith Development*, 67.

57 Ibid., 65–67.

58 Grbich, *Qualitative Data Analysis*, 35.

59 Silences of more than two seconds.

60 See Zembylas and Michaelides, 'The Sound of Silence', 207.

61 Poland and Pederson, 'Reading Between the Lines', 296–297.

62 Zembylas and Michaelides, 'The Sound of Silence', 207.

63 Brita L. Gill-Austern, 'Pedagogy Under the Influence of Feminism and Womanism', in *Feminist and Womanist Pastoral Theology*, ed. Bonnie Miller-McLemore and Brita Gill-Austern (Nashville: Abingdon Press, 1990), 152.

64 Tina Miller, 'Shifting Layers of Professional, Lay and Personal Narratives: Longitudinal Childbirth Research', in *Feminist Dilemmas*, ed. Ribbens and Edwards, 58–71.

65 Mary Field Belenky *et al.*, *Women's Ways of Knowing: The Development of Self, Voice, and Mind* (New York: Basic Books, 1986).

66 Ibid., 23–34.

67 Ibid., 35–51.

68 Ibid., 52–86.

69 Ibid., 87–130.

70 Ibid., 131–152.

71 Ibid., 68.

11 Song of a voiceless person

Using the poetry of Menna Elfyn in a study of Welsh women's identity and religion

Manon Ceridwen James

Introduction

In this chapter I explore how I used poetry as a qualitative method within a project researching the impact and extent of religion on the social and personal identities of Welsh women. I describe how a reflection on the work of one writer (in this case, the poet Menna Elfyn) can be an effective method in gaining an in-depth perspective on the lives of women, and is particularly relevant within practical and feminist theological research, given the key role that literature (especially fiction and poetry) has played within feminist theology. I then describe the themes that arose within Elfyn's work and how they help to interpret the nature of female engagement with faith in Wales, and what this project can offer feminist theology as a discipline.

If ideographic knowledge, rather than generalizable information, is important within qualitative research then one poet's perspective can enhance our knowledge of a particular phenomenon or culture. The principle that the particular can illuminate the general is important within practical theology and feminist theology as well as qualitative research.[1] Interdisciplinary approaches are also seen as useful within qualitative methodologies in order to gain a rich, in-depth understanding of human experience.[2]

Within the wider project I utilized a practical theology 'critical conversation'[3] approach bringing my own experience, the experience of women shared through narrative interviews, the socio-religio-historical context of Wales and the published writings of significant Welsh women into dialogue with each other. I particularly wanted to investigate the extent and nature of the impact of the dominant religious traditions on how Welsh women thought and felt about themselves and the social groupings to which they belong. I conducted thirteen narrative life story research conversations with women between the ages of 30 and 55 from a variety of (mainly Christian)[4] religious backgrounds and practices. Instead of conducting further interviews, I decided to deepen the data by interrogating it with the poetry of Menna Elfyn as one of the most well-known female poets writing in Welsh.

I analysed the research conversations through identifying the themes that emerged using an approach informed by discourse analysis, and the concept of 'figured worlds'[5] in particular the stereotypes, archetypes, metaphors, social norms, idealized behaviours and values held in common by the participants. In this chapter I argue that the analysis of 'found' creative materials, such as poetry, can make a useful contribution within an eclectic methodology and that this analysis can be a way of accessing and exploring women's voices within feminist theological research.

Poetry as a feminist theological research strategy

Using a body of work to learn more about a culture seems both familiar and innovative. Within cultural studies, reflecting on literature and its context is common, as is analysing records, writings and other artefacts within histori-cal research.[6] However, using poetry for research investigation is rare, though there has been some interest in developing research poems – using the poetic form in presenting data.[7] Song lyrics[8] have also been used within Welsh studies in order to enrich the most recent volume looking at gendered lives in Wales. Furman and colleagues[9] argue that analysing poetry can be a rich method of gaining knowledge about experiences, in revealing knowledge about both the context and subjectivity of the poet. Slee[10] argues that poetry has similarities to ethnography, in that both attend to the detail and sacredness of human life, and has the potential for meaningful and rich research into human experience.[11]

Pryce[12] used poetry in order to stimulate deep reflection on the nature and experiences of ordained ministry and argued that poetry 'may be particularly good for getting under the surface of things to explore underlying emotions, feelings and intuitions, and for detecting subtleties of meaning, pattern and sig-nificance in situations'.[13] Qualitative research and poetry therefore share similar concerns, in particular a curiosity and attentiveness to the depth of human experience.

Fiction, and to a certain extent poetry, has also been highly influential within feminist theology and spirituality, providing a parallel set of sacred texts for women,[14] as well as a challenge and impetus for action.[15] It could be argued that the natural home for feminist theology has not been the academy but crea-tive writing, liturgy and preaching.[16] Creative and reflective writing have also provided methods for those with stigmatized identities to reflect theologically and to find an authentic voice, denied them by traditional doctrinal theol-ogy.[17] This is true of Wales, where there has been a lively and long tradition of women writing poetry in English and Welsh since the fifteenth century, even if publically poetry in Wales has been dominated by men.[18]

By bringing the voice of Menna Elfyn into dialogue with my research par-ticipants I was able to attend more profoundly to the metaphors, tropes and patterns within Welsh women's experiences and their relationship with reli-gion. Given that literature has been one of the few spaces available for Welsh women to develop their theological voice, this is also one way of bringing an authentic Welsh female voice to the table of feminist theology. I now explore briefly the data that emerged from the research interviews – what was the nature and impact of religion on women's social and personal identities?

Findings from the research interviews

All the women I interviewed spoke about Christianity as a carrier of a Welsh social identity, especially in its Free Church form, even if they themselves were not religious. Repression and respectability are significant character-istics of this influence, what one of my research participants called 'the fear of what Mrs Jones down the road might say'. They reported a decisive shift in the influence of religion on the different generations. For their own mothers, institutional religion had formed a crucial part of their figured worlds, but this was being rejected by them, particularly as an influence on moral values. In fact, the Churches were harshly criticized for hypocrisy and even the women who were committed churchgoers regarded institutional religion as almost irrelevant to their faith lives, especially to their decisions about behaviour or doctrine.

The women did not seem to lack confidence or agency, as I had expected. They told stories of how their experiences of national and local church could be misogynistic and oppressive and also how local churches, clergy and espe-cially personal faith could be empowering and supportive. Resilience was not linked to religious beliefs. Although some women ascribed their high sense of self-esteem to their own relationship with the divine (but never institu-tional religion), the non-religious or occasional churchgoers were no less agentic or resilient. One key aspect of the women's strength was humour, which many of them utilized both to cope with difficult experiences and also to resist misogyny.

Several of the women reported that their relationships with their mothers were crucial to the formation of their own personal identities; in my question about Welsh role models several commented that their mother was their hero-ine. Often their transition into motherhood, for some seen as a transition into adulthood, was empowering rather than oppressive.

The archetype of the Strong Woman, linked to the Welsh Mam, was seen by many of the women as a particularly Welsh stereotype and this seemed operative within their world view. This trope seemed more linked to Wales' industrial heritage than religion – the woman running the home while her husband was at the quarry or down the coal mine. The women's life stories exemplified this strength and resilience and I was impressed with the courage of the women who had faced difficult circumstances, even tragedy and abuse, and had not only withstood these difficulties but had overcome them, utilizing them for their own development and in order to help others.

I was interested to find out whether the characteristics of this figured world were more widely shared within Wales, a set of discourses where the Strong Woman was an inspiring trope, mothers were significant, and motherhood a potentially empowering experience. A repressive chapel culture seemed to have been highly significant for the women as they grew up but was in the process of being rejected by them. Would these themes also be reflected in the writings of Menna Elfyn?

Menna Elfyn: a case study

I chose Menna Elfyn because she is regarded as one of the most 'dominant female' voices in Welsh language poetry at the end of the twentieth century.[19] She is also considered to be the 'best known Welsh language poet internationally'[20] and is the most published female writer working through the medium of Welsh.[21] She is a language activist and campaigner and was imprisoned twice for non-violent protest and has brought 'a radical wave of feminism into traditional Welsh society'[22] through her writing.

Her work has been translated into several languages (most notably English) and in translation her work is known globally. However, the fact that her work has been translated has caused controversy and it has been suggested that she has had to seek other avenues and audiences for her work because of her 'ostracization' by the 'exclusive male club' of Welsh poets.[23] Lloyd-Morgan comments that she is unaware of any other poet who has been as influential as Elfyn in articulating Welsh women's experiences.[24] However, Marks[25] observes that there is very little exploration of her work and her own treatment in an epistolary book length literary critical work is the only sustained examination of Elfyn's poetry apart from brief book chapters or journal articles.

For my study of her work I used the same reflective approach, influenced by discourse analysis, which I had used for analysing my interviews, and in particular looking out for religious themes. I found that confidence/agency, religion/faith and language/voice emerged as significant themes in her work. Elfyn reports that she was a shy child, unwilling to speak at the family dinner table and had a speech impediment which affected her confidence.[26] This struggle to find a voice has been important in her development as a feminist and Aaron comments that Elfyn has become 'the recognised spokeswoman of Welsh language feminist protest'[27] as evidenced by the following poem, which explores gaining agency as a woman through the process of growing up:

> I was humbly feminine
> now I am bold,
> I was spinelessly girlish
> now I am strong,
> I was powerlessly passive
> like my voiceless sex,
> I was contentedly restless
> through the centuries of rape.
>   But,
>   watch
>   your step,
>   brother![28]

Writing in a preface to an early collection, Elfyn maintains that there is not a definitive female mindset. Although she acknowledges that there are experiences that are characteristically female, for example birth, menstruation and hysterectomies, she does not consider that there are particularly male or female styles of writing, nor writing that is characteristic of a particular nation. It has been patriarchy that has attempted to restrict women and their identities by imposing the tropes of Eve/Mary on them.[29]

Religion

This reference to religious figures could indicate that Elfyn sees religion as central to female oppression. However, her treatment of religion and faith is more complex. Thomas says about her that she has an 'ambivalent relationship to [that] Nonconformist culture which is apparent in all her writing'.[30] Although her entry in the *Cambridge Companion to Women's Writing in English* states that 'religion dances under the surface of her work',[31] she does not refer to religion as a major theme in her own work, for a PhD by publication. In this, a personal reflection on her own work, she identified Wales, children (and motherhood), women, people and places as her major areas of exploration.[32]

In her poems there are echoes of the two dominant Christian traditions: first, the liturgical tradition of Anglicanism and Catholicism and second, the Nonconformist tradition. References to both traditions are often related to agency, voice and discourse. There are also some references to Eastern religious traditions. In the poem 'Hymn to a Welshman', a praise poem in honour of R. S. Thomas, a priest is the one 'who read the Word / on their behalf', rendering the nation passive; however the 'voiceless' and 'hoarse-voiced choir' of the Welsh's spokesperson is a 'poet'.[33] Likewise, religion and freedom / captivity are important themes; for example in her volume *Cell Angel*, her prison cell is a place of contemplation influenced by both Eastern and Western spirituality.[34]

God in Elfyn's prison in 'Psalm to the Little Gap in the Cell Door'[35] is not the Christian God of her upbringing but the earth goddess Gaia, whose eye is the eye-hole in the prison door. This eye is 'an open door', a signifier of freedom, where the prison officers look at her as the prisoner while she, in turn, looks at them, recognizing the divine in them, prisoner and prison officer alike.

Her father was a Congregationalist minister and there is reference to this in her poem 'The Small Communion',[36] where she describes the act of playing with his home communion set ('he was the only man I knew had a little set of cups without handles, who played at houses'). This poem is partnered with another, called 'The Big Communion'[37] where she describes a church service at HMP Pucklechurch and her incredulity at the simplistic teaching and insensitivity of the priest:

> He gave out
>
> to them that God was not like a one-armed bandit
> in an arcade. Seriously, that's what he said.
>
> He was pretty brusque. 'Don't expect
> to put money in and hit the handy jackpot
>
> as you offer a prayer'.[38]

Later she describes how they were all on their knees 'not expecting anything – / nothing at all / That's what he said wasn't it?'[39] Humorously she comments in her notes in 'Perffaith Nam / Perfect Blemish' that the large crowd at the prison for communion 'may have something to do with the wine'.[40]

The title poem of her collection *Cell Angel* reflects her experience of meeting a young male prisoner and she contrasts him with the other young men who perform in choirs in large churches: 'God's no more there / than here, the in the angel cell'.[41]

If a prison cell can be an ambivalent place of contemplation and freedom as well as restriction and captivity, her poems about chapel buildings and life are more unambiguously critical. It is clear she regards the chapel as a 'patriarchal institution'.[42] In her two significant satirical poems about chapels, one pokes fun at the Welsh obsession with cleanliness being next to godliness and the other is a poem that satirizes the discourse of women being asked to 'stay behind' to make the tea.

In 'Cleaning the Chapel',[43] Elfyn elaborates on a comment the minister Eifion Powell made once in a sermon that a chapel member had translated 'Holy Spirit' in the English into the 'Clean Spirit' in Welsh.[44] The poem suggests affectionately but humorously that the Celts, unlike other 'saints' turning to 'sackcloth and ashes' had a much more clean attitude to religion, 'stripping down to the skin / to wash, bathe and sing / in baths they called chapels'.[45] The poem is resonant with the values of Welsh respectability and of the role of the woman in keeping a clean house – the Spirit like a 'charwoman armed with a duster'.[46]

'Will the Ladies Please Stay Behind'[47] is angrier and less affectionate in tone. She names and critiques the damaging assumptions and its 'will the ladies please stay behind' discourse of male leadership and female service within church life. It represents a call for women to stand up to the men who are making them 'stay behind' and restrict their own faith and leadership. She contrasts the voicelessness of the women in the present with the vision of speaking a new empowered liturgy that even challenges Christ himself.

A service.
Us in the sheepfold.
The deacons ranked, facing us,
bald, thoughtful.
Him in the pulpit says,
'Thanks to the women
        who served ...'
Yes, served at the grave,
        wept, by the cross ...
'And will the ladies' – the women –
        'please
                stay behind?'

Behind –
we're still behind,
still waiting,
serving,
smiling … still dumb …
the same two thousand years ago
       as today.

But the next time they say it
from the seat too big for women,
'Will the ladies, etc.'
what about singing out (all together now!)
in a chant, a new psalm,
a lesson being recited –

'Listen here, little masters,
if Christ came back today

he'd definitely be making
       His own cup of tea.'

Her satire has been a significant voice challenging the dominant patriarchal discourses of the churches in Wales and is an example of how a poetic theology can both critique dominant voices and empower women (and men).

Liturgy, voice and voicelessness

Liturgy is a key theme in Elfyn's work and one that has not received much attention by scholars. Often, as in the above poem, it is linked to voice and agency and is offered as a dissenting discourse. Several of her poems have liturgical names, particularly in translation, for example, 'Matins', 'Litany on the Beginning of a Burial', 'In Praise of the Moon',[48] as well as the poems already mentioned (though the Welsh titles for these poems are less liturgical in style).

In the poem, 'Song of a Voiceless Person to British Telecom',[49] translated by R. S. Thomas, liturgy is again used as a form of dissenting discourse. When the poet is told to 'speak up' when she speaks in Welsh to a BT call handler, she realizes that the request is actually for her to speak in English and not in Welsh. She reflects on this and her voicelessness:

No pronunciation, no annunciation,
inflection. I am infected
with dumbness. I can neither lampoon,
sing in tune; much less can I
intone. My grace-notes

are neither music nor mumble.
I am not heard at Evening Prayer
nor at triumphal Matins.

Welsh speakers have been rendered 'mutes, Trappists'.[50] However the final but one stanza imagines how the poet will retort next time, using the biblical language of 1 Corinthians 13:

So the next time I am commanded
to 'speak up'
deferring to the courtesy
that is our convention,
with like courtesy I will require the operator
to 'pipe down';
and like 'sounding brass'
I will suggest the superfluousness of barbed wire,
since our language has berylled wares.

In one of her early poems, 'Angladd',[51] she expresses the pain of not being able to mark the death of her miscarried baby through any form of ritual,[52] which again is a form of silencing, though the poet eventually finds a voice to eulogize the lost baby in the second stanza.[53] A recurring theme in her poems that utilize liturgical vocabulary is that it eventually provides a dissenting voice where the poet is able to challenge the dominant discourse.

Her latest volume, *Murmur* also contains several allusions to liturgy and services. The collection opens with the poem 'Ghazal: Loss',[54] which is situated at a gravestone, described as an 'altar / of this tearful stone'. The next poem 'Babysitting in the Crematorium'[55] also has loss and ritual as a theme but with an element of hope in the timelessness of a child's sleep. A found poem 'Visitor'[56] recounts the conversation of a relative who tells the story of a couple found making love in the chapel gallery during a communion service ('Think of the cheek of it / we always keep the place unlocked, / we chapel people are much too good / for scoundrels like him. / He was one of eight, too, / each with a different surname . . .).[57] The collection ends with a poem to her father on his death and the final verse is resonant with one of the most famous Welsh graces that children recite in school, proclaiming her thankfulness, having recognized in the earlier stanza that:

Verses never leave me;
daughter of the Manse,
I had to learn the longest verse
without understanding that the smallest
is enough for a residue of prayer.[58]

This is perhaps the clearest acknowledgement by Elfyn herself of the influence of religious discourse within her poetry. Her utilization of liturgical and religious metaphors for the experience of feeling silenced and of speaking a stigmatized and sometimes subjugated language as a mother tongue, deepens our understanding of the experience of bilingual women in Wales, as well as reflecting an ambivalent experience of religion where it can be both empowering and silencing.

Religion and women

Although her satirical poems are critical of religion's treatment of women, her sequence 'Theology of Hair',[59] which she regards as exemplifying her exploration of women's experience,[60] is more serious in tone. The sequence starts with exploring the experience of being in a chapel and seeing an array of female heads arousing in the poet a desire to touch and play with them. She suggests that this is not erotic, but innocent,[61] though a major theme in the sequence is to question why female hair is so threatening to patriarchal religion.

For Elfyn, male sexuality and the desire to control women, particularly within a religious context, has led women to a lonely and alienating place.[62] In one poem in the sequence, 'A God-Problem',[63] Elfyn is more outspokenly critical and hair is referred to as symbolic of the violence that religion has inflicted on women:

> Standing before your altar,
> in my worst nightmares, I see
> a woman, shorn, being drowned as a witch,
> each single hair plucked out;[64]

This dilemma leads the poet to question Jesus directly:

> Jesus, what would you say today
> to women who wear veils?
> Is there a place for us in your sanctum?[65]

The poem ends with a longing to hear the story of the woman who washed Jesus' feet, drying them with her hair, an action that no-one, not even Jesus, stopped. However, the treatment of women by religion has caused the poet to have 'A God Problem' and in this Elfyn seems to align herself with a feminist or even post-feminist critique of Christianity. In 'Hairdresser'[66] there is a humorous treatment of gender difference, using Biblical language and metaphor self-consciously in the rhythms and length of the lines.[67] An important facet of Elfyn's exploration of women's experience is that of motherhood, which also appears in this sequence too.

Motherhood

Elfyn is regarded as the first Welsh poet who has written honestly about the subject of miscarriage and her early volume *Stafelloedd Aros*[68] is regarded as radical and groundbreaking, as well as deeply moving.[69] Elfyn herself considers motherhood as an important theme within her work (as I have already mentioned); she explores the experience not only in terms of her own motherhood but also as a daughter and, in the notion of 'Mother Tongue' (sequence IV in 'Theology of Hair'[70]), she combines a reference to the Welsh language with the particular bond between mother and daughter:

> The old language between mother and daughter.
>
> At times of sickness she'd be there,
> her palm flat on my forehead,
> chasing a curl away ... [71]

This is not an idealized image, as the poet talks about how she would cringe when her mother did this when she was younger. Generally, her discussion of motherhood is one that turns the concept on its head,[72] for example, she uses the mythical domestic voice of motherhood to condemn war.[73] This voice is arguably one of the most characteristic voices and identity within her work.[74] Motherhood for her is infused with loss, joy and guilt[75] as well as connection, and is also a spur to pacifism, radicalization and protest.[76] Her poetic exploration of this theme expresses the complexity and ambivalence of women's experience of motherhood and how it can become a potential gateway into a new form of empowerment.

Elfyn's work in dialogue with my findings

Women's engagement with religion

The research participants and the poetic voice in Menna Elfyn's work share a similar figured world, where religion is seen as repressive and occasionally patriarchal and silencing. Elinor was born (as she put it) in an 'unmarried mother's home' in the 1960s and was brought up by her grandmother, who she had thought was her mother. Her birth father was the minister's son, and the 'secrets and dynamics going round' both families had an impact on her and in particular her birth mother's sense of self. Elinor said:

> my birth mother, my sister, was made to feel unclean and dirty and she had lots of issues due to that and I think in those days that's what people did – you went to chapel and you had to be like this and had to be like that.

Sera, a chapelgoer, also spoke about how her father was shamed because of the sermons railing against the evils of drink, when he would often enjoy a pint. He was 'made to feel' bad because of this. However, she also laughingly told me the account of clearing out her chapel and coming across yellowing 'pledge' cards of several of their friends and neighbours promising to be teetotal whereas they were all known to be social drinkers. Yet this repressive culture is changing; although Sera is unable to be open about her sexuality completely, she has been supported privately as a lesbian by successive ministers in her small village chapel.

Where the women had a personal faith it was an individual relationship with God, held in parallel with an institutional religion that they engaged with on their own terms. Similarly Elfyn in her writing is affectionate towards the Church and its rituals (as seen in 'The Small Communion'), acknowledges its impact, but engages with it critically, rejecting what is unhelpful (God as a one-armed bandit) and embracing a more personal, even pluralist, faith where God is more present in a prison cell than in a Cathedral, and is Gaia as well as the Christian God. Similarly, the women I interviewed also utilized faith and religion in order to construct their identity and for their personal empowerment, with agency and skilfulness.

Another similarity between Elfyn's engagement with religion in her writings and the experience of the women recounted in interviews was in the use of humour as a dissenting discourse. Her satirical voice resonated with the humour of the women who laughed as they critiqued the attempts of men to diminish or control them, whether they were ministers, preachers or ex-husbands.

Voice and voicelessness

The metaphor of speaking and being silenced was also a relevant one for the research participants. Bethan spoke about her shyness, derived in part from the fear of others' disapproval leading her not to say anything at all rather than saying the wrong thing. However she also saw this in positive terms, as it stopped her from 'gabbling' when she spoke and encouraged her to be careful of what she said. Some participants spoke about finding a voice, for example Marged, who spoke publically and bravely in a meeting, offering to help with the male role of parking at a conference rather than 'staying behind' (echoing the words of the poem) to help to organize the refreshments.

Bons-Storm's influential study of Dutch women's engagement with the Church found that they were unable to share with their pastors the negative aspects of family life such as ambivalence about motherhood, and felt silenced.[77] However in Elfyn's work we see taboo subjects such as miscarriage explored, and the ambivalence within motherhood articulated. Walton suggests that the boundary between literature and theology can be a fruitful space where difficult experiences can be explored and theology challenged by the 'silenced, the absent and the unbearable'.[78] Elfyn's poetry has demonstrated this in her writing. Similarly, the women in my sample spoke honestly about difficult experiences, particularly that of relationship breakdown, loss and abuse, one participant even mentioning the woman with a black eye as a Welsh female stereotype. Yet, Welsh women were not seen as disempowered by the women in my study, nor in Elfyn's work. Several of the women described the process by which they had found confidence and agency, and above all considered themselves and other Welsh women as resilient.

Mothers and motherhood: the Strong Woman

The trope of the Strong Woman, closely linked to the stereotype of the Welsh Mam who emerged in my research conversations, is very present in Elfyn's work both in terms of her empowered dissenting poetic voice and the significance given to motherhood (and daughterhood). Motherhood in her work is reimagined as an ambivalent experience of loss, connection and even political action.

Bethan described motherhood as a gateway into self-determination and adulthood. Similarly Hannah spoke about motherhood as an enriching and life-changing experience. In answer to my question, who was their Welsh female role model or heroine, many of the women's first answer was to simply say their mothers. Even though the mothers had attempted to socialize them into the respectable identity informed by Welsh religious values, they also inspired in them an agency that the next generation was able to more fully realize. Marged described how her mother had hissed at her to sit down when she had stood up to make a speech at her wedding, but still said this about her:

> Mam was a minister's wife and took an interest but she wasn't the stereotype. She worked full-time and I remember her saying that when she got married, she was young, and she said she was her own person and I'm not just a minister's wife. I think she'd said in her first chapel when she married at about 24, 'and we welcome Mrs Robert Jones' and she said 'it's enough for me having taken on his surname I don't want to take on his first name as well. My name is Mrs Elinor Jones!'

The theme of Welsh women as strong was echoed in the lives of the participants and made explicit in what they said. For example, Lucy commented:

> Yes, I think we are strong. I think we are independent, I think we are opinionated but in a good way ... I think we have an identity that there is an underlying strength within the community which owes in no small part to the women within it. I think Welsh women are strong.

Hannah also described a process of growing in confidence, of empathizing with others and being a generally stronger person in recent years despite the experience of divorce and being neglected by her parents:

So I'm independent and I must say in the last two years I am getting stronger and stronger and stronger as a person. I'm getting confident of doing … I feel that I could do anything that I wanted if I put my mind to it.

Conclusion

In this chapter I have argued that a case study looking at poetry can provide deep reflection on a research question. This can enrich findings gained from other qualitative research methods as part of an eclectic approach and within the discipline of practical theology, where poetry can become an important contributor to a 'critical conversation'.

If, as Walton suggests, the boundary between literature and theology can be a fruitful space where difficult experiences and meaning-making can be explored,[79] then Elfyn's poetry has demonstrated this in writing about taboo subjects such as miscarriage and imprisonment. Motherhood is also reimagined as an experience of loss and personal and political empowerment. Her work has shown the potential for the construction of a Welsh feminist theology that utilizes satire, creativity and imagination in order to empower and inspire women in their engagement with religion and the world, to stand up for themselves and for the rights of others who are oppressed. This was reflected in the life stories of the women I interviewed who spoke about and exemplified in their lives the trope of the Strong Woman.

Welsh women's engagement with religion is complex. While my participants reported attempts to silence and control them, they also described finding voice and agency. Within discourse analysis, attentiveness to metaphors and archetypes is an important way of understanding human experience, and an important trope for the women I interviewed was that of the Strong Woman. The poetry of Menna Elfyn, sharing the same figured world as my research participants, shows how a deeper reflection on the trope of the Strong Woman, and a reimagining of how she would speak and act (as in the chanting of a psalm telling Jesus to make his own cup of tea) can further empower women as agents within their social world.

Notes

1 See, for example, Judith Plaskow and Carol Christ, ed., *Weaving the Visions: New Patterns in Feminist Spirituality* (New York: Harper Collins, 1989), 5; John Swinton and Harriet Mowat, *Practical Theology and Qualitative Research* (London: SCM Press, 2006), 43; Tom Wengraf, 'Uncovering the General from Within the Particular: From Contingencies to Typologies in the Understanding of Cases', in *The Turn to Biographical Methods in Social Science: Comparative Issues and Examples*, ed. Prue Chamberlayne, Joanna Bornat and Tom Wengraf (London: Routledge, 2000), 161.
2 Norman K. Denzin and Yvonna S. Lincoln, *The SAGE Handbook of Qualitative Research*, 4th ed. (Thousand Oaks, CA: Sage, 2011), 6; John W. Creswell, *Qualitative*

Inquiry and Research Design: Choosing Among Five Approaches, 3rd ed. (Thousand Oaks, CA: Sage, 2013), 45.

3 James Woodward and Stephen Pattison, ed., *The Blackwell Reader in Pastoral and Practical Theology* (Oxford: Blackwell, 2000), 7.

4 According to The Welsh Government, Knowledge and Analytic Services *2011 Census: First Results for Ethnicity, National Identity and Religion for Wales. Statistical Bulletin* (2012), Cardiff, accessed 7 November 2016. http://cdn.basw.co.uk/ upload/basw_111853-3.pdf, only 57.6 per cent of the Welsh population identified as Christian and 32.1 per cent as no religion. Islam, the next most popular religion has 1.5 per cent adherents. My participants identified as Christian or non-religious.

5 James P. Gee, *An Introduction to Discourse Analysis: Theory and Method*, 3rd ed. (New York and London: Routledge, 2011), 70.

6 Shulamit Reinharz, *Feminist Methods in Social Research* (New York: Oxford University Press, 1992), 146.

7 See Rich Furman, Cynthia Lietz and Carol L. Langer, 'The Research Poem in International Social Work: Innovations in Qualitative Methodology'. *International Journal of Qualitative Methods* 5, no. 3 (2006): 1–8.

8 Dawn Mannay, ed., *Our Changing Land: Revisiting Gender, Class and Identity in Contemporary Wales* (Cardiff: University of Wales Press, 2016).

9 Rich Furman *et al.*, 'Expressive, Research and Reflective Poetry as Qualitative Inquiry: a Study of Adolescent Identity', *Qualitative Research* 7, no. 3 (2007): 303.

10 Nicola Slee, *Women's Faith Development: Patterns and Processes* (Aldershot: Ashgate, 2004), 176. See also Slee, '(W)riting like a Woman: In Search of a Feminist Theological Poetics', in *Making Nothing Happen: Five Poets Explore Faith and Spirituality*, Gavin D'Costa *et al.* (Farnham: Ashgate, 2014), 10.

11 Slee, '(W)riting) Like a Woman', 10.

12 Mark Pryce, 'The Poetry of Priesthood: A Study of the Contribution of Poetry to the Continuing Ministerial Education of Clergy in the Church of England' (DProf thesis, University of Birmingham, 2014).

13 Pryce, 'The Poetry of Priesthood', 30.

14 Dawn Llewellyn, *Reading, Feminism, and Spirituality: Troubling the Waves* (Basingstoke: Palgrave Macmillan, 2015), 10.

15 Llewellyn, *Reading, Feminism, and Spirituality*, 12. Also Anna Fisk, *Sex, Sin, and Our Selves: Encounters in Feminist Theology and Contemporary Women's Literature.* (Eugene, OR: Pickwick, 2014), xvii.

16 Fisk *Sex, Sin and Our Selves*, 5; Llewellyn, *Reading, Feminism and Spirituality*, 18.

17 Heather Walton, *Literature, Theology and Feminism* (Manchester: Manchester University Press, 2007), 26.

18 Katie Gramich and Catherine Brennan, *Welsh Women's Poetry 1460–2001: An Anthology* (Dinas Powys: Honno Press, 2003), xvii; Menna Elfyn, *O'r Iawn Ryw: Blodeugerdd o Farddoniaeth* (Dinas Powys: Honno Press, 1991), v.

19 Katie Gramich, *Twentieth-Century Women's Writing in Wales: Land, Gender, Belonging* (Cardiff: University of Wales Press, 2007), 151.

20 British Council for Literature, *Writers: Menna Elfyn*, accessed 31 May 2016, https:// literature.britishcouncil.org/writer/menna-elfyn.

21 Menna Elfyn, 'Barddoniaeth Menna Elfyn: Pererindod Bardd' (PhD thesis, University of Wales, Trinity St. David, 2010).

22 Gramich, *Twentieth-Century Women's Writing*, 153.

23 Tudur Hallam, 'When a Bardd Meets a Poet: Menna Elfyn and the Displacement of Parallel Facing Texts', in *Slanderous Tongues: Essays on Welsh Poetry in English 1970–2005*, ed. Daniel G. Williams (Bridgend: Seren, 2010), 89–111.

24 Quoted in Rhiannon Marks, *Pe Gallwn, Mi Luniwn Lythyr: Golwg Ar Waith Menna Elfyn* (Cardiff: University of Wales Press, 2013), 6.

25 Marks, *Pe Gallwn Mi Luniwn Lythyr*.

26 Elfyn, *Pererindod Bardd*, 5, 6.

27 Jane Aaron, 'Women in Search of a Welsh Identity', *Scottish Affairs* 18 (Winter 1997), 73.

28 Aaron's own translation. Elfyn in Aaron, 'Women in Search of a Welsh Identity', 73, 74.

29 Elfyn, *O'r Iawn Ryw*, v.

30 M. Wynn Thomas, 'The Place of Gender in the Poetry of Gillian Clarke and Menna Elfyn', *Sheer Poetry: Resources on Poetry by the Poets Themselves*, accessed 31 May 2016, www.sheerpoetry.co.uk/advanced/dissertations/the-place-of-gender-in-the-poetry-of-gillian-clarke-and-menna-elfyn.

31 D. Morley, 'Menna Elfyn', in *The Cambridge Guide to Women's Writing in English* ed. Lorna Sage (Cambridge: Cambridge University Press, 1999), 218.

32 Elfyn, *Pererindod Bardd*, 3.

33 Menna Elfyn, *Perfect Blemish/Perffaith Nam: New and Selected Poems 1995–2007* (Newcastle Upon Tyne: Bloodaxe, 2007), 225–226.

34 Morley, *Menna Elfyn*, 8.

35 Menna Elfyn, *Cell Angel* (Newcastle Upon Tyne: Bloodaxe, 1996), 25.

36 Ibid., 167.

37 Ibid., 169.

38 Ibid., 169.

39 Ibid., 169.

40 Elfyn, *Perfect Blemish*, 295.

41 Elfyn, *Cell Angel*, 21.

42 Marks, *Pe Gallwn Mi Luniwn Lythyr*, 217.

43 Elfyn, *Perfect Blemish*, 171.

44 Ibid., 295.

45 Ibid., 171.

46 Ibid., 171.

47 Menna Elfyn, *Eucalyptus – Detholiad o Gerddi Selected Poems 1978–1994* (Llandysul: Gwasg Gomer, 1995), 17.

48 Elfyn, *Perfect Blemish*.

49 Elfyn, *Eucalyptus*, 7, 9.

50 Ibid., 7.

51 Angladd means 'funeral' in Welsh, from Menna Elfyn, *Stafelloedd Aros* (Llandysul: Gwasg Gomer, 1978).

52 Marks, *Pe Gallwn*, 91.

53 Elfyn, *Stafelloedd Aros*, 38

54 Menna Elfyn, *Murmur* (Newcastle Upon Tyne: Bloodaxe, 2012), 11.

55 Ibid., 13.

56 Ibid., 57.

57 Ibid., 57.

58 Ibid., 125.

59 Elfyn, *Cell Angel*, 57–69.

60 Elfyn, *Pererindod Bardd*, 57.

61 Ibid., 57.

62 Ibid., 58.
63 Elfyn, *Perfect Blemish*, 53.
64 Ibid., 53.
65 Ibid., 53.
66 Ibid., 57.
67 Elfyn, *Pererindod Bardd*, 60.
68 Waiting rooms in Welsh.
69 Marks, *Pe Gallwn*, 87.
70 Elfyn, *Perfect Blemish*, 55, 57.
71 Ibid., 55, 57.
72 Marks, *Pe Gallwn*, 98.
73 Ibid., 98.
74 Ibid., 87.
75 Elfyn, *Pererindod Bardd*, 10–14.
76 Marks, *Pe Gallwn*, 220.
77 Riet Bons-Storm, *The Incredible Woman: Listening to Women's Silences in Pastoral Care and Counselling* (Nashville: Abingdon, 1996).
78 Walton, *Literature, Theology and Feminism*, 36.
79 Walton *Literature, Theology and Feminism*, 35.

Part IV

Practising reflexivity

12 Reflexivity, identity and the role of the researcher

Jenny Morgans

Introduction

As the experiences and expectations of emerging adults are shifting, along with changes in the university culture, understanding how faith is formed and reformed in young adults is important. Higher education is a particular context informing this process, presenting those who attend with new experiences and opportunities in what is often an intense time of transition. With this in mind, I set out to understand the gendered practices of congruence and intentionality in terms of women's faith and identity development at university.

I interviewed twenty-one Christian women, all first-year university students at the same higher education institution, most of whom were away from home for the first time. I located the women through attending Christian student societies and student-majority churches, as well as through posting requests on relevant social media groups, asking female freshers if they wished to be interviewed. I attempted to practise reflexivity, a key feminist characteristic, throughout the design and development of my research. As I began my data production,[1] my initial feelings and reflections as well as my identity then as a PhD candidate and an ordinand in the Church of England were significant to my research development. Four encounters in particular stand out as forcing me to re-evaluate my role as a researcher and reflect on my identity. These encounters were significant in both challenging and informing my understanding and practise of reflexivity.

In this chapter, then, I engage critically with these four encounters, placing them in dialogue with relevant literature, interview transcripts and entries into my research journal. I introduce my own reflections on reflexivity as immensely useful, yet ongoing and difficult, before closely examining the four encounters. The first considers the researcher as distinct from a mentor, teacher or role-model, based on a conversation at the end of my interview with Ashley.[2] The second analyses my interview with Danielle, an interview where I found myself having to hold my tongue despite some deep worries about her. The following two situations were tricky encounters arising from events that I attended with the aim of finding interviewees. They surprised me into reflecting on the researcher's role and values in the research design, so I consider these alongside one another. I then look at the place of prayer in research, considering its usefulness in the light of my four encounters. Finally, I consider different approaches to the role of the researcher, and in particular explain my preference for the researcher as 'friendly stranger' based on my own experiences.

My research journal was a significant tool in my work, and the decision to include sections of it here highlights the importance of the place of emotion in the reflexive process of data production. It also intentionally foregrounds my doubts and emotions as I responded to encounters with female Christian freshers relatively recently to my own experiences as an undergraduate, and later when I continued to reflect on these encounters at deeper levels as I became more experienced.

Reflexivity: useful, ongoing and hard

Reflexivity is defined by Fonow and Cook as

> the tendency of feminists to reflect upon, examine critically, and explore analytically the nature of the research process ... to gain insight into the assumptions about gender relations underlying the conduct of inquiry ... including an exploration of the investigator's reactions to doing the research.[3]

While it is agreed that reflexivity is vital to the work of feminist research, there are different opinions about why this is so, and different understandings of what it looks like in practice. Warnings about research that fails to take reflexivity seriously need heeding – otherwise, as well as having an impact on the quality and reliability of research, researchers can also do harm to those they are researching, and to themselves. As Etherington cautions in her substantial work on reflexivity: 'Unacknowledged negative thoughts and feelings may block our ability to hear participants clearly or may influence how we make sense of what we are hearing'.[4]

It was not out of this fear that I was keen to pursue reflexivity in my own research, but out of a positive desire for my holistic well-being and an integration of my work and self. I was aware that, following my previous work with students as well as my own experience as a student, the research had sought me out and 'chosen' me. The experience of female students felt like something I was *called* to research, that I *needed* to do following on from experiences that I had had. I was also excited that reflexive research would involve recognizing and celebrating the presence of my emotions and multiple identities as a person: as a liberal/progressive Christian training for ministry, as a woman and a feminist, as someone leaving behind her twenties, as an academic and as a holistic human being. It gave me confidence knowing that my prior experiences and knowledge could be taken seriously. I also knew that working reflexively brought limitations, that my research would reveal only as much as I could see, hear, and comprehend. I took heed of Ramazanoglu's warning that 'from the start, your project will incorporate your own values, . . . your theory, . . . your ontology, . . . your epistemology'.[5] Yet I hoped and suspected that I had achieved a commitment to what Ferguson calls 'poking around and prodding within' our theories and positionalities.[6]

However, I had underestimated how *useful* reflexivity would be throughout my research, in helping me to understand what it was that I was actually doing, and in negotiating the relationships that I had with the students that I worked with. Reflexivity enabled me to understand implicit decisions that I had made, to analyse more deeply the experiences that I had had, and to shape more intentionally the future of the project. It has enabled me to practise some self-care when I have had deep feelings, and offered me encouragement in difficult periods.

I had also not considered how *ongoing* a task reflexivity would prove, as I dwell on these four encounters some time after they occurred. This reflexive 'identity work' took on a different shape through each of the research stages – finding interviewees, interviewing, data analysis and writing up. But, even more challenging has been the need to continue to engage with these events on increasingly deeper 'levels' alongside developments and changes in my own life. I have transitioned from an ordinand to a minister, and moved from being a new researcher to one with more experience. This has required significant reflection, and while it has always been rewarding, it has sometimes left me feeling vulnerable and 'raw' in the process.

Moreover, I had not considered how *hard* this would be, how being reflexive would expose my exercise of power, would deeply affect my sense of self as I attempted a difficult balancing of my different identities, and would blur the boundaries placed around my researcher role. These encounters highlighted tensions between my researcher role and other aspects of my identity, and I had to reflect on where the boundaries were as I negotiated developments in my own identity – or rather *identities* – and the messiness and self-critique that this reflexivity involves. I reconsidered what feminist research ethics involved and how best to negotiate them in the immediacy of a research encounter, calling into question my own implicit assumptions and viewpoints. Moreover, much of the emotion that comes through in my research journal came from the initial desire to rescue and teach these young women, as I know I needed others to rescue and teach me when I was in the same position, and the reflections here come from my own tensions and dilemmas when the researcher's role makes this teaching ethically untenable. With Pillow and Mayo, I found:

> Finding a balance as an observer-participant – when to wear the researcher hat and when to become involved by giving your opinion, providing help, or actively leading a project – is difficult and specific to each research context ... and we may often find we are unprepared.[7]

In fact, the more reflexive I aspired to be, the more I was convinced with Richardson that there is 'no resolution to the problem of speaking for others'.[8]

Researcher, not mentor

My very first interview shook some of my assumptions and made me reconsider my role as a researcher and how reflexive I actually was. It threw up questions about ethics and power, forcing me to consider carefully my own positionality. I had previously understood the basis of research ethics as the intention to do no harm, and not to influence the women that I interviewed more than happened organically from their experience of the interview. However, my encounter with Ashley showed me that this was a more complex and difficult aim than I had first considered.

Ashley was an articulate new Christian from a conservative Anglican church. While aware of the importance of 'feminist issues', Ashley had been unable to answer my questions about the impact of her own gender in her faith-life, and this seemed to surprise her. She also was not sure what she thought of her church's refusal to allow women to lead worship or preach.

Out of a desire to be as transparent as possible in my research, at the end of each formal interview I conducted I gave the women an opportunity to ask me questions. Many women asked nothing, while others wanted to know more about my research goals or findings. Ashley, however, turned some of the questions I had asked her back to me, asking what my own thoughts about being a woman at church were. I disclosed that I was training to be a priest, and thus from a different church tradition to her own. She was genuinely interested in my experience. Soon we were talking about feminist theology – a term she had never heard before – and she was asking me to recommend some reading. How could I be authentic to myself, honest to her, but keep to my role and ethics as a researcher?

In the conversation, I was thinking 'should I be saying this about myself to Ashley? Should I be influencing her?' I (perhaps misleadingly[9]) took comfort in the knowledge that the 'official' or 'formal' interview was over, and that I had my 'data', which would not be adulterated by our conversation. I also reasoned that in the conversation, I might learn more about Ashley, which would add to the things that she had already told me. As Ashley recognized she could learn from my knowledge and experience, my speech had the potential to move the relationship to a different level, raising ethical questions. My role slipped from researcher to teacher, mentor, or perhaps even role model. I felt uncomfortable with this, but I could not prevent it, because I felt that I had some responsibility to help Ashley that I could not define. I wanted her to encounter feminist theology as an undergraduate and for it to have the same transformative impact that it had had on me nearly fifteen years earlier. I wanted to show what Mies terms 'conscious partiality',[10] but I was struggling to find what this meant for me here.

A second level of reflexivity occurred after the interview, when in my research journal I wrote:

I wanted to be honest/transparent about my motives and my own experience. I clearly put across ideas that Ashley hadn't experienced before ... I saw so much potential in her that clearly wasn't flourishing for her at the moment. But I think that compared to where I was at that age, she is miles further on.

At the end of each 'formal' interview, where I asked the women questions, I left my electronic device recording (with their permission) until the student left. In transcribing, I listened carefully to the informal conversation that followed, including any questions they asked me, because I knew that sometimes the women might disclose further information here. It seemed important to me to pay full attention to the end of the exchange, in a prayerful 'paying of minute attention to every word spoken by research participants, to the inflection, nuance . . . as well as to the researcher's own part in the interchange'.[11] Following the interview with Ashley, transcribing my own passionate and muddled speech, trying to articulate my own thoughts about being a Christian woman was a steep learning curve, giving me empathy with the women I interviewed but shaking my own confidence in the process. As Etherington writes:

> [I]t is inevitable that issues of power come into focus and require us constantly to scrutinize and interrogate our own positions, views, and behaviours, turning back onto ourselves the same scrupulous lens through which we examine the lives of our participants.[12]

I still have doubts about my behaviour in this conversation. When my position as an ordinand and my church background went against her own conservative tradition, was I right be so honest about it, and so clearly keen to influence her own position by explaining my own opinion and suggesting literature she could read? Letherby writes, 'Researchers' multiple identities as people are as relevant to the research process and product as the personhood of respondents'.[13] Was I self-indulgent in allowing my identities as a liberal Christian and as an ordinand come so freely to the fore?

The work of DeVault and Gross acknowledges some of these same tensions. They advocate for 'strategic disclosure' in the building of rapport, calling for data production to be 'a collaborative moment of making knowledge' between women with common interests. They also advise a deep listening in the interview, 'allowing that information to affect you, baffle you, haunt you, make you uncomfortable, and take you on unexpected detours'.[14] This enables me to understand my questions around this conversation with Ashley not as a blip but as central to my research aims.

The researcher and holding silence

Moschella argues that when studying people's spiritual lives, extra care must be taken. We need to bring honesty and transparency about our motives to the research encounter, and reverence to our research relationships.[15] The second encounter I will explore, my interview with Danielle, taught me just how true this is.

Danielle, a lesbian from a conservative evangelical church, told me about the different responses she had received from Christians who knew about her sexuality, including some very negative reactions from friends:

> [I]t's a bit stressful especially coz two of my best mates are Christians and they just don't get it they're like 'oh you can't do that you shouldn't do that it's not what God wants' and the amounts of arguments and debates we had over it, I don't really tell people back home at church I didn't tell anyone, yeah, it's just kind of that thing of being judged.[16]

She was relieved, however, after attending a youth event where she heard that the Bible taught that homosexuality was acceptable as long as any relationships were not consummated. In response, this was how she was living at the time of the interview. She seemed to have accepted this position for herself, and portrayed positive feelings about it:

> Before (the event) ... I was trying to kind of move away from (being a lesbian) and just kind of be straight, and, and then when I went there I was just kind of like 'this is okay' so when people say stuff now I'm like 'well have you actually read the Bible? Do you know that much about it or are you just saying it because that's what you hear other people saying?'

The interview was deeply upsetting for me. Letherby writes that researchers need to understand our respondents' worldview for us to listen to what they're saying. However, sometimes we will hear things that are difficult for us to accept or agree with, and in those situations we have to manage our dislike of their attitudes, however uncomfortable this is. And even when the interviewee discusses difficult situations, she continues by reminding us that, 'research relationships are *not* counselling relationships . . . [A]lthough as researcher we may feel that we want to "help" our respondents, it is important to acknowledge that such feelings may reflect our own needs . . . rather than those of respondents'.[17]

Pillow and Mayo argue that discomfort is as powerful as knowing.[18] However, I struggled with this. In my discomfort, I wanted to help Danielle to see that there are other ways of interpreting the Bible, and signpost her to more inclusive churches and ministers. I also wanted to advise her to stop seeing her 'friends'. Of course I did none of these things, and I had to remind myself that these desires said more about me than about Danielle. Moschella writes that patient listening, while sounding simple, is actually difficult to sustain. Instead, lapsing into a mode of giving advice, becoming an expert (or pretending to be one) is easier.[19] This was the case for me in Danielle's interview because of the extent to which I was worried about her. In my entry in my research journal afterwards, I wrote, 'While she was talking I was thinking "I'm struggling to give her my full attention because my heart is breaking"'.

I hoped that Danielle would question me at the end of the interview, as Ashley had, and give me an opportunity to share something of my own views. While the conversation with Ashley had made me uncomfortable, I realized that it was preferable to having to listen to things I found difficult in silence. To my disappointment she did not ask, but perhaps that was best since it meant that I maintained my researcher distance and did not have the opportunity to influence her views. Of course it was not my place to tell her that I considered her own views somehow incorrect or invalid.

My research journal reflects how emotional I felt following the interview, with my thoughts muddled up and tripping over one another:

> Had the saddest interview ever with Danielle ... She is celibate! And in a celibate relationship! I'm so sad, I just wanted to give her a hug and talk to her about ... queer theology ... It wouldn't surprise me if she has some sort of mental health crisis and leaves the church in a number of years. So sad! I just wanted her to meet some of my gay Christian friends. I'm so judgemental! Maybe she'll be fine! I'm so worried for her, it's really damaging! She seemed to have internalized it all though ... It was quite confusing ... I am so sad for her. How can her church at home not know she's gay!

Reading this journal back, I am struck by the number of exclamation marks. I was upset and angry. I was aware I was being arrogant for making assumptions and judgements, assuming that my own theological position was correct and that Danielle's and those of her Christian networks were wrong, harmful and not sustainable. It was my worries based on this assumption, not on Danielle's words, that prevented me from listening and sufficiently engaging with her viewpoint.

I recognize now that I was feeling maternalistic towards Danielle, and Etherington highlights how this can be deeply patronizing, and thus unhelpful. She writes that with the feminist aim

> to provide a platform for the voices of those who have been marginalized or victimized, ... (t)here is a danger that we report the voices of participants, either as powerless victims incapable of acts of resistance or as heroic stories of innocents who have overcome powerful destructive forces.[20]

Danielle did not articulate herself in these terms at all, and nor should I so represent her.

In writing my journal, I was also reminded of something that a priest had suggested to me. He had said that the researcher's role was in some ways similar to a priest's in that there needs to be 'a priestly emptying of self'. I wrote: 'I can't force myself, my theology, my views onto her. I just have to be empty and listen'. I realize now that this was a stance of contemplative prayer in the research relationship, which I explore below.

My anger needed much closer examination. I had to engage in theological reflection on LGBTI rights, and how my theology impinged on my role as researcher. Pillow and Mayo write that advocacy is one of feminist research's key aims.[21] While racism and sexism are generally agreed injustices, many Christians from Danielle's tradition would not recognize LGBTI rights. Thus, in this case, what researcher advocacy for these rights looks like is blurred. Josselson writes:

> I would worry most if I stopped worrying, stopped suffering for the dis-junction that occurs when we try to tell the Other's story ... It is with our anxiety, dread, guilt, and shame that we honour our participants. To do this work we must contain these feelings rather than deny, suppress, or rationalize them.[22]

While this quotation is helpful, I realized that I needed to do more than 'con-tain' my feelings in an air of pseudo-detachment. It is in this space that I found prayer to be significant, as I explore later.

The researcher in tricky encounters

The following two encounters resulted from Christian events that I attended in order to meet potential interviewees. Attending these meetings proved to be the most successful method of locating participants, however, I did not expect the events to have the impact upon me and upon my research that they did. I attended these events 'lightly', but I was forced to reflect on them in a much more reflexive manner. The two encounters demonstrated in different ways how reflexivity is intrinsic to the research development process, in which I learnt a lot about myself and my implicit values in relation to others – the first with an individual woman, and the second with a group/institution.

After an event at a Christian student society (Society A), I spoke with Madison, who was not a potential interviewee. She shared with me her difficul-ties with a large conservative evangelical student society (Society B). Madison also asked me how I was experiencing attending the different societies, and what I was discovering in my interviews. Afterwards, I wrote in my journal:

> I was a bit worried about how I was going to handle it ... [Madison] was especially interested in hearing about Society B. She said that she had some damaging experiences there ... I tried to be diplomatic and gentle. I wish afterwards I had a better conversation with her about what I really thought. It's hard being a researcher at these things. I want Madison to know that my theology is much more inclined in her direction, but like-wise I don't want Society B to know that! ... There's some unresolved anger there. I hope she's ok.

Again, as with Danielle, I was concerned about Madison's well-being, but I knew that I could be more honest with Madison in a one-to-one setting because the conversation would not directly influence my data. I said something to her like: 'well you probably know that the theology at Society A is closer to what I think than when I go to Society B', and to my surprise she replied saying: 'I don't really know what your theology is, you don't say much about it'. I thought that I had been more open than I had been, but I was not sure which approach would have been better, or in which approach I would have held more integrity. I wondered again about the complexities of self-disclosure, and I was aware that Madison and I were not talking as 'friends' but in a different context.

My second example came following my third visit at Society B. I received a message via social media from the society's president asking me to cease attending meetings. It explained that the leadership team considered my research to go against their evangelistic mission, and my attendance at the society to distract students from this mission. My initial reaction to the message is evident in my entry in my research journal:

> I feel winded, like I've been punched in the stomach … The message hints that I've been slipping under their radar when I'd tried to be completely transparent about what I've been doing … And I'm worried about the two Society B participant interviews I've got coming up … what if Society B stops them being involved? … It feels really unjust … I feel so vulnerable.

I felt that Society B had misunderstood both my research and my purpose in attending the meetings, despite my honesty both by email before I had visited, and with the society each time I attended. It was difficult not to take the message personally. I was confronted with the power that the society's student committee had over my research concerning how I accessed and was viewed by their attendees. This led to the feeling of powerlessness.

In a measured reply, I agreed to stop attending the meetings, and I attempted to explain my research. I said:

> I do not use Society B meetings to talk to people about my research, but only to find students who would be willing to participate. My research does not take place at Society B meetings. Students can choose for themselves whether being involved is part of their discipleship or not … I hope that this has cleared up some of the misunderstanding.

This message exchange, and my discontinued attendance at Society B, was a useful exercise in being made to feel some of the vulnerability that Society B were experiencing. An important area of being reflexive is being honest about dead-ends and admitting to mistakes.[23] I realized that I had made assumptions about how Society B had understood my research, and felt uneasy when the president played the important role of 'holding researchers accountable to those with whom they research'.[24]

I later considered why I felt such a physical reaction, of being 'punched in the stomach'. The rejection from the society came not in response to my initial verbal request for access, but as a direct reaction to my embodied physical presence in the meetings. The *idea* of my research was not considered a problem or threat. Society B's problem lay with *me*, and my actual physical and emotional presence in the group. It was the 'otherness' that my presence embodied that reflects something about the depth of challenge that Society B felt. In a further level of reflexivity here, however, I became clear that I othered Society B as much as they othered me. Similar to my experience of hearing Danielle's opinions, this was a further opportunity to learn how to deal with differing worldviews. Of course the society had the right to bar me as the outsider/ researcher. The power struggle with Society B's leadership revealed values implicit in my research, in my very embodied self, that were perhaps incompatible with Society B's conservative approach to Christianity, values that I had not disclosed to the society (or to any of the societies – as my conversation with Madison confirmed).

This led me to reflect further on my journal entry. Had Society B really misunderstood my research? Perhaps if my research presence and activity began to challenge the leadership of Society B, then maybe the leaders did 'understand' something of where it might lead – perhaps with criticism of the society and their approach. It was something of my own power and presence as a researcher that made them feel threatened.

Despite their differences, there are some similarities with how being reflexive on these two encounters helped me to understand more about myself as a researcher, and about the research project itself. As Madison showed interest in my experiences, and as Society B questioned my approach, in both encounters I became the 'researched',[25] and it was this experience that forced me to carry out further reflexivity. In particular, I pondered the uncomfortable place that a researcher holds as neither 'insider' nor 'outsider'. Researchers are often referred to as 'outsiders/within',[26] detailing the complexities of the researcher gaining access because of aspects of her identity or experiences shared with those being researched. I wanted to say to both Madison and Society B 'I am like you', but I could not reveal all aspects of my identity and I did not intend this to be deceptive. I also recognized the many ways in which I could say 'I am not like you'.[27]

In some encounters and interviews, the parts of my identity that made me an insider were the same parts that rendered me an outsider in others. It was the negotiation of these different identities that resulted in Madison's observation of my tight-lipped behaviour. Throughout my conversation with her, I crossed a fraught and complicated boundary line – back and forth. My own experience as a young Christian woman perhaps could have enabled me to feel like an insider, but instead I felt distanced as I clung to my role as researcher. There are a number of reasons for this – including not wanting to have a detrimental impact on my data production and not wanting overly to influence

Madison. I did not want to appear 'unprofessional', or to compromise in any way the interviewees that I was meeting.

Hesse–Biber and Piatelli attempt to unite insider/outside relationships, but recognize that this is hindered by the fluid and shifting nature of identity. They find that the researcher cannot recognize her insider/outsider position at the outset, but only discovers it *during* the research. Moreover, others will also define us and our role on a shifting basis, and I discerned something of this in both encounters. It is not merely a question of whether we are in or out, since both the similarities and differences between self and those we research are subject to negotiation. Hesse–Biber and Piatelli write:

> After eighteen months in the field, I am neither insider nor outsider. My research identity remains and interacts with my other identities, sometimes acting as an asset and other times a hindrance ... It is the multiple aspects of our identity ... that shape our research experience, and this identity continuously shifts throughout the research process.[28]

Further to reflecting on the researcher's positionality in this way, I can now see that in my responses to both Madison and to Society B, I was attempting to extend 'reflexivity outward . . . from analysing my own self-presentation to also considering how I am being defined and why'.[29] While I could not control how others viewed me, I could try to influence the image they held by negotiating with them my researcher role, rather than imposing it.

I had decided early in the project design not to use participant observation as a research method. Instead, I had entered Society B's space with a purely transactional understanding. However, on further reflection, I reconsidered my response to their message. I had the surprising realization that *of course* attending the meetings was part of my research, adding to my picture of the Christian societies and thus the students that I was interviewing – something that Madison had also picked up. Participating in the meetings had made the interviews possible. Society B had recognized this before I had, and this realization helped me to understand why Society B had responded in this way.

Researching, praying, being

Slee writes that research and prayer have many of the same characteristics:

> As in prayer, so in research ... We have to learn to focus all our attention on the other and to get ourselves and our egos out of the way. At the same time, we need to know how to use ourselves – feelings, body, intelligence, intuition – to assist our listening.[30]

As reflexivity is a useful, ongoing and hard path to tread, prayer proved to me a vital tool in navigating that journey. Being reflexive about my emotions, values, behaviour, researcher role, and identities involved some difficult work. I have had to be emotionally astute and academically rigorous at a time when my own personal formation and transition has been intense. This has combined with the depth of feeling and personal connection I have felt with Ashley, Danielle, Madison and the 'rejection' from Society B. It is at these times in particular that I have discovered the importance of prayer and fostering my own spirituality in the research process. In being unable to intervene myself, in the inappropriateness of teaching or rescuing the women, I have had to trust that God is at work in and around the lives of the students. This has not been an attempt to manipulate the women's lives from afar, but instead is a contemplative prayer of longing. Since advocacy is a goal of feminist research, advocacy with God has enabled me to act without acting. It has enabled me simply to *be* with my worries for others, my doubts of my own behaviour and the rawness of my own emotion, and to offer them to the eternal Other. I am learning that praying about those I research is a transformative and hopeful practice for my very being.

Researchers as friendly strangers

It seems that in these four encounters, it has been the blurring of the *role* of the researcher that has forced reflexivity and required further consideration. In reflecting further, I have discovered with DeVault and Gross that '[r]esearch relations are never simple encounters, innocent of identity and lines of power'.[31]

What was my role, and how did it shift in the different encounters that I have explored, and in many others besides? Other feminist researchers offer suggestions and models. Reinharz evaluates different approaches including those that find helpful a distance between the researcher and the researched, and cites Evans and Zimmerman's emphasis on the interviewer being a 'stranger'. She advocates 'avoiding control over others and developing a sense of connectedness with people', while avoiding a 'superficial friendliness'.[32] Other scholars call for intimacy, integrity and self-disclosure in building a framework of 'friendship' or genuine relationship for interviewing and research.[33]

My own experiences as recounted here most resonate with that of Letherby. She observes that research of a personal nature 'often prompts a temporary closeness initiated by shared experience', which can feel like friendship for the duration of the interview. She proposes researchers take the role of 'friendly strangers'.[34] This approach enabled me to share with Ashley my experiences of feminist theology in answering her questions while also maintaining some distance; to care deeply about Danielle while remaining silent; to show some honesty with Madison about my research findings while not becoming her 'friend'; and to hope that Society B did not think too negatively of me while resisting taking their critique to heart. Being a friendly stranger enabled me to evaluate situations reflexively, ethically, pastorally, personally and 'academically/scientifically' – all in the research role.

Conclusion

Being reflexive in these four encounters changed me and my research. Not only did reflexivity clarify my research aims and process, it helped to shape it. I began to understand that reflexivity could add a rich additional layer to my data production, changing the shape and nature of my project.

I am also learning how to be respectfully open with those I disagree with. I am not powerless in how others see me, but with integrity and honesty I am becoming aware of the place of my value judgements in the different stages of research. Where I was initially patronizing, disrespectful and arrogant in my views and behaviour, I now hope that I have learnt from others calling me to account – both allies and those with different understandings. By allowing my emotions to come to the surface, I have been able to affirm and understand them, but also analyse their origin and critique their underlying assumptions. This has helped me to reflect further on myself as researcher and as woman.

Being reflexive ensured my accountability to those I researched, and kept me aware of my own power and bias. It continues to show me ways that the research is both shaped by me, and continues to shape me. On a more personal note, being reflexive has helped me to practise self-care and enabled me to stay focussed on the bigger picture.

While reflexivity is indeed constantly ongoing and hard, it is immensely rewarding, both in terms of our work and our own understanding of our role and positionality in the messiness of research. All these things, I believe, have both enabled me to be a better researcher, and have improved the quality and nature of my research.

Notes

1 I use the term 'data production' rather than 'data collection', rejecting the notion that social realities are simply 'there' for researchers to find. Caroline Ramazanoglu with Janet Holland, *Feminist Methodology: Challenges and Choices* (London: Sage, 2002), 154.
2 I use pseudonyms for the students.
3 Mary Margaret Fonow and Judith A. Cook, eds, *Beyond Methodology: Feminist Scholarship as Lived Research* (Bloomington: Indiana University Press, 1991), 2.
4 Kim Etherington, *Becoming a Reflexive Researcher: Using Our Selves in Research* (London: Jessica Kingsley, 2004), 128.
5 Ramazanoglu with Holland, *Feminist Methodology*, 149, 157.
6 Kathy Ferguson, *The Man Question: Visions of Subjectivity in Feminist Theory* (Berkeley: University of California Press, 1993), ix.
7 Wanda S. Pillow and Cris Mayo, 'Feminist Ethnography: Histories, Challenges and Possibilities', in *The Handbook of Feminist Research: Theory and Practice*, ed. Sharlene Nagy Hesse-Biber, 2nd ed. (London: Sage, 2012), 187–205, 195.
8 Laurel Richardson, *Fields of Play: Constructing an Academic Life* (New Brunswick, NJ: Rutgers University Press, 1997), 58.
9 Especially since changing the interviewee is not actually an aim of feminist research. See Pillow and Mayo, 'Feminist Ethnography', 197.
10 Maria Mies, 'Towards a Methodology for Feminist Research', in *Social Research: Philosophy, Politics and Practice*, ed. Martyn Hammersley (London: Sage, 1993), 68.

11 Nicola Slee, 'Feminist Qualitative Research as Spiritual Practice: Reflections on the Process of Doing Qualitative Research', in *The Faith Lives of Women and Girls*, ed. Nicola Slee, Fran Porter and Anne Phillips (Farnham: Ashgate, 2013), 19.

12 Etherington, *Becoming a Reflexive Researcher*, 226.

13 Gayle Letherby, *Feminist Research in Theory and Practice* (Buckingham: Open University Press, 2003), 143–144.

14 Marjorie L. DeVault and Glenda Gross, 'Feminist Qualitative Interviewing: Experience, Talk and Knowledge', in *The Handbook of Feminist Research: Theory and Practice*, ed. Sharlene Nagy Hesse-Biber, 2nd ed. (London: Sage, 2012), 206–236.

15 Mary Clark Moschella, *Ethnography as a Pastoral Practice: An Introduction* (Cleveland, OH: Pilgrim Press, 2008), 87.

16 I have removed many repetitions of the word 'like' from Danielle's quotations, to help the text flow.

17 Letherby, *Feminist Research*, 127–128. Author's emphasis.

18 Pillow and Mayo, 'Feminist Ethnography', 198.

19 Moschella, *Ethnography*, 12–13.

20 Etherington, *Becoming a Reflexive Researcher*, 210.

21 Pillow and Mayo, 'Feminist Ethnography', 195–197.

22 Ruthellen Josselson, *Ethics and Process in the Narrative Study of Lives*, Vol. 4 (London: Sage, 1996), 70.

23 Nicola Slee, *Women's Faith Development: Patterns and Processes* (Aldershot: Ashgate, 2004), 52; Susan Shooter, *How Survivors of Abuse Relate to God: The Authentic Spirituality of the Annihilated Soul* (Farnham: Ashgate, 2012), 40.

24 Sharlene Nagy Hesse-Biber and Deborah Piatelli, 'The Feminist Practice of Holistic Reflexivity', in *The Handbook of Feminist Research: Theory and Practice*, ed. Sharlene Nagy Hesse-Biber, 2nd ed. (London: Sage, 2012), 559.

25 Ibid., 567.

26 Patricia Hill Collins, 'Learning From the Outsider Within: The Sociological Significance of Black Feminist Thought', in *Beyond Methodology*, ed. Fonow and Cook (Bloomington: Indiana University Press), 35–59; Juanita Johnson-Bailey, 'The Ties that Bind and the Shackles that Separate: Race, Gender, Class and Color in a Research Process', *The International Journal of Qualitative Studies in Education* 12, no. 6 (1999): 659–670; Pillow and Mayo, 'Feminist Ethnography', 194.

27 See Catherine K. Riessman, 'When Gender Is Not Enough: Women Interviewing Women', *Gender and Society* 1 (1987): 172–207.

28 Hesse-Biber and Piatelli, 'The Feminist Practice of Holistic Reflexivity', 559, 562–563.

29 Ibid., 559

30 Nicola Slee, 'Feminist Qualitative Research', 19.

31 DeVault and Gross, 'Feminist Qualitative Interviewing', 215.

32 Shulamit Reinharz, *Feminist Methods in Social Research* (New York: Oxford University Press, 1992), 20–27, 68.

33 For example, Ann Oakley, *The Sociology of Housework* (Oxford: Martin Robertson, 1974); Denise Anne Segura, 'Chicana and Mexican Women at Work: The Impact of Class, Race and Gender on Occupational Mobility', *Gender and Society* 3 (1989): 37–52; Anne Phillips, *The Faith of Girls: Children's Spirituality and Transition to Adulthood* (Farnham: Ashgate, 2011), 61.

34 Letherby, *Feminist Research*, 109, 129.

13 Writing the self

Using the self in feminist theological research

Jan Berry

Introduction

When I first embarked on my doctorate my supervisor made a comment about research as a journey. It was this metaphor that inspired my imagination and sustained me through the lengthy, demanding and exciting process of part-time doctoral research. It gave me a greater sense of personal involvement, a realization that research was not simply about objective knowledge, but about my personal engagement and potential for change, growth and development.

During my teaching of research methods in contextual and practical theology I have increasingly drawn on feminist sources to stress the importance of using the self and of reflexivity in the research process. In supervising and sharing in collaborative dialogue with students and other researchers, self-awareness and the dynamics of relationships have been key elements in shaping and sharing ideas, and in the process of interpretation and writing. While I write as a feminist working within the broad discipline of practical theology, I have found that engagement with other disciplines in contextual theology has enriched my understanding and enabled my feminist perspective to contribute to a wider debate. In this chapter I draw together my own experience in writing, teaching and supervising, alongside published and unpublished research to examine the use of the self in feminist theological research. I explore the issues and power dynamics involved, and some of the theological implications of writing the self that have become increasingly central in feminist theological research.

The self as research instrument

Traditional views on research, based on a scientific model, stressed the need for objectivity and detachment. However, since Oakley's groundbreaking article[1] arguing that the detachment of the researcher could constitute an abuse of power, there has been an increasing recognition of the importance of the researcher as an instrument within the research process, particularly within qualitative research methodology: 'All phases of research are impacted by the researcher. Especially important is the idea that it is through his or her eyes and ears that questions are formulated and data are identified, collected, analysed and interpreted'.[2]

Within feminist theological research, for some this has led to a desire to make women's experience visible, arguing for recognition and a privileging of women's experience as a key category that shifts the hermeneutic process. The argument that those who are oppressed have a particular and valid form of knowledge goes back to Marxist standpoint theory: for example, Hartsock argues that 'women's lives make available a particular and privileged vantage point on male supremacy'.[3] This has been taken up in liberation theology in what is often called 'the epistemological privilege of the poor':

> In other words, theologies of liberation require that we not only make 'an option for the poor', but that we also accept the 'epistemological privilege of the poor'. This implies an epistemological paradigm shift in which the poor and marginalised are seen as the primary dialogue partners of theology.[4]

While not all women are economically poor, feminist liberation theologians claim that women experience structural and interlocking forms of oppression, and therefore that the concept of epistemological privilege is relevant and appropriate in feminist theory and theology:

> Far from engaging in a disinterested, objective, ahistorical enterprise, feminists who theorize women's oppression do so from the inside. They theorize it at the same time they stand in it – as inside experts. ... Her place on the inside gives her privileged access to knowledge about oppression.
>
> Feminist theorists refer to this as the epistemological privilege of the oppressed.[5]

The relativism of postmodernity, which recognizes a plurality of voices, texts and stories, challenges the concept of privileged readings; if there is no grand narrative, or universal norm, then how can one reading be privileged against another? Evans recognizes this difficulty, but argues that there is still a place for the concept of a privileged reading, and that in fact 'there must be one, for feminism to make its claims'.[6]

Women's experience is not a heterogeneous whole, but a diversity of interweaving and conflicting voices from women of colour, women with disabilities, lesbian, queer and trans women. Nevertheless, the initial recognition that theology is not founded on universal, assumed norms but originates in contexts of particularity and oppression underlies the importance of naming experience and making the self visible in theological research and reflection. This is certainly true of much feminist research, which focuses on experiences of women that have been consequent on patriarchal oppression or rendered invisible by it.[7]

The recognition of particularity and what Haraway[8] calls 'situated knowledge' is a strong element in postmodernity. The breaking down of the sense of a grand narrative, and the valuing of particular, individual or collective stories has resulted in a multiplicity of voices and a resistance to categorizing them hierarchically. It therefore becomes part of the research process to identify the writer's perspective, to locate her or his work within a context and to write from a personal and/or cultural perspective. In feminist theology – and in contextual and practical theology – it has become increasingly common to begin with an autobiographical introduction that locates the writer, and talks about interest and motivation for choosing a particular topic. There is also a strong emphasis, particularly in feminist theology, on reflexivity, in which the researcher shows an awareness of her own impact on the research process and its effect on her own understanding and experience. As a feminist researcher, therefore, I am committed to methodologies that give a particular place to the voices and experiences of women on the margins, using a liberationist perspective to privilege their experience, while making my own bias and conviction an integral part of my writing.

A problematic self

However, we cannot assume that in research and writing we have access to a raw, unmediated self. Increasingly postmodernism has stressed that the self is fluid, constructed in relation with others, and in relation to gender, culture and ethnicity. The self is not an essential whole, but is shifting, fragmented and fluid. What emerges of the self in research and writing is a glimpse or snapshot constructed in a particular moment of time. In that sense, as Walton argues, even non-fiction is a narrative construction and therefore 'fictive'.[9] Fisk argues that talking of 'stories' may be more helpful in reminding us that there are many different ways of expressing 'self', and says of her own writing:

> Rather a multitude of different stories could be told in a survey of the same young life; a multitude of different voices adopted, different masks worn. In writing about myself I am creating certain versions of myself. It is not pretence, but it is artifice.[10]

The self that is constructed in feminist theological research is a particular and situated self – distinct from the self of home and family, of journals and diaries, of intimate and even professional relationships. These selves may overlap, interact and collide – but always there is an element of mediation, of storytelling, or in Fisk's word, 'artifice'.

While ethical considerations in relation to qualitative research have focused on the power of the researcher, and her responsibility to care for her participants, to write honestly of personal struggles, challenges and delights exposes the writer in a way that could be embarrassing or even painful.

In Behar's book *The Vulnerable Observer* she uses personal and autobiographic narrative to reflect on issues of death, ethnicity and her Cuban heritage. She recognizes that this approach to methodology makes her and her readers vulnerable, but defends it as a skilled and essential form of anthropology: 'Writing vulnerably takes as much skill, nuance and willingness to follow through on all the ramifications of a complicated idea as does writing invulnerably and distantly'.[11]

To bring a critical reflection to one's own personal and vulnerable experiences can be painful, and sometimes can only be attempted from some distance in time. Walton says of her writing about her experience of infertility:

> It was too painful, and my feelings about it were too strong and chaotic. It was only when I had achieved some kind of perspective that I was ready to begin communicating. Having achieved this 'distance' I found that the writing process did not make me feel vulnerable or miserable – it was actually empowering.[12]

But as Walton suggests, the reflexive element can itself be therapeutic. Many researchers choose a topic that in some way or another resonates with their own experience, and the process of hearing, reflecting on and interpreting others' stories can become a way of making sense and meaning out of painful experiences. Etherington writes of her own personal and reflective writing (although acknowledging that she did not take this risk until well-established in her career) that it 'has changed my sense of the experiences I have written about and strengthened me in the process'.[13]

In writing of the self it is impossible to tell one's own story without telling the stories of others. The 'self' does not exist in isolation, but is shaped and constructed by interweaving relationships. Our own stories are also the stories of the others with whom we interact. To write of personal experience means writing about others, and this may make them vulnerable too: 'Because your identity is already disclosed, the identities of others connected to you sometimes become transparent to the broader audience and other times to smaller circles of your acquaintance'.[14]

How far is it legitimate to tell stories of one's childhood that include the stories of parent and siblings, or stories of growth, conflict and development that include friends, partners or colleagues? Walton argues that there is a need for 'respectful care',[15] and reminds us that theological writing is often engaging with sensitive and potentially painful topics, wrestling with the dilemmas of human frailty and struggle. But ultimately, it is almost impossible to be honest about one's own story and experience without involving others, and for writing of the self this raises ethical issues that go beyond the protocols and procedures of ethical committees.

The trajectory of using self

There are a number of different levels at which personal narrative or conviction is used in research. Often at the beginning of a piece of work an autobiographical introduction sets the scene and shows the researcher's motivation.

In accordance with the academic convention that writing must be impersonal and objective, this is left behind as the thesis or paper proceeds, and there is little further evidence of the person and self of the researcher. In feminist theology, however, acknowledging the perspective and bias of the author is an essential element in locating the work within a particular and specific context. The experiential and autobiographical elements can be interwoven throughout the work of writing. Increasingly within feminist theological research there is an awareness that this is not only legitimate, but valuable and perhaps even essential for reflexive writing, in which the voice and experience of the researcher is present throughout the work. Such reflexivity makes the researcher's process transparent in the research design and methodology, and the analysis and interpretation of data, and also shows the impact the research has had on her.

Thornton interweaves her own experience as a narrative thread through her thesis on motherhood as a rite of passage. She began her research with a focus on alternative ceremonies to baptism, but through her initial interviews and her own experience of becoming a mother, the focus of her research changed to place an emphasis on the transition into motherhood: 'I became interested from both a personal and research perspective in hearing more stories of women who had become mothers through childbirth and what rituals, if any, they had found or created to help them through this transition'.[16]

In *Proverbs of Ashes*, Parker and Brock interweave their stories of abuse and ethnicity with theological reflection and critique that speak powerfully of self. They tell how they began to attempt to write a book on the doctrine of the atonement, using academic argument and stories of experiences of others, but came to realize that they could not leave out their own stories: '[t]he mask of objectivity, with its academic, distanced tone, hid the lived character of our theological questions and our theological affirmations'.[17]

These writers are not only telling their own stories, but reflecting back on the way the process of research has impacted on them. The practice of reflexivity requires reflecting not only on the data that has been gathered, but on the researcher's own role in the process, and the way in which the research has impacted on her own understanding and development. Etherington defines it as 'the capacity of the researcher to acknowledge how their own experiences and contexts (which might be fluid and changing) inform the process and outcomes of inquiry'.[18] The experience and self of the researcher is renegotiated in the engagement with the experiences and selves of others, in a process of reshaping and construction of meaning in which both share. Increasingly reflexivity is recognized as an important critical tool, demanding a disciplined self-awareness that makes the presence of the self in the research visible and transparent to the reader.

In reflexivity the writer not only shares her own interpretation and analysis of the material she has gathered, but also makes visible and transparent the impact that the process of research and writing has had on her. Davies argues that this needs to be done with a strong critical awareness – it can lead to self-absorption and a breaking down of the boundaries between author and text, which leads to the research becoming simply about itself.[19] However, a genuine reflexivity, which shares with honesty the researcher's journey, self-questioning and dilemmas in the research process, brings the research and its methodology to life, and shows how the researcher herself grows, develops, and is vulnerable within the process. In my own thesis I wrote: 'Throughout my working with this material the idea of reflexivity is one that has excited and moved me. Research, for me, is about personal involvement, and my awareness of my own position, reactions and development is crucial'.[20]

Etherington, writing from the perspective of counselling research, draws parallels with the disciplined self-awareness and reflexivity that is required in therapeutic work.[21] While there is a clear distinction between the research interview and the counselling encounter, those trained in therapeutic disciplines are encouraged to reflect critically and with awareness on their own emotional processes, and this is a skill that is essential for the qualitative or reflexive researcher.

Reflexivity makes clear that research is a relational process. Unlike the false rapport to which Oakley alludes,[22] some feminist researchers are working with participants who are known to them, and where there is a high level of trust. Sometimes making the research element of the relationship specific can be problematic, and Thornton talks honestly of the dilemmas she encountered in engaging in conversation with friends while doing her research into mother-hood. She uses the term 'researched friends' to reflect the awkwardness and dilemmas that she experienced in trying to negotiate the tensions between being a friend or a researcher:

> However, the group I found it most difficult to protect against being harmed were the group I chose to call 'researched friends'; the people I approached for interview or consent because I already knew their story. I found these situations much more difficult to navigate, and therefore more time consuming, and I chose to give the group a clumsy title to reflect this tension.[23]

Reflexivity can help to address the power imbalance between the researcher and the research participants. Rather than the impersonal authorial/authoritarian voice commenting on and interpreting others' stories, reflexivity shows a process of co-construction of knowledge, in which researcher and researched share together. It gives research participants what Chopp has called 'narrative agency', which allows them to 'intentionally create their lives in relation to their culture, their bodies, their individual experiences, and their Christian communities';[24] it shows how their stories have contributed to the growing knowledge and understanding of the researcher. A reflexive methodology, in which the intersubjectivity of researcher and participants is acknowledged and made visible, strengthens the sense of a collaboration that recognizes the agency and active participation of both.

Some feminist researchers, however, go beyond recounting their own experiences, or making their presence visible and transparent. Autoethnography takes the experience of the researcher and analyses it as part of the data. It has been defined as 'an approach to research and writing that seeks to describe and systematically analyze (*graphy*) personal experience (*auto*) in order to understand cultural experience (*ethno*)'.[25]

This is more than autobiography, in that it goes beyond personal narrative, and focuses on an examination and analysis of culture. In feminist theological writing, often the cultural aspects are less apparent; rather autoethnography is used to reflect on aspects of women's culture, or particular groups or collective experience. Walton's definition includes this wider use of the term in a way that is appropriate to feminist theological research: '[a]utoethnography is a way of using personal experience to investigate a particular issue or concern that has wider cultural or religious significance'.[26]

Baker describes how, in her research on the theology of adolescent girls, she used autoethnography as a method, listening to their stories as 'an anthropologist entering a foreign land',[27] but also making visible her own participation and presence, and interweaving her own stories with that of the girls in her research:

> I became convinced that in order to hold carefully the stories of adolescent females – stories about death, race, gender, bodies, God – I had to tell carefully some of the stories from my own experience. In autoethnography I found a method which enabled me to do so.[28]

In recognizing the difference between her own experience and that of the girls, and the power dynamics involved, she compares the process to 'slipping through a barbed wire fence', a crossing of borders that makes powerful use of narrative, and of metaphors drawn from anthropological writing. 'My fantasy trip to this other world takes me across a border – the border between white girls lying in bed and brown bodies, dancing, singing, and entering space not seen by an overseer'.[29]

Bacon, in her article on feminist theology in relation to attitudes to the body and weight loss, tells of her participation in a slimming group over a period of fifteen months,[30] but does not reflect on her own experiences of the group or ways in which the experience impacted on her. In a later article, however, she adopts a more autoethnographic approach. She reflects on the dissonance implied in challenging dualist thinking while leaving her own bodily experience out of the research; building in her own experience as an integral part of her methodology, she emphasizes that she was there not simply as an observer, but as a participant, with a genuine concern for her own weight loss:

> It seemed to me, however, that seeking to rise above my own body and its contradictory desires only reinvested with new power the body/mind dualism feminists have long since tried to critique, not least within Christian theology. Consequently, I decided to include myself in the research as a participant.[31]

Woolley, in looking at women's practices of silence, included within her data her own responses to her interview questions.[32] While her research is not fully autoethnographic, she engaged with her own perceptions and understandings as part of the dialogue with her research data:

> [A]s individual and communal practices of silence form part of my spiritual life, it felt appropriate to 'hear my own voice', as Jane Ribbens suggests, and expose my own perceptions of silence to the same consideration I was asking other women to allow me to make.[33]

Chang, working in the field of education, has written on using autoethnography as a research method, drawing out its distinctive nature alongside autobiography and other forms of self-narrative, and setting out its benefits and pitfalls.[34] She argues that it is particularly useful in multicultural settings, and that it gives researchers easy and immediate access to data that they could not gain in any other way. Engaging in the process, as with reflexivity, can be transformative. It can, however, have its dangers – in particular, it can too easily become simply a personal narrative, focused on the individual without sufficient analysis of the surrounding context; and it needs to be combined with other data, so that there is not simply a reliance on memory, which can be selective.

Ellis *et al.* and Walton recognize that there are two main forms that autoethnography can take. One they describe as analytic autoethnography, which is critical, realist and attempts a systematic analysis of personal experience alongside other data. The other focuses on the construction of a literary narrative, seeking to evoke feelings and responses in the reader, in ways that Walton argues are particularly appropriate for theological writing: 'Evocative autoethnographic writing can also convey the complexity and ambiguity of our religious selves. Schooled in traditions of Bible reading, preaching and liturgy, we are already imbued with a sense of the purpose and power of evocative language forms'.[35]

The use of the self in supervision

Although much has been written about the use of the self in choosing a topic, in methodology, and in analysis and interpretation of data, very little has been written about the role of the self in the relationship between researcher and supervisor. For most research students this is a key relationship, and the dynamics may affect the successful completion (or otherwise) of the thesis or dissertation. Yet often this element of the research process is invisible to the reader other than in an expression of gratitude or appreciation in the acknowledgements at the beginning of a thesis, or of a book based on doctoral research. Etherington argues that little research has been done on the supervisory relationship, particularly from the perspective of the student, and goes on to tell her own story, and that of some of her own supervisory work with students, in order to analyse the importance of reflexivity in the relationship.

In the beginning of the process, finding the right person to supervise the research can be key. As well as the match of subject area, there needs to be a compatibility, a level of trust that can form the basis for sharing work over a number of years. Etherington describes negotiating a supervisory relationship in a way similar to counselling or therapy, 'exploring the expectations and hopes of the relationship in terms of themes such as: inspiration, honesty and respect, limits and boundaries, mutuality and power-sharing, challenge, managing difficulty and change, checking out responsibilities, and negotiating times to meet'.[36]

In supervision, I find myself not only engaging with the subject matter of the dissertation or thesis that I am supervising, but also with the feelings, emotions and processes of the researcher, sensing where energy and enthusiasm lie, being alongside in a sense of isolation or 'stuckness', or helping someone to clarify ideas and themes. My own sense of self and my interaction with the other becomes one of the methodological tools I use in my practice of supervision. The dynamics of the supervisory relationship are not only about expertise or engagement with the topic, but about a relationship in which two people (or more, if there is a supervisory team) work together to explore knowledge and meaning.

Part of the supervisory experience is helping students to explore and focus on appropriate methodologies. For one of my students, from a Transylvanian background, the whole notion of qualitative and reflexive research was new. For him, academic research had always been seen as objective and text-based, with no room for self or experience. A particular conversation in supervision marked a significant methodological turn in his research.

Working with research students on methodology can be a learning process for the supervisor too. I was introduced to autoethnography by a student attempting to research conflict resolution in Madagascar. Due to the political situation there, he was unable to find research participants willing to take the risks of being interviewed. Uncertain how to progress, he made himself the subject of his research, exploring his own hybrid identity as a way in to formulating a theological understanding of conflict and its resolution that would be relevant to his own context.[37]

For another of my students, her research involved field work with people working with gender-based violence in Uganda. As she conducted this element of her research, she became aware of a difficult dynamic. As a woman she was treated with a lack of respect and often felt marginalized; however, her commitment to respecting local culture and customs made this difficult to challenge. My own research has largely been with women from a similar social and educational background to my own, and so from her I am learning more about the ambivalences and dynamics involved in research with 'the other'. Inevitably there is a power dynamic at work within the supervisory relationship. At the beginning of the research the supervisor is likely to be perceived by the research student as being a powerful authority (although new supervisors may actually be feeling nervous and apprehensive about the responsibility).

Etherington argues for a model that is based on shared power: '[t]he model I am proposing is one of power-sharing, both parties being able to acknowledge their expertise, albeit the students being at an earlier stage of development'.[38]

In feminist research methodology there is an intention to make the relationship as far as possible one of mutuality, with an understanding of the research process as a shared journey, in which the supervisor may be a guide, but is increasingly a companion who walks alongside. There comes a point, however, in which I find myself saying to the researcher: 'You've found your voice'. There is a sense that the researcher 'owns' the material – she is no longer simply analysing what she has read, but adding her distinctive contribution. While as a supervisor I still accompany and support, the relationship has changed as her confidence and expertise have grown.

A reflexive supervisor is changed by the process too. She explores subjects and topics that are new to her – the nature of doctoral research in particular, with its requirement for originality, means that often the student will be venturing into unknown territory. But the supervisor also invests in the research process, sharing the sense of frustration or discovery, of triumph when a piece of work is successfully completed, and disappointment when it is not. Walton writes of her feelings after a successful PhD viva for one of her students:

> My student was wonderful. A deeply spiritual and also funny, witty and clever person. She answered all the questions with thoughtfulness and perception. I was very proud of her. So the results were delivered, the forms all signed, and there was a great sense of achievement and completeness to it all.[39]

While such emotional investment in the process of the supervision is rewarding, it is also costly for the supervisor. Like many others, I find the demands of supervision and teaching, and the investment in it, are often in tension with my own research interests and my own hopes and expectations for research. Retaining a sense of autonomy, of my own participation and agency in research, is difficult; and sometimes I can feel that my own 'research self' is in danger of becoming submerged by the demands of academic life. This is not simply an issue of time pressures, however great they are, but of an expending of emotional energy in which my sense of my own work and reflective space seems to be crowded out.

Theological reflection

In looking at the use of self in feminist theological research we are not only exploring the personal and interpersonal dynamics of the research process – we are also touching on important themes in feminist theology.

To talk of using the self in feminist theological research raises questions about the value we place on self. A feminist theological understanding of self begins with the conviction that we are all, male and female, made in the image of God. This means taking our female selves seriously, recognizing the female as of worth and as a site of divine revelation. It critiques theological views that urge women to be submissive, to subject themselves to male authority, and encourages a recognition of self-valuing and self-worth. Moreover, it is an embodied understanding, rejecting the dualism that sees the bodily and material as less worthy than the spiritual, and instead affirming a holistic view of body, emotion and spirit in an integrated whole. Therefore, to affirm the use of our selves in our research is to reject the dualistic compartmentalism that separates out academic research as a category that is separate from the rest of life. Feminist theological research is an embodied, emotional, intellectual and spiritual journey. The different strands may feel messy and tangled, but all must be there, and we strive to integrate them into a celebration of the wholeness of our embodied female lives. To undertake research entails a certain level of self-belief – we must believe that we have something to explore and to say. There will be times in the research process when self-belief struggles – we doubt ourselves, our capacity, our ability, and whether we have anything worthwhile to say. But we are sustained by a recognition of the value of all that we bring – not only in terms of our intellectual capability, but our life experience, our relationships, and our selves made in the image of the divine.

Female voices and wisdom have often been silenced in patriarchal theology. Research is a process of giving voice to that which has been silenced in ourselves and in others – it is a process, in Morton's words, of 'hearing into speech'.[40] Through the reviewing and critiquing of the work of other scholars, through the transcribing of interviews, through the coding and analysis of data, the researcher arrives at a point where her own critique and interpretation come through strongly – she is writing with confidence and authority, so that her voice is being heard. In much qualitative feminist research, there is a genuine desire to hear the voices of research participants, and to share their experiences and stories. Often feminist researchers are choosing to carry out research with people whose voices would not readily be heard, particularly in the world of academic theology, for example, Shooter writing of her research among survivors of abuse and their experiences of God[41] or Phillips researching the faith development of young girls.[42] But in that process our own voices must not be lost. Working with research data brings us into conversation and dialogue in which ultimately we are responsible for the process of interpretation: the researcher is finding her own voice.

The process of data gathering, analysis and interpretation involves power dynamics, and the themes of power, mutuality and vulnerability run through feminist theology. Feminists have critiqued the power-over model of patriarchy, with its elements of hierarchy and domination, and have instead argued for mutuality and an openness and a vulnerability to the other. The research process tends to locate power with the researcher, and feminist researchers are keen to address this imbalance as far as possible, giving power and voice back to the participants, although recognizing that sometimes this may be an impossible ideal.[43] But the use of self in research also makes visible the vulnerability of the researcher, from the beginnings of data gathering through to a form of writing that is honest about self-doubt and questioning, about personal pain and struggle, about the cost of the research or writing process. In making herself visible in her research, the female researcher embodies that sense of mutuality and vulnerability seen in an incarnate God/Christa.[44]

Feminist theological research is a relational process: the relationships between researcher and research participants, between the researcher and her supervisor(s), among the researcher and her peers interweave in shifting patterns and dynamics. In these embodied relationships we see a reflected glimpse of the interrelatedness of trinity, the dance of Creator, Christ/Christa, Spirit/Sophia. Human relationships become a site of the revelation of divine mutuality and interrelatedness.

Feminist research is a journey of faith, in which the faith and understanding of the researcher grows and is challenged, flourishes or struggles with the intricacies of the process and her interaction with her material. Sometimes it is a journey of questioning and doubt, sometimes there are moments of new insight and revelation. Parts of the journey are a grind, like plodding through mud; others are exciting, full of anticipation or inspiration. It is a journey not simply of the mind or intellect, but also of the spirit.

Conclusion

The use of the self in feminist research is not an optional extra, it is at the heart of the research process. This is not masked by the fiction of the detached, neutral observer, but is incorporated and made visible at every stage of the research and writing process. In this, feminist theological research is congruent with themes and values that lie at the core of feminist theology. It is a journey of self-affirmation, of mutuality and vulnerability, of relatedness with God/ess and self and other – a journey of faith.

Notes

1 Ann Oakley, 'Interviewing Women: A Contradiction in Terms', in *Turning Points in Qualitative Research: Tying Knots in a Handkerchief*, ed. Yvonna S. Lincoln and Norman K. Denzin (Walnut Creek, CA: Altamira Press, Rowman & Littlefield, 2003), 243–263.

2 Marilyn Lichtman, *Qualitative Research for the Social Sciences* (Thousand Oaks, CA: Sage, 2014), 31.

3 Nancy C. M. Hartsock, 'The Feminist Standpoint: Developing the Ground for a Specifically Feminist Historical Materialism', in *Feminism and Methodology: Social Science Issues*, ed. Sandra Harding (Milton Keynes: Open University Press, 1987), 159.

4 Gerald West, 'The Bible and the Poor: A New Way of Doing Theology', in *The Cambridge Companion to Liberation Theology*, ed. Christopher Rowland (Cambridge: Cambridge University Press, 1999), 131.

5 Serene Jones, *Feminist Theory and Christian Theology: Cartographies of Grace* (Minneapolis: Fortress Press, 2000), 74–75.

6 Judith Evans, *Feminist Theory Today: An Introduction to Second-Wave Feminism* (London: Sage, 1995), 126.

7 See, for example: Susan Shooter, *How Survivors of Abuse Relate to God: The Authentic Spirituality of the Annihilated Soul* (Farnham: Ashgate, 2012), or Anne Phillips, *The Faith of Girls: Children's Spirituality and Transition to Adulthood* (Farnham: Ashgate, 2011).

8 Donna Haraway, 'Situated Knowledge: The Science Question in Feminism and the Privilege of Partial Perspective', in *Turning Points in Qualitative Research: Tying Knots in a Handkerchief*, ed. Yvonna S. Lincoln and Norman K. Denzin (Walnut Creek, CA: Altamira Press, Rowman & Littlefield, 2003), 243–263.

9 Heather Walton, *Writing Methods in Theological Reflection* (London: SCM Press, 2014), xxv.

10 Anna Fisk, *Sex, Sin and Our Selves: Encounters in Feminist Theology and Contemporary Women's Literature* (Eugene, OR: Pickwick, 2014), 16.

11 Ruth Behar, *The Vulnerable Observer: Anthropology That Breaks Your Heart* (Boston: Beacon Press, 1996), 13.

12 Walton, *Writing Methods*, xxix.

13 Kim Etherington, *Becoming a Reflexive Researcher: Using Our Selves in Research* (London: Jessica Kingsley, 2004), 142.

14 Heewon Chang, *Autoethnography as Method* (Walnut Creek, CA: Left Coast Press, 2008), 68.

15 Walton, *Writing Methods*, xxx.

16 Jill Thornton, 'Moments Marked: An Exploration into the Ways in which Women are Choosing to Mark Aspects of their Rite of Passage into Motherhood' (PhD diss., University of Manchester, 2015), 41–42.

17 Rebecca N. Brock and Rita A. Parker, *Proverbs of Ashes: Violence, Redemptive Suffering, and the Search for What Saves Us* (Boston: Beacon Press, 2001), 6.

18 Etherington, *Becoming a Reflexive Researcher*, 31–32.

19 Charlotte Aull Davies, *Reflexive Ethnography: A Guide to Researching Self and Others*, 2nd ed. (Abingdon: Routledge, 2008), 9–10.

20 Jan Berry, *Ritual Making Women: Shaping Rites for Changing Lives* (London: Equinox, 2009), 55.

21 Etherington, *Becoming a Reflexive Researcher*, 31–32.

22 Oakley, 'Interviewing Women'.

23 Thornton, 'Moments Marked', 31.

24 Rebecca Chopp, *Saving Work: Feminist Practices of Theological Education* (Louisville: Westminister John Knox Press, 1995), 31.

25 Carolyn Ellis, Tony E. Adams and Arthur P. Bochner, 'Autoethnography: An Overview'. *Forum Qualitative Sozialforschung/Forum: Qualitative Social Research* 12, no. 1, Art. 10 (2010): 1. Authors' emphasis, accessed July 26 2016, http://nbn-resolving.de/urn:nbn:de:0114-fqs1101108.

26 Walton, *Writing Methods*,, xxxi–xxxii.

27 Dori Grinenko Baker, *Doing Girlfriend Theology: God-Talk with Young Women*. (Cleveland, OH: Pilgrim Press, 2005), 21–22.

28 Dori Grinenko Baker, 'Future Homemakers and Feminist Awakenings: Autoethnography as a Method in Theological Education and Research', *Religious Education* 96, no. 3 (2001): 395–407.

29 Baker, *Doing Girlfriend Theology*, 118–119.

30 Hannah Bacon, 'Expanding Bodies, Expanding God: Feminist Theology in Search of a Fatter Future', *Feminist Theology* 21, no. 3 (2013): 309–326.

31 Hannah Bacon, 'Fat, Syn and Disordered Eating: The Dangers of Powers of Excess', *Fat Studies* 4, no. 2 (2015): 92–111, accessed 13 May 2016, doi:10.1080/21604851.2015.1016777

32 This was a method also used in Nicola Slee's doctoral research: see Nicola Slee, *Women's Faith Development: Patterns and Processes* (Aldershot: Ashgate 2004), 53.

33 Alison Woolley, 'Women Choosing Silence: Transformational Practices and Relational Perspectives' (PhD diss., University of Birmingham, 2015), 146–147.
34 Chang, *Autoethnography as Method*, 56–57.
35 Walton, *Writing Methods*, 5–6.
36 Etherington, *Becoming a Reflexive Researcher*, 173.
37 Alfred Randriamampionona, 'Difference as Ferment for the Hybrid Church: Analysis of Conflict within the Hybrid Nature of the Church and Society' (PhD diss., University of Manchester, 2012).
38 Etherington, *Becoming a Reflexive Researcher*, 171.
39 Walton, *Writing Methods*, 83.
40 Nelle Morton, *The Journey is Home* (Boston: Beacon Press 1985), 210.
41 Shooter, *Survivors of Abuse.*
42 Phillips, *The Faith of Girls.*
43 Marjorie L. DeVault, *Liberating Method: Feminist and Social Research* (Philadelphia: Temple University Press, 1999).
44 Christa is the term used by feminist theologians to denote a female image of Christ. See for example: Nicola Slee, *Seeking the Risen Christa* (London: SPCK, 2011).

Bibliography

Aaron, Jane. 'Women in Search of a Welsh Identity'. *Scottish Affairs* 18 (Winter 1997): 69–81.

Åkerström, Jeanette and Elinor Brunnberg. 'Young People as Partners in Research: Experiences from an Interactive Research Circle with Adolescent Girls'. *Qualitative Research* 13, no. 5 (2002): 528–545.

Allan, G. 'A Critique of Using Grounded Theory as a Research Method'. *Electronic Journal of Business Research Methods* 2, no. 1 (2003): 1–10.

Alvizo, Xochital. 'The Listening Guide: A Practical Tool for Listening Deeply to the Body of Christ'. *Perspectivas* 13 (Spring 2016): 99–106. Accessed 4 August 2016. http://perspectivasonline.com/downloads/the-listening-guide-a-practical-tool-for-listening-deeply-to-the-body-of-christ-5/#_ftn21.

American Psychological Association. *Report of the APA Taskforce on the Sexualization of Girls, Executive Summary*. Accessed 1 November 2016. www.apa.org/pi/women/programs/girls/report-summary.pdf.

Ammerman, Nancy T. *Sacred Stories, Spiritual Tribes: Finding Religion in Everyday Life*. Oxford: Oxford University Press, 2014.

Ammerman, Nancy T. and Roman R. Williams. 'Speaking of Methods: Eliciting Religious Narratives through Interviews, Photos, and Oral Diaries'. *Annual Review of the Sociology of Religion* 3 (2012): 117–134.

Atkinson, Maxwell and John Heritage. 'Jefferson's Transcript Notation'. In *The Discourse Reader*, edited by Adam Jaworski and Nicolas Coupland, 158–166. London: Routledge, 1999.

Attenborough, David, (Presenter) and B. Appleby (Producer), 'The Silk Spinners' [Television series episode]. In M. Salisbury (Series Producer), *Life in the Undergrowth*. London: BBC, 2005.

Attride-Stirling, Jennifer. 'Thematic Networks: An Analytical Tool for Qualitative Research'. *Qualitative Research* 1, no. 3 (2001): 385–405.

Aune, Kristin. 'Feminist Spirituality as Lived Religion: How UK Feminists Forge Religio-Spiritual Lives'. *Gender and Society* 29, no. 1 (2015): 122–145.

Bacon, Hannah. 'Expanding Bodies, Expanding God: Feminist Theology in Search of a Fatter Future', *Feminist Theology* 21, no. 3 (2013): 309–326.

Bacon, Hannah. 'Fat, Syn and Disorderd Eating: The Dangers of Powers of Excess'. *Fat Studies* 4, no. 2 (2015): 92–111. Accessed 13 May 2016. doi:10.1080/2160485 1.2015.1016777.

Baker, Dori Grinenko. 'Future Homemakers and Feminist Awakenings: Autoethnography as a Method in Theological Education and Research'. *Religious Education* 96, no. 3 (2001): 395–407.

Baker, Dori Grinenko. *Doing Girlfriend Theology: God-Talk with Young Women*. Cleveland, OH: Pilgrim Press, 2005.

Banks, Marcus. *Using Visual Data in Qualitative Research*. London: Sage, 2008.

Bates, Charlotte. 'Video Diaries: Audio-Visual Research Methods and the Elusive Body'. *Visual Studies* 28 (2013): 29–37.

Bates, Laura. *Girl Up*. London: Simon & Schuster, 2016.

Beaman, Lori G. and Peter Beyer. 'Betwixt and Between: A Canadian Perspective on the Challenges of Researching the Spiritual but Not Religious'. In *Social Identities: Between the Sacred and the Secular*, edited by Abby Day, Giselle Vincett and Christopher Cotter, 127–142. Farnham and Burlington, VT: Ashgate, 2013.

Becker, Howard S. 'Afterword: Photography as Evidence, Photographs as Exposition. In *Picturing the Social Landscape: Visual Methods and the Sociological Imagination*, edited by Caroline Knowles and Paul Sweetman, 193–197. London: Routledge, 2004.

Beeching, Vicky. 'Trolling & Feminism'. In *FaithinFeminism.com: Conversations on Religion and Gender Equality*. Accessed 30 April 2016. http://faithinfeminism.com/online-trolling-and-feminism.

Behar, Ruth. *The Vulnerable Observer: Anthropology That Breaks Your Heart*. Boston: Beacon Press, 1996.

Belenky, Mary Field, Blythe McVicker Clinchy, Nancy Rule Goldberger and Jill Mattuck Tarule. *Women's Ways of Knowing: The Development of Self, Voice, and Mind*. New York: Basic Books, 1986.

Berry, Jan. *Ritual Making Women: Shaping Rites for Changing Lives*. London: Equinox, 2009.

Bian, Lin, Sarah-Jane Leslie and Andrei Cimplan. 'Gender Stereotypes about Intellectual Ability Emerge Early and Influence Children's Interests'. *Science* 355, no. 6323 (January 2017): 389–391. Accessed 27 January 2017. http://science.science mag.org/content/355/6323/389.

Bons-Storm, Riet. *The Incredible Woman: Listening to Women's Silences in Pastoral Care and Counselling*. Nashville: Abingdon Press, 1996.

Bourdieu, Pierre. *Distinction: A Social Critique of the Judgement of Taste*. Translated by Richard Nice. London: Routledge, 1984.

Bourdieu, Pierre and Loïc Wacquant. *An Invitation to Reflexive Sociology*. Cambridge: Polity Press, 1992.

Bowman, Marion. 'Christianity, Plurality and Vernacular Religion in Early Twentieth-Century Glastonbury: A Sign of Things to Come?' In *Christianity and Religious Plurality*, edited by Charlotte Methuen, Andrew Spicer and John Wolffe. Volume 51 of *Studies in Church History*, 302–321. Woodbridge: Boydell, 2015.

Brandes, Sigal Barak and David Levin. '"Like My Status": Israeli Teenage Girls Constructing their Social Connections on the Facebook Social Network'. *Feminist Media Studies* 14, no. 5 (2014): 743–758. Accessed 1 March 2016. doi: 10.1080/14680777.2013.833533.

Brearley, Laura. 'Exploring the Creative Voice in an Academic Context', *The Qualitative Report* 5, no. 3/4 (2000). Accessed 1 May 2017. http://nsuworks.nova.edu/tqr/vol5/iss3/2/.

Brierley, Peter and David Longley. *UK Christian Handbook*. 1992/1993 ed. London: Marc Europe, 1991.

Brinkmann, Svend. *Qualitative Interviewing: Understanding Qualitative Research.* New York: Oxford University Press, 2013.

Brison, Susan J. 'Trauma Narratives and the Remaking of the Self'. In *Acts of Memory: Cultural Recall in the Present,* edited by Mieke Bal, Jonathan Crewe and Leo Spitzer, 39–54. Hanover: Dartmouth College, 1999.

British Council for Literature. *Writers: Menna Elfyn.* Accessed 31 May 2016. https://literature.britishcouncil.org/writer/menna-elfyn.

Brown, Callum G. *The Death of Christian Britain: Understanding Secularization 1800–2000.* London and New York: Routledge, 2001.

Brown, Charis, Carolyn Costley, Lorraine Friend and Richard Varey. 'Capturing their Dream: Video Diaries and Minority Consumers'. *Consumption Markets and Culture* 13 (2010): 419–436.

Brown, Lyn Mikel and Carol Gilligan. *Meeting at the Crossroads: Women's Psychology and Girls' Development.* New York: Ballantine Books, 1992.

Brock, Rita N. and Rebecca A. Parker. *Proverbs of Ashes: Violence, Redemptive Suffering, and the Search for What Saves Us.* Boston: Beacon Press, 2001.

Burger, Thomas. *Max Weber's Theory of Concept Formation: History, Laws and Ideal Types.* Durham, NC: Duke University Press, 1976.

Cameron, Helen, Deborah Bhatti, Catherine Duce, James Sweeney and Clare Watkins. *Talking about God in Practice: Theological Action Research and Practical Theology.* London: SCM, 2010.

Cameron, Helen and Catherine Duce. *Researching Practice in Ministry and Mission: A Companion.* London: SCM, 2013.

Campbell-Reed, Eileen R. and Christian Scharen. 'Ethnography on Holy Ground: How Qualitative Interviewing is Practical Theological Work'. *International Journal of Practical Theology* 17, no. 2 (2013): 232–259.

Carli, Linda. 'Gendered Communication and Social Influence'. In *The Sage Handbook of Gender and Psychology,* edited by Michelle K. Ryan and Nyla R. Branscombe, 199–215. London: Sage, 2013.

Cartledge, Mark. *Practical Theology: Charismatic and Empirical Perspectives.* London: Paternoster, 2003.

Cartledge, Mark. *Encountering the Spirit: The Charismatic Tradition.* London: DLT, 2006.

Chandler, Siobhan. 'The Social Ethic of Religiously Unaffiliated Spirituality'. *Religion Compass* 2, no. 2 (2008): 240–256.

Chang, Heewon. *Autoethnography as Method.* Walnut Creek, CA: Left Coast Press, 2008.

Chaplin, Elizabeth. 'My Visual Diary'. In *Picturing the Social Landscape: Visual Methods and the Sociological Imagination,* edited by Caroline Knowles and Paul Sweetman, 35–48. London: Routledge, 2004.

Charmaz, Kathy. 'Stories and Silences: Disclosures and Self in Chronic Illness'. *Qualitative Inquiry* 8, no. 3 (2002): 302–328.

Chase, S. E. 'Taking Narrative Seriously: Consequences for Method and Theory in Interview Studies'. In *Interpreting Experience: The Narrative Study of Lives, Volume 3,* edited by Ruthellen Josselson and Amia Lieblich, 1–26. London: Sage, 1995.

Cherrington, Jim and Beccy Watson. 'Shooting a Diary, Not Just a Hoop: Using Video Diaries to Explore the Embodied Everyday Contexts of a University Basketball Team'. *Qualitative Research in Sport and Exercise* 2 (2010): 267–281.

Cheruvallil-Contractor, Sariya, Tristram Hooley, Nicki Moore, Kingsley Purdam and Paul Weller. 'Researching the Non-Religious: Methods and Methodological Issues, Challenges and Controversies'. In *Social Identities between the Sacred and the Secular,* edited by Abby Day, Giselle Vincett and Christopher Cotter, 173–189. Farnham and Burlington, VT: Ashgate, 2013.

Children's Research Centre. Accessed 7 December 2016. www.open.ac.uk/research projects/childrens-research-centre.

Chopp, Rebecca. *The Power to Speak: Feminism, Language, God.* New York: Crossroad, 1989.

Chopp, Rebecca. *Saving Work: Feminist Practices of Theological Education.* Louisville: Westminster John Knox Press, 1995.

Chopp, Rebecca. 'Theology and Poetics of Testimony'. In *Converging on Culture: Theologians in Dialogue with Cultural Analysis and Criticism*, edited by Delwin Brown, Sheila Greeve Davaney and Kathryn Tanner, 56–70. Oxford: Oxford University Press, 2001.

Chopp, Rebecca S. and Sheila Greeve Davaney, eds. *Horizons in Feminist Theology.* Minneapolis: Fortress Press, 1997.

Christ, Carol. 'Weaving the Fabric of Our Lives'. *Journal of Feminist Studies in Religion* 13, no. 1 (1997): 131–136.

Clark, Alison, Rosie Flewitt, Martyn Hammersley and Martin Robb, eds. *Understanding Research with Children and Young People.* Oxford and London: The Open University and Sage, 2014.

Clarke, Simon. 'Ideal Type: Conceptions in the Social Sciences'. In *International Encyclopedia of the Social and Behavioral Sciences*, edited by N. J Smelser and P. B. Baltes, 7139–7148. Amsterdam and Oxford: Elsevier, 2001.

Coates, Jennifer. *Women Talk: Conversation Between Friends.* Oxford: Blackwell, 1996.

Coates, Jennifer. 'Women's Friendships, Women's Talk'. In *Gender and Discourse* edited by Ruth Wodak, 245–262. London: Sage, 1997.

Coates, Jennifer. *Women, Men and Language: A Sociolinguistic Account of Gender Differences in Language.* 3rd ed. Abingdon: Routledge, 2016.

Coleman, Monica A. with C. Yvonne Augustine. 'Blogging as Religious Feminist Activism: Ministry To, Through, With, and From'. In *Feminism and Religion in the 21st Century: Technology, Dialogue, and Expanding Borders*, edited by Gina Messina-Dysert and Rosemary Radford Ruether, 20–33. New York and Abingdon: Routledge, 2015.

Collins, Helen. 'Weaving Worship and Womb: A Feminist Practical Theology of Charismatic Worship from the Perspective of Early Motherhood'. PhD diss., University of Bristol, 2017.

Collins, P. H. 'Learning from the Outsider Within: The Sociological Significance of Black Feminist Thought'. In *Beyond Methodology: Feminist Scholarship as Lived Research*, edited by M. M. Fonow and J. Cook, 35–59. Bloomington: Indiana University Press, 1991.

Couture, Pamela. 'Weaving the Web: Pastoral Care in an Individualistic Society'. In *Through the Eyes of Women: Insights for Pastoral Care*, edited by Jeanne Stevenson-Moessner, 94–106. Minneapolis, MN: Fortress Press, 1996.

Creswell, John W. *Qualitative Inquiry and Research Design: Choosing Among Five Approaches.* 3rd ed. Thousand Oaks, CA: Sage, 2013.

Daly, Mary. *Gyn/Ecology: The Metaethics of Radical Feminism.* London: Women's Press, 1979.

Daly, Mary. *Beyond God the Father: Towards a Philosophy of Women's Liberation.* London: Women's Press, 1986.

Davie, Grace. *Religion in Britain Since 1945: Believing Without Belonging.* Oxford: Blackwell, 1994.

Davie, Grace. 'Vicarious Religion: A Methodological Challenge'. In *Everyday Religion*, edited by N. Ammerman, 21–35. Oxford & New York: Oxford University Press, 2007.

Davies, Charlotte Aull. *Reflexive Ethnography: A Guide to Researching Self and Others*. 2nd ed. Abingdon: Routledge, 2008.

Denzin, Norman K. and Yvonna S. Lincoln. *The SAGE Handbook of Qualitative Research*. 4th ed. Thousand Oaks, CA: Sage, 2011.

Department for Education. Accessed 1 February 2017. www.gov.uk/government/organisations/department-for-education.

DeVault, Marjorie L. 'Talking and Listening from Women's Standpoint: Feminist Strategies for Interviewing and Analysis'. *Social Problems* 37, no. 1 (1990): 96–116.

DeVault, Marjorie L. *Liberating Method: Feminist and Social Research*. Philadelphia: Temple University Press, 1999.

DeVault, Marjorie L. 'Talking and Listening from Women's Standpoint: Feminist Strategies for Interviewing and Analysis'. In *Qualitative Research*, Vol. 4, edited by A. Bryman and R. G. Burgess, 86–111. London: Sage, 1999.

DeVault, Marjorie. L. and G. Gross. 'Feminist Qualitative Interviewing: Experience, Talk and Knowledge'. In *The Handbook of Feminist Research: Theory and Practice*, 2nd ed., edited by S. N. Hesse-Biber, 206–236. London: Sage, 2012.

Doucet, Andrea and Natasha S. Mauthner. 'Feminist Methodologies and Epistemology'. In *21st Century Sociology: A Reference Handbook*, Vol. 2, edited by Clifton D Bryant and Dennis L Peck, 36–42. Thousand Oaks, CA: Sage, 2007.

Douglas, D. 'Inductive Theory Generation: A Grounded Approach to Business Inquiry'. *Electronic Journal of Business Research Methods* 2, no. 1 (2003): 47–54.

Douglas, Jack D. *Creative Interviewing*. Beverley Hills and London: Sage, 1985.

Dunlop, Sarah and Philip Richter. 'Visual Methods'. In *Religion and Youth*, edited by Sylvia Collins-Mayo and Pink Dandelion, 209–216. Farnham: Ashgate, 2012.

Dunlop, Sarah and Peter Ward. 'Narrated Photography: Visual Representations of the Sacred among Young Polish Migrants in England'. *Fieldwork in Religion*, 9 (2014): 30–52.

Dunne, Gillian A. *The Different Dimensions of Gay Fatherhood: Exploding the Myths*. Accessed 30 April 2016. www.lse.ac.uk/genderinstitute/pdf/gayfatherhood.pdf.

Eccles, Janet B. 'Speaking Personally: Women Making Meaning through Subjectivised Belief'. In *Religion and the Individual: Belief, Practice, Identity*, edited by A. Day, 19–32. Aldershot and Burlington, VT: Ashgate, 2008.

Eckert, Penelope and Sally McConnell-Ginet. *Language and Gender*. 2nd ed. Cambridge: Cambridge University Press, 2013.

Elfyn, Menna. *Stafelloedd Aros*. Llandysul: Gwasg Gomer, 1978.

Elfyn, Menna. *O'r Iawn Ryw: Blodeugerdd o Farddoniaeth*. Dinas Powys: Honno Press, 1991.

Elfyn, Menna. *Eucalyptus – Detholiad o Gerddi Selected Poems 1978–1994*. Llandysul: Gwasg Gomer, 1995.

Elfyn, Menna. *Cell Angel*. Newcastle Upon Tyne: Bloodaxe, 1996.

Elfyn, Menna. *Perfect Blemish/Perffaith Nam New and Selected Poems 1995–2007*. Newcastle Upon Tyne: Bloodaxe, 2007.

Elfyn, Menna. 'Barddoniaeth Menna Elfyn: Pererindod Bardd'. PhD thesis, University of Wales, Trinity St. David, 2010.

Elfyn, Menna. *Murmur*. Newcastle Upon Tyne: Bloodaxe, 2012.

Elliot, Esther. 'Worship Time: The Journey Towards the Sacred and the Contemporary Christian Charismatic Movement in England'. PhD thesis, University of Nottingham, 1999.

Ellis, Carolyn, Tony E. Adams and Arthur P. Bochner. 'Autoethnography: An Overview'. *Forum Qualitative Sozialforschung/Forum: Qualitative Social Research* 12, no. 1, Art. 10 (2011): 1. Accessed 26 July 2016. http://nbn-resolving.de/urn:nbn:de:0114-fqs1101108

Emerson, Robert, Rachel Fretz and Linda Shaw. *Writing Ethnographic Fieldnotes.* Chicago: Chicago University Press, 2011.

Emmison, Michael, Philip Smith and Margery Mayall. *Researching the Visual.* 2nd ed. London: Sage, 2012.

Esim, Simel. 'Can Feminist Methodology Reduce Power Hierarchies in Research Settings?' *Feminist Economics* 3 (1997): 137–139.

Etherington, Kim. *Becoming a Reflexive Researcher: Using Our Selves in Research.* London: Jessica Kingsley, 2004.

Evans, Judith. *Feminist Theory Today: An Introduction to Second-Wave Feminism.* London: Sage, 1995.

Ferguson, K. *The Man Question: Visions of Subjectivity in Feminist Theory.* Berkeley: University of California Press, 1993.

Finch, Janet. '"It's Great to Have Someone to Talk To": Ethics and Politics of Interviewing Women'. In *Social Research: Philosophy, Politics and Practice* edited by Martyn Hammersley, 166–180. London: Sage, 1993.

Fisk, Anna. *Sex, Sin and Our Selves: Encounters in Feminist Theology and Contemporary Women's Literature.* Eugene, OR: Pickwick, 2014.

Fonow, M. M. and J. A. Cook, eds. *Beyond Methodology: Feminist Scholarship as Lived Research.* Bloomington: Indiana University Press, 1991.

Foucault, Michel. *The History of Sexuality.* Vol. 1. London: Penguin, 1978.

Fuller, Robert C. *Spiritual But Not Religious: Understanding Unchurched America.* New York: Oxford University Press Inc, 2001.Furman, Rich, Carol L. Langer, Christine S. Davis, Heather P. Gallardo and Shanti Kulkarni. 'Expressive, Research and Reflective Poetry as Qualitative Inquiry: a Study of Adolescent Identity'. *Qualitative Research* 7, no. 3 (2007): 301–315. Accessed 1 May 2017. https://sites.ualberta.ca/~iiqm/backissues/5_3/PDF/furman.pdf.

Furman, Rich, Cynthia Lietz and Carol L. Langer. 'The Research Poem in International Social Work: Innovations in Qualitative Methodology', *International Journal of Qualitative Methods* 5, no. 3 (2006): 1–8.

Furman, Rich, Carol L. Langer, Christine S. Davis, Heather P. Gallardo and Shanti Kulkarni. 'Expressive, Research and Reflective Poetry as Qualitative Inquiry: a Study of Adolescent Identity.' *Qualitative Research* 7.3 (2007): 301–315. Accessed May 1, 2017. https://sites.ualberta.ca/~iiqm/backissues/5_3/PDF/furman.pdf.

Gallacher, Lesley-Anne and Michael Gallagher. 'Methodological Immaturity in Childhood Research? Thinking through "Participatory Methods"'. *Childhood* 15, no. 4 (2008): 499–516.

Gee, James, P. *An Introduction to Discourse Analysis: Theory and Method.* 3rd ed. New York and London: Routledge, 2011.

Gerson, Kathleen and Ruth Horowitz. 'Observation and Interviewing: Options and Choices in Qualitative Methods'. In *Qualitative Research in Action*, edited by Tim May, 199–224. London: Sage, 2002.

Gibran, Kahlil. *The Prophet.* London: Heinemann, 1926.

Gill-Austern, Brita L. 'Pedagogy Under the Influence of Feminism and Womanism'. In *Feminist and Womanist Pastoral Theology*, edited by Bonnie Miller-McLemore and Brita Gill-Austern, 149–168. Nashville: Abingdon Press, 1990.

Gilligan, Carol. *In a Different Voice: Psychological Theory and Women's Development.* Cambridge, MA: Harvard University Press, 1982.

Gilligan, Carol, Renee Spencer, M. Katherine Weinberg and Tatiana Bertsch. 'On the *Listening Guide:* A Voice-Centred Relational Method'. In *Qualitative Research in Psychology: Expanding Perspectives in Methodology and Design*, edited by Paul M. Camic, Jean E. Rhodes and Lucy Yardley, 157–172. Washington, DC: American Psychological Association, 2003.

Girlguiding Girls' Attitudes Survey. Accessed 6 December 2016. www.girlguiding.org.uk/social-action-advocacy-and-campaigns/research/girls-attitudes-survey.

Glaser, B. G. *Theoretical Sensitivity: Advances in the Methodology of Grounded Theory*. Mill Valley, CA: Sociology Press, 1978.

Glaser, B. G. *Basics of Grounded Theory Analysis: Emergence vs Forcing*. Mill Valley, CA: Sociology Press, 1992.

Glaser, B. G. and A. L. Strauss. *The Discovery of Grounded Theory*. 4th ed. New Brunswick, NJ: Aldine Transaction, 2009.

Gluck, S. B. and S. Armitage. 'Reflections on Women's Oral History: An Exchange'. *Frontiers: A Journal of Women Studies* 19, no. 3 (1998): 1–11.

Gluck, S. B. and D. Patai. *Women's Words: The Feminist Practice of Oral History*. New York: Routledge, 1991.

Graham, Elaine. 'Review of *The Faith Lives of Women and Girls*, edited by N. Slee, F. Porter and A. Phillips'. *Journal of Beliefs & Values* 35, no. 3 (2014): 383–385. Accessed 2 August 2016. doi: 10.1080/13617672.2014.980076.

Graham, Elaine and Margaret Halsey, ed. *Life Cycles: Women and Pastoral Care*. London: SPCK, 1993.

Graham, Elaine, Heather Walton and Frances Ward. *Theological Reflection: Methods*. London: SCM Press, 2005.

Gramich, Katie. *Twentieth-Century Women's Writing in Wales: Land, Gender, Belonging*. Cardiff: University of Wales Press, 2007.

Gramich, Katie and Catherine Brennan. *Welsh Women's Poetry 1460–2001: An Anthology*. Dinas Powys: Honno Press, 2003.

Grbich, Carol. *Qualitative Data Analysis: An Introduction*. Thousand Oaks, CA: Sage, 2007.

Grbich, Carol. *Qualitative Data Analysis: An Introduction*. 3rd ed. London: Sage, 2013.

Green, Laurie. *Let's Do Theology: Resources for Contextual Theology*. London: Bloomsbury Academic, 2012.

Guite, Malcolm. *Faith, Hope and Poetry: Theology and the Poetic Imagination*. Farnham: Ashgate, 2010.

Guite, Malcolm. *Word in the Wilderness*. Norwich: Canterbury Press, 2014.

Hallam, Tudur. 'When a Bardd Meets a Poet: Menna Elfyn and the Displacement of Parallel Facing Texts'. In *Slanderous Tongues: Essays on Welsh Poetry in English 1970–2005*, edited by Daniel G. Williams, 89–111. Bridgend: Seren, 2010.

Haraway, Donna. 'Situated Knowledges: The Science Question in Feminism and the Privilege of Partial Perspective'. In *Turning Points in Qualitative Research: Tying Knots in a Handkerchief*, edited by Yvonna S. Lincoln and Norman K. Denzin, 243–263. Walnut Creek, CA: Altamira Press, Rowman & Littlefield, 2003.

Harding, Sandra. 'Introduction: Is There a Feminist Methodology?' In *Feminism and Methodology: Social Science Issues*, edited by Sandra Harding, 1–14. Milton Keynes: Open University Press, 1987.

Harris, Catherine, Lucy Jackson, Lucy Mayblin, Aneta Oiekut and Gill Valentine. '"Big Brother Welcomes You": Exploring Innovative Methods for Research with Children and Young People Outside of the Home and School Environments'. *Qualitative Research* 15, no. 5 (2015): 583–599.

Harris, Catherine and Gill Valentine. 'Childhood Narratives: Adult Reflections on Encounters with Difference in Everyday Spaces'. *Children's Geographies* (2017): 1–12. Accessed 4 January 2017. doi: 10.1080/14733285.2016.1269153.

Hart, Roger. *Children's Participation: From Tokenism to Citizenship*. Florence: UNICEF, 1992.

Hartsock, Nancy C. M. 'The Feminist Standpoint: Developing the Ground for a Specifically Feminist Historical Materialism'. In *Feminism and Methodology: Social Science Issues*, edited by Sandra Harding, 157–180. Milton Keynes: Open University Press, 1987.

Hay, David and Kate Hunt. *Understanding the Spirituality of People Who Don't Go to Church: A Report on the Findings of the Adults' Spirituality Project at the University of Nottingham*. Nottingham: University of Nottingham, 2000.

Hay, David with Rebecca Nye. *The Spirit of the Child*. Rev. ed. London and Philadelphia: Jessica Kingsley, 2006.

Hays, Sharon. *The Cultural Contradictions of Motherhood*. London: Yale University Press, 1996.

Heelas, Paul and Linda Woodhead. *The Spiritual Revolution: Why Religion Is Giving Way to Spirituality*. Malden, MA and Oxford: Blackwell, 2005.

Heller, David. *The Children's God*. Chicago and London: Chicago University Press, 1986.

Herbert, George. 'The Flower'. Accessed 25 April 2017. www.poetryfoundation.org/poems-and-poets/poems/detail/50700.

Herring, Susan C., Inna Kouper, Lois Ann Scheidt and Elijah Wright. 'Women and Children Last: The Discursive Construction of Weblogs'. *Into the Blogosphere* (2004). Accessed 30 October 2015. http://hdl.handle.net/11299/172825.

Hesse-Biber, Sharlene N. 'The Practice of Feminist In-Depth Interviewing'. In *Feminist Research Practice: A Primer*, edited by Sharlene N. Hesse-Biber and Patricia L. Leavy, 111–148. London: Routledge, 2007.

Hesse-Biber, Sharlene N., ed. *The Handbook of Feminist Research: Theory and Praxis*. 2nd ed. London: Sage, 2012.

Hesse-Biber, Sharlene N. 'Feminist Approaches to in-Depth Interviewing'. In *Feminist Research Practice: A Primer*, edited by Sharlene Hesse-Biber, 2nd ed., 182–232. London: Sage, 2014.

Hesse-Biber, S. N. and D. Piatelli. 'The Feminist Practice of Holistic Reflexivity'. In *The Handbook of Feminist Research: Theory and Practice* edited by S. N. Hesse-Biber, 2nd ed., 557–582. London: Sage, 2012.

Hogan, Linda. *From Women's Experience to Feminist Theology*. Sheffield: Sheffield Academic Press, 1995.

Holliday, Ruth. 'Reflecting the Self'. In *Picturing the Social Landscape: Visual Methods and the Sociological Imagination*, edited by Caroline Knowles and Paul Sweetman, 49–64. London: Routledge, 2004.

Holm, Gunilla. 'Visual Research Methods: Where Are We and Where Are We Going?' In *Handbook of Emergent Methods*, edited by Sharlene N. Hesse-Biber and Patricia Leavy, 325–341. London: The Guilford Press, 2008.

Isherwood, Lisa. *The Fat Jesus: Feminist Exploration in Boundaries and Transgressions*. London: Darton, Longman & Todd, 2007.

Johnson-Bailey, J. 'The Ties that Bind and the Shackles that Separate: Race, Gender, Class and Color in a Research Process'. *The International Journal of Qualitative Studies in Education* 12, no. 6 (1999): 659–670.

Jones, Serene. *Feminist Theory and Christian Theology: Cartographies of Grace*. Minneapolis: Fortress Press, 2000.

Josselson, R. *Ethics and Process in the Narrative Study of Lives*, Vol. 4. London: Sage, 1996.

Jovchelovitch, Sandra and Martin W. Bauer. 'Narrative Interviewing'. In *Qualitative Research with Text, Image and Sound: A Practical Handbook*, edited by Martin W Bauer and George Gaskell, 57–74. London: Sage, 2000.

Kamberelis, George and Greg Dimitriadis. 'Focus Groups: Strategy, Articulations of Pedagogy, Politics and Inquiry'. In *Collecting and Interpreting Qualitative Materials* edited by Norman K. Denzin and Yvonna S. Lincoln, 375–401. London: Sage, 2008.

Kara, Helen. *Creative Research Methods in the Social Sciences: A Practical Guide*. Bristol: Policy Press, 2015.

Keenan, Michael, Andrew K. T. Yip and Sarah-Jane Page. 'Exploring Sexuality and Religion using an Online Questionnaire'. In *Innovative Methods in the Study of Religion*, edited by Linda Woodhead. Oxford: Oxford University Press, forthcoming.

Kellett, Mary. 'Small Shoes, Big Steps! Empowering Children as Active Researchers'. *American Journal of Community Psychology* 46 (2010): 195–203.

Kendall, J. 'Axial Coding and the Grounded Theory Controversy'. *Western Journal of Nursing Research* 21, no. 6 (1999): 743–757.

Kiegelmann, Mechthild. 'Making Oneself Vulnerable to Discovery: Carol Gilligan in Conversation with Mechthild Kiegelmann'. *Forum Qualitative Sozialforschung/ Forum: Qualitative Social Research* 10, no. 2 (2009). Accessed 3 August 2016. www.qualitative-research.net/index.php/fqs/article/view/1178/2718#g5.

Kindon, Sara, Rachel Pain and Mike Kesby. *Participatory Action Research Approaches and Methods: Connecting People, Participation and Place*. Abingdon: Routledge, 2007.

Kittay, Eva Feder. *Love's Labor: Essays on Women, Equality, and Dependency*. New York and London: Routledge, 1999.

Kittay, Eva Feder, Bruce Jennings and Angela A. Wasunna. 'Dependency, Difference and Global Ethic of Longterm Care'. *Journal of Political Philosophy* 13, no. 2 (2005): 443–469.

Knowles, Caroline and Paul Sweetman. 'Introduction'. In *Picturing the Social Landscape: Visual Methods and the Sociological Imagination*, edited by Caroline Knowles and Paul Sweetman, 1–17. London: Routledge, 2004.

Knox, Francesca Bugliani and David Lonsdale, ed. *Poetry and the Religious Imagination: The Power of the Word*. Farnham: Ashgate, 2015.

Kolb, David. *Experiential Learning: Experience as the Source of Learning and Development*. Englewood Cliffs, NJ: Prentice Hall, 1984.

Korn, Jenny Ungbha and Tamara Kneese. 'Guest Editors' Introduction: Feminist Approaches to Social Media Research: History, Activism, and Values'. *Feminist Media Studies* 15, no. 4 (2015): 707–710. Accessed 1 March 2016. doi: 10.1080/14680777.2015.1053713.

Kvale, Steinar. InterViews: *An Introduction to Qualitative Research Interviews*. Thousand Oaks, CA: Sage, 1996.

Laird, Joan. 'Women and Stories: Restorying Women's Self-Constructions'. In *Women in Families: A Framework for Family Therapy*, edited by Monica McGoldrick, Carol M. Anderson and Froma Walsh, 427–450. New York: Norton, 1991.

Lakoff, R. T. *Language and Woman's Place*. New York: Harper & Row, 1975.

Langer, Carol L. and Rich Furman. 'Exploring Identity and Assimilation: Research and Interpretive Poems', *Forum: Qualitative Social Research* 5, no. 2 (2004). Accessed 1 May 2017. www.qualitative-research.net/index.php/fqs/rt/printerFriendly/609/1319.

Langer, Carol L. and Rich Furman, 'The Tanka as a Qualitative Research Tool: A Study of a Native American Woman'. *Journal of Poetry Therapy* 17 (2004): 165–171.

Lanzetta, Beverly J. *Radical Wisdom: A Feminist Mystical Theology*. Minneapolis: Fortress Press, 2005.

Lartey, Emmanuel. 'Practical Theology as a Theological Form'. In *The Blackwell Reader in Pastoral and Practical Theology*, edited by James Woodward and Stephen Pattison, 128–134. Oxford: Blackwell, 2000.

Lash, Nicholas. *Holiness, Speech and Silence*. Aldershot: Ashgate, 2004.

Lawler, Steph. 'Narrative in Social Research'. In *Qualitative Research in Action*, edited by Tim May, 242–258. London: Sage, 2002.

Lawless, E. 'Women's Life Stories and Reciprocal Ethnography as Feminist and Emergent'. *Journal of Folklore Research* 28, no. 1 (1991): 35–60.

Leavy, Patricia. *Method Meets Art: Arts-Based Research Practice*. 2nd ed. New York: The Guilford Press, 2015.

Lee, Raymond M. and Claire M. Renzetti. 'The Problems of Researching Sensitive Topics'. In *Researching Sensitive Topics*, edited by Claire M. Renzetti and Raymond M. Lee, 3–13. London: Sage, 1993.

Letherby, Gayle. *Feminist Research in Theory and Practice*. Buckingham: Open University Press, 2003.

Lichtman, Marilyn. *Qualitiative Research for the Social Sciences*. Thousand Oaks, CA: Sage, 2014.

Lipscomb, Anna and Irvine Gersch. 'Using a "Spiritual Listening Tool" to Investigate How Children Describe Spiritual and Philosophical Meaning Making in their Lives'. *International Journal of Children's Spirituality* 17, no. 1 (2012): 5–23.

Litosseliti, Lia. *Gender and Language: Theory and Practice*. Abingdon: Routledge, 2013.

Livedifference. 'Living with Difference in Europe: Making Communities Out of Strangers in an Era of Super Mobility and Super Diversity'. Accessed 7 December 2016. http://livedifference.group.shef.ac.uk.

Llewellyn, Dawn. *Reading, Feminism, and Spirituality: Troubling the Waves*. Basingstoke: Palgrave Macmillan, 2015.

Lloyd, Genevieve. *The Man of Reason: 'Male' and 'Female' in Western Philosophy*. London: Routledge, 1993.

Lövheim, Mia. 'Young Women's Blogs as Ethical Spaces'. *Information, Communication & Society* 14, no. 3 (2011): 338–354. Accessed 26 October 2015. doi: 10.1080/1369118X.2010.542822.

Lunnay, Belinda, Joseph Borlagdan, Darlene McNaughton and Paul Ward. 'Ethical Use of Social Media to Facilitate Qualitative Research'. *Qualitative Health Research*, 25, no. 1 (2015): 99–109. Accessed 1 March 2016. doi: 10.1177/1049732314549031.

McGrath, Alister. *Christian Theology: An Introduction*. 5th ed. Oxford: Blackwell, 2011.

McGuire, Meredith B. 'Embodied Practices: Negotiation and Resistance'. In *Everyday Religion: Observing Modern Religious Lives*, edited by Nancy Ammerman, 187–200. Oxford and New York: Oxford University Press, 2007.

McGuire, Meredith B. *Lived Religion: Faith and Practice in Everyday Life*. Oxford: Oxford University Press, 2008.

Mann, Chris and Fiona Stewart. *Internet Communication and Qualitative Research: A Handbook for Researching Online*. London: Sage, 2000.

Mannay, Dawn, ed. *Our Changing Land: Revisiting Gender, Class and Identity in Contemporary Wales*. Cardiff: University of Wales Press, 2016.

Massey, Doreen. 'Reflections on Gender and Geography'. In *Social Change and the Middle Classes*, edited by Tim Butler and Mike Savage, 330–344. London: UCL Press, 1995.

Massey, Kate. 'How Does the Experience of South Warwickshire Churchgoing Women, Who Feel Dually Called to Both Motherhood and Career, Help Us to Understand the Ideals of Motherhood as Expressed in Their Church and Community? To What Extent Does Their Faith Help Them in Balancing Dual Callings?' MA diss., University of Birmingham, 2013.

Marks, Rhiannon. *Pe Gallwn, Mi Luniwn Lythyr: Golwg Ar Waith Menna Elfyn.* Cardiff: University of Wales Press, 2013.

Mauthner, Melanie. 'Bringing Silent Voices into a Public Discourse: Researching Accounts of Sister Relationships'. In *Feminist Dilemmas in Qualitative Research: Public Knowledge and Private Lives,* edited by Jane Ribbens and Rosalind Edwards, 39–57. London: Sage, 1998.

Mauthner, Natasha and Andrea Doucet. 'Reflections on a Voice-Centred Relational Method: Analysing Maternal and Domestic Voices'. In *Feminist Dilemmas in Qualitative Research: Public Knowledge and Private Lives,* edited by Jane Ribbens and Rosalind Edwards, 119–146. London: Sage, 1998.

Mazzei, Lisa. 'Inhabited Silences: In Pursuit of a Muffled Subtext'. *Qualitative Inquiry* 9, no. 3 (2003): 355–368.

Messina-Dysert, Gina. '#FemReligionFuture: The New Feminist Revolution in Religion'. In *Feminism and Religion in the 21st Century: Technology, Dialogue, and Expanding Borders,* edited by Gina Messina-Dysert and Rosemary Radford Ruether, 9–19. New York and Abingdon: Routledge, 2015.

Messina-Dysert, Gina and Rosemary Radford Ruether, eds. *Feminism and Religion in the 21st Century: Technology, Dialogue, and Expanding Borders.* New York and Abingdon: Routledge, 2015.

Mies, M. 'Towards a Methodology for Feminist Research'. In *Social Research: Philosophy, Politics and Practice,* edited by M. Hammersley, 64–82 London: Sage, 1993.

Miles, M. B. and A. M. Huberman. *Qualitative Data Analysis: An Expanded Sourcebook.* 2nd ed. London: Sage, 1994.

Miller, Tina. 'Shifting Layers of Professional, Lay and Personal Narratives: Longitudinal Childbirth Research'. In *Feminist Dilemmas in Qualitative Research: Public Knowledge and Private Lives,* edited by Jane Ribbens and Rosalind Edwards, 58–71. London: Sage, 1998.

Miller-McLemore, Bonnie. *Also a Mother: Work and Family as Theological Dilemma.* Nashville: Abingdon Press, 1994.

Miller-McLemore, Bonnie J. 'The Living Human Web: Pastoral Theology at the Turn of the Century'. In *Through the Eyes of Women: Insights for Pastoral Care,* edited by Jeanne Stevenson-Moessner, 9–26. Minneapolis: Fortress Press, 1996.

Miller-McLemore, Bonnie. 'The Subject and Practice of Pastoral Care as a Practical Theological Discipline: Pushing Past the Nagging Identity Crisis to a Poetics of Resistance'. In *Liberating Faith Practices: Feminist Practical Theologies in Context,* edited by D. M. Ackerman and Riet Bons-Storm, 175–198. Leuven: Peeters, 1998.

Miller-McLemore, Bonnie, ed. *The Wiley-Blackwell Companion to Practical Theology.* Malden, MA and Oxford: Wiley Blackwell, 2014.

Miller-McLemore, Bonnie J. and Brita L. Gill-Austern, eds. *Feminist and Womanist Pastoral Theology.* Nashville: Abingdon Press, 1999.

Minister, K. 'A Feminist Frame for the Oral History Interview'. In *Women's Words: The Feminist Practice of Oral History,* edited by S. B. Gluck and D. Patai, 27–42. New York: Routledge, 1991.

Montgomery, David. *Sing a New Song: Choosing and Leading Praise in Today's Church.* Edinburgh: Rutherford House and Handsel Press, 2000.

Morgan, David L. *Focus Groups as Qualitative Research.* London: Sage, 1997.

Morley, D. 'Menna Elfyn'. In *The Cambridge Guide to Women's Writing in English*, edited by Lorna Sage, 217–218. Cambridge: Cambridge University Press, 1999.

Morley, Janet. *The Heart's Time*. London: SPCK, 2011.

Morton, Nelle. *The Journey is Home*. Boston: Beacon Press, 1985.

Moschella, Mary Clark. *Ethnography as a Pastoral Practice: An Introduction*. Cleveland, OH: The Pilgrim Press, 2008.

Muers, Rachel. *Keeping God's Silence: Towards a Theological Ethics of Communication*. Oxford: Blackwell, 2004.

Muir, Stewart and Jennifer Mason. 'Capturing Christmas: The Sensory Potential for Data from Participant Produced Video'. *Sociological Research Online* 17 (2012). Accessed 1 May 2016. www.socresonline.org.uk/17/1/5.html.

Myers, Benjamin. 'Theology 2.0: Blogging as Theological Discourse'. *Cultural Encounters* 6, no. 1 (2010): 47–60. Accessed 18 July 2016. www.academia.edu/5793572/Theology_2.0_Blogging_as_Theological_Discourse.

Nairn, Karen, Jenny Munro and Anne B. Smith. 'A Counter-Narrative of a "Failed" Interview'. *Qualitative Research* 5, no. 2 (2005): 221–244.

Nesbitt, Eleanor. 'Researching 8- to 13-year-olds' Perspectives and their Experience of Religion'. In *Researching Children's Perspectives*, edited by Ann Lewis and Geoff Lindsay, 135–149. Buckingham & Philadelphia: Open University Press, 2000.

NHS Confederation. Accessed 6 December 2016. www.nhsconfed.org/news/2016/09/the-adult-psychiatric-morbidity-survey.

Nye, Rebecca. 'Psychological Perspectives on Children's Spirituality'. PhD thesis, University of Nottingham, 1998.

Oakley, Ann. *The Sociology of Housework*. Oxford: Martin Robertson, 1974.

Oakley, Ann. 'Interviewing Women: A Contradiction in Terms'. In *Doing Feminist Research*, edited by H. Roberts, 30–61. London: Routledge, 1981.

Oakley, Ann. 'Interviewing Women: A Contradiction in Terms'. In *Turning Points in Qualitative Research: Tying Knots in a Handkerchief*, edited by Yvonna S. Lincoln and Norman K. Denzin, 243–263. Walnut Creek, CA: Altamira Press, Rowman & Littlefield, 2003.

Oakley, Mark. *The Splash of Words*. Norwich: Canterbury Press, 2016.

Oswald, Alice. *Dart*. London: Faber & Faber, 2010.

Ota, Cathy. 'Stories Told and Lessons Learned: Meeting Beliefs, Values and Community through Narrative and Dialogue'. *Journal of Beliefs and Values* 21, no. 2 (2000): 189–201.

Oxford Dictionaries Online. Accessed 30 April 2016. www.oxforddictionaries.com.

Page, Sarah-Jane. 'Double Scrutiny at the Vicarage: Clergy Mothers, Expectations and the Public Gaze'. In *Angels on Earth: Mothering, Religion and Spirituality*, edited by Vanessa Reimer, 17–38. Bradford: Dementer Press, 2016.

Page, Sarah-Jane and Andrew K. T. Yip. 'Gender Equality and Religion: A Multi-Faith Exploration of Young Adults' Narratives'. *European Journal of Women's Studies* (2016). Advanced access. doi: 10.1177/1350506815625906.

Paintner, Christine Valtners. *Eyes of the Heart: Photography as Christian Contemplative Practice*. Notre Dame, IN: Sorin Books, 2013.

Parker, Evelyn L., ed. *The Sacred Selves of Adolescent Girls: Hard Stories of Race, Class, and Gender*. Cleveland, OH: The Pilgrim Press, 2006.

Parr, Janet. 'Theoretical Voices and Women's Own Voices: The Stories of Mature Women Students'. In *Feminist Dilemmas in Qualitative Research: Private Lives and Public Texts*, edited by Jane Ribbens and Rosalind Edwards, 87–102. London: Sage, 1998.

Pattison, Stephen. 'Some Straw for the Bricks: A Basic Introduction to Theological Reflection'. *Contact* 99 (1989): 2–9.

Pease, Bob. *Undoing Privilege: Unearned Advantage in a Divided World*. London: Zed Books, 2011.

Percy, Emma. 'Reverend Mother: How Insights from Mothering can Inform the Practice of Leadership in the Church' (Part 1). *Modern Believing* 44, no. 2 (2003): 33–44.

Percy, Emma. 'Reverend Mother: How Insights from Mothering can Inform the Practice of Leadership in the Church' (Part 2). *Modern Believing* 44, no 3, (2003): 24–36.

Percy, Emma. *What Clergy Do Especially When It Looks Like Nothing*. London: SPCK, 2014.

Phillips, Anne. *The Faith of Girls: Children's Spirituality and Transition to Adulthood*. Farnham: Ashgate, 2011.

Piela, Anna. *Muslim Women Online: Faith and Identity in Virtual Space*. Abingdon: Routledge, 2012.

Pillow, W. S. and C. Mayo. 'Feminist Ethnography: Histories, Challenges and Possibilities'. In *The Handbook of Feminist Research: Theory and Practice*, edited by S. N. Hesse-Biber, 2nd ed., 187–205. London: Sage, 2012.

Pink, Sarah. *Doing Visual Ethnography*. London: Sage, 2007.

Plaskow, Judith and Carol Christ, ed. *Weaving the Visions: New Patterns in Feminist Spirituality*. New York: Harper Collins, 1989.

Plummer, Ken. *Telling Sexual Stories: Power, Change and Social Worlds*. London: Routledge, 1995.

Poindexter, C. C. 'Meaning from Methods: Re-Presenting Narratives of an HIV-Affected Care-Giver', *Qualitative Social Work* 1 (2002): 59–78.

Poland, Blake and Ann Pederson. 'Reading Between the Lines: Interpreting Silences in Qualitative Research'. *Qualitative Inquiry* 4, no. 2 (1998): 293–312.

Porter, Fran. 'Faith and Feminism: Women's Christian Faith Experience in Northern Ireland'. DPhil thesis, University of Ulster, 1999.

Porter, Fran. *Changing Women, Changing Worlds: Evangelical Women in Church, Community and Politics*. Belfast: Blackstaff, 2002.

Porter, Fran. *It Will Not Be Taken Away from Her: A Feminist Engagement with Women's Christian Experience*. London: Darton Longman & Todd, 2004.

Porter, Fran. *Women and Men After Christendom: The Dis-Ordering of Gender Relationships*. Milton Keynes: Paternoster, 2015.

Prendergast, Monica, Carl Leggo and Pauline Sameshima, eds. *Poetic Inquiry: Vibrant Voices in the Social Sciences*. Rotterdam: Sense, 2009. Accessed 1 May 2017. www.sensepublishers.com/media/765-poetic-inquiry.pdf.

Procter-Smith, Marjorie. *In Her Own Rite: Constructing Feminist Liturgical Tradition*. Nashville, TN: Abingdon Press, 1990.

Prosser, Jon and Andrew Loxley. ESRC National Centre for Research Methods Review Paper: Introducing Visual Methods (2008). Accessed 1 April 2014. http://eprints.ncrm.ac.uk/420/1/MethodsReviewPaperNCRM-010.pdf.

Pryce, Mark, ed. *Literary Companion to the Lectionary: Readings Throughout the Year*. London: SPCK, 2001.

Pryce, Robin Mark. 'The Poetry of Priesthood: A Study of the Contribution of Poetry to the Continuing Ministerial Education of Clergy in the Church of England'. DProf thesis, University of Birmingham, 2014. Accessed 10 May 2017. http://etheses.bham.ac.uk/5772

Punch, K. F. *Introduction to Social Research: Quantitative and Qualitative Approaches*. London: Sage, 2005.

Ramazanoglu, Caroline with Janet Holland. *Feminist Methodology: Challenges and Choices*. London: Sage, 2002.

Randriamampionona, Alfred. 'Difference as Ferment for the Hybrid Church: Analysis of Conflict within the Hybrid Nature of the Church and Society'. PhD diss., University of Manchester, 2012.

Rath, Jean. 'Poetry and Participation: Scripting a Meaningful Research Text with Rape Crisis Workers'. *Forum: Qualitative Social Research* 13, no. 1 (2012): 13. Accessed 1 May 2017. www.qualitative-research.net/index.php/fqs/article/view/1791/3312.

Redman, Matt. *10,000 Reasons*. Integrity Music UK and Hillsong, 2011.

Reinharz, Shulamit. *Feminist Methods in Social Research*. New York: Oxford University Press, 1992.

Ribbens, Jane. 'Interviewing – an "Unnatural Situation"?' *Women's Studies International Forum* 12, no. 6 (1989): 579–592.

Ribbens, Jane and Rosalind Edwards, eds. *Feminist Dilemmas in Qualitative Research: Public Knowledge and Private Lives*. London: Sage, 1998.

Richardson, Laurel. *Fields of Play: Constructing an Academic Life*. New Brunswick, NJ: Rutgers University Press, 1997.

Richardson, Laurel. 'Poetic Representation of Interviews'. In *Postmodern Interviewing*, edited by Jaber F. Gubrium and James A. Holstein, 187–201. New York: Sage, 2003.

Riessman, C. K. 'When Gender Is Not Enough: Women Interviewing Women'. *Gender and Society* 1 (1987): 172–207.

Ross, Maggie. *Silence: A User's Guide*. London: Darton, Longman & Todd, 2014.

Ruether, Rosemary Radford. Introduction to *Feminism and Religion in the 21st Century: Technology, Dialogue, and Expanding Borders*, edited by Gina Messina-Dysert and Rosemary Radford Ruether, 1–6. New York and Abingdon: Routledge, 2015.

Rukeyser, Muriel. *The Book of the Dead*. Accessed 25 April 2017. http://murielrukeyser.emuenglish.org/writing/the-book-of-the-dead/.

Saville-Troike, Muriel. 'The Place of Silence in an Integrated Theory of Communication'. In *Perspectives on Silence*, edited by Deborah Tannen and Muriel Saville-Troike, 3–18. Norwood, NJ: Ablex, 1985.

Schmidt, Leigh Eric. *Restless Souls: The Making of American Spirituality. From Emerson to Oprah*. New York: HarperCollins, 2005.

Schofield Clark, Lynn and Jill Dierberg, 'Digital Storytelling and Collective Religious Identity in a Moderate to Progressive Youth Group'. In *Digital Religion*, edited by Heidi A. Campbell, 147–154. London: Routledge, 2012.

Segundo, Juan Luis. *The Liberation of Theology*. Maryknoll, NY: Orbis Books, 1982.

Segura, D. 'Chicana and Mexican Women at Work: The Impact of Class, Race and Gender on Occupational Mobility'. *Gender and Society* 3 (1989): 37–52.

Sellers, T. S., K. Thomas, J. Batts and C. Ostman. 'Women Called: A Qualitative Study of Christian Women Dually Called to Motherhood and Career'. *Journal of Psychology and Theology* 33, no. 3 (2005): 198–209.

Sevenhuijsen, Selma. *Citizenship and the Ethic of Care: Feminist Considerations on Justice, Morality and Politics*. London and New York: Routledge, 1998.

Shakman Hurd, Elizabeth. *Expert Religion: The Politics of Religious Difference in an Age of Freedom and Terror*. Badia Fiesolana, Italy: RSCAS, 2015.

Shier, Harry. 'Pathways to Participation: Openings, Opportunities and Obligations'. *Children and Society* 15 (2001): 107–117.

Shooter, Susan. *How Survivors of Abuse Relate to God: The Authentic Spirituality of the Annihilated Soul*. Farnham: Ashgate, 2012.

Silverman, David. *Doing Qualitative Research: A Practical Handbook*. London: Sage, 2010.

Skeggs, Beverley. *Formations of Class and Gender*. London: Sage, 1997.

Slee, Nicola. *Women's Faith Development: Patterns and Processes*. Aldershot: Ashgate, 2004.

Slee, Nicola. *Seeking the Risen Christa*. London: SPCK, 2011.

Slee, Nicola. 'Feminist Qualitative Research as Spiritual Practice: Reflections on the Process of Doing Qualitative Research'. In *The Faith Lives of Women and Girls*, edited by Nicola Slee, Fran Porter and Anne Phillips, 13–24. Farnham: Ashgate, 2013.

Slee, Nicola. '(W)riting like a Woman: In Search of a Feminist Theological Poetics'. In *Making Nothing Happen: Five Poets Explore Faith and Spirituality*, by Gavin D'Costa, Eleanor Nesbitt, Mark Pryce, Ruth Shelton and Nicola Slee, 9–47. Farnham: Ashgate, 2014.

Slee, Nicola, Fran Porter and Anne Phillips, eds. *The Faith Lives of Women and Girls*. Farnham: Ashgate, 2013.

Smail, Tom, Andrew Walker and Nigel Wright. *Charismatic Renewal*. London: SPCK, 1995.

Smith, Christine. *Weaving the Sermon: Preaching in a Feminist Perspective*. Louisville: John Knox Press, 1989.

Sprague, Joey. *Feminist Methodologies for Critical Researchers: Bridging Differences*. 2nd ed. Lanham, MD: Rowman & Littlefield, 2016.

Stacey, Judith. 'Can there be a Feminist Ethnography?' *Women's Studies International Forum* 11 (1988): 21–27.

Stern, Daniel. *The Present Moment in Psychotherapy and Everyday Life*. New York: W. W. Norton, 2004.

Storm, Ingrid. 'Halfway to Heaven: Four Types of Fuzzy Fidelity in Europe'. *Journal for the Scientific Study of Religion* 48, no. 4 (2009): 702–718.

Strauss, A. L. and J. M. Corbin. *Basics of Qualitative Research: Techniques and Procedures for Developing Grounded Theory*. 1st ed. London: Sage, 1988; 2nd ed. London: Sage, 1998.

Stringer, Martin D. 'The Sounds of Silence: Searching for the Religious in Everyday Discourse'. In *Social Identities between the Sacred and the Secular*, edited by Abby Day, Giselle Vincett and Christopher R. Cotter, 161–171. Farnham and Burlington, VT: Ashgate, 2013.

Swinton, John and Harriet Mowat. *Practical Theology and Qualitative Research*. London: SCM Press, 2006.

Tacey, David. *The Spirituality Revolution: The Emergence of Contemporary Spirituality*. Hove and New York: Brunner-Routledge, 2004.

Tamminen, Kalevi. *Religious Development in Childhood and Youth*. Helsinki: Suomalainen Tiedeakatemia, 1991.

Taylor, Yvette and Ria Snowdon. 'Mapping Queer, Mapping Me: Visualizing Queer Religious Identity'. In *Globalized Religion and Sexual Identity*, edited by Heather Shipley, 295–312. Leiden: Brill, 2014.

Tedlock, Dennis. *The Spoken Word and the Work of Interpretation*. Philadelphia: University of Pennsylvania Press, 1983.

Thomas, M. Wynn. 'The Place of Gender in the Poetry of Gillian Clarke and Menna Elfyn'. *Sheer Poetry: Resources on Poetry by the Poets Themselves*. Accessed 31 May 2016. www.sheerpoetry.co.uk/advanced/dissertations/the-place-of-gender-in-the-poetry-of-gillian-clarke-and-menna-elfyn.

Thompson, Judith with Stephen Pattison and Ross Thompson. *SCM Study Guide to Theological Reflection*. London: SCM, 2008.

Thorne, Helen. *Journey to Priesthood: An In-Depth Study of the First Women Priests in the Church of England*. Bristol: Centre for Comparative Studies in Religion and Gender, 2000.

Thornton, Jill. 'Moments Marked: An Exploration into the Ways in which Women Are Choosing to Mark Aspects of their Rite of Passage into Motherhood'. PhD diss., University of Manchester, 2015.

Thornton, Leslie-Jean. '"Time of the Month" on Twitter: Taboo, Stereotype and Bonding in a No-Holds-Barred Public Arena'. *Sex Roles* 68 (2013): 41–54. Accessed 30 April 2016. doi: 10.1007/s11199-011-0041-2.

'Top 100 UK Universities on Social Media'. *Rise*. Accessed 30 April 2016. www.rise. global/top-uk-universities/r/2435899

Tracy, David. 'The Foundations of Practical Theology'. In *Practical Theology: The Emerging Field in Theology, Church and World*, edited by Don S. Browning, 61–72. New York: Harper & Row, 1983.

Tronto, Joan C. *Moral Boundaries: A Political Argument for an Ethic of Care*. New York and London: Routledge, 1993.

Veling, Terry. *Practical Theology: 'On Earth as It Is in Heaven'*. Maryknoll, NY: Orbis Books, 2005.

Voas, David. 'The Rise and Fall of Fuzzy Fidelity in Europe'. *European Sociological Review* 25, no. 2 (2009): 155–168.

Walton, Heather. *Literature, Theology and Feminism*. Manchester: Manchester University Press, 2007.

Walton, Heather. 'Poetics'. In *The Wiley Blackwell Companion to Practical Theology*, edited by Bonnie J. Miller-McLemore, 173–182. Malden, MA and Oxford: Wiley-Blackwell, 2012.

Walton, Heather. *Writing Methods in Theological Reflection*. London: SCM Press, 2014.

Walton, Heather. *Not Eden: Spiritual Life Writing for this World*. London: SCM, 2015.

Ward, Hannah and Jennifer Wild. *Guard the Chaos: Finding Meaning in Change*. London: Darton, Longman & Todd, 1995.

Ward, Pete. *Selling Worship: How What We Sing Has Changed the Church*. Milton Keynes: Paternoster, 2005.

Wasey, Kim. 'Being in Communion: A Qualitative Study of Young Lay Women's Experiences of the Eucharist'. ThD thesis, University of Birmingham, 2013. http://etheses.bham.ac.uk/3980/.

Wasey, Kim. 'Standing Together: Loving the Communion Queue!'. *Women in Communion Blog*, 2 October 2015. Accessed 30 April 2016. https://womenincommunion.wordpress.com/2015/10/02/standing-together-loving-the-communion-queue.

Wasey, Kim. 'Circles of Communion'. *Women in Communion Blog*, 5 October 2015. Accessed 30 April 2016. https://womenincommunion.wordpress.com/2015/10/05/circles-of-communion.

Wasey, Kim. 'Communion: A Time to Stop'. *Women in Communion Blog*, 7 October 2015. Accessed 30 April 2016. http://womenincommunion.wordpress.com/2015/10/07/communion-a-time-to-stop.

Watts, Jacqueline. '"The Outsider Within": Dilemmas of Qualitative Feminist Research Within a Culture of Resistance'. *Qualitative Research* 6, no. 3 (2006): 385–402.

Webster, Alison R. *Found Wanting: Women, Christianity and Sexuality*. London: Cassell, 1995.

Welsh Government, Knowledge and Analytic Services. *2011 Census: First Results for Ethnicity, National Identity and Religion for Wales. Statistical Bulletin.* Cardiff, 2012. Accessed 7 November 2016. http://cdn.basw.co.uk/upload/basw_111853-3.pdf.

Wengraf, Tom. 'Uncovering the General from within the Particular: From Contingencies to Typologies in the Understanding of Cases'. In *The Turn to Biographical Methods in Social Science: Comparative Issues and Examples,* edited by Prue Chamberlayne, Joanna Bornat and Tom Wengraf, 141–164. London: Routledge, 2000.

West, Gerald. 'The Bible and the Poor: A New Way of Doing Theology'. In *The Cambridge Companion to Liberation Theology,* edited by Christopher Rowland, 129–152. Cambridge: Cambridge University Press, 1999.

Westmarland, Nicole. 'The Quantitative/Qualitative Debate and Feminist Research: A Subjective View of Objectivity'. *Forum Qualitative Sozialforschung/Forum: Qualitative Social Research* 2, no. 1, Art. 13 (2001). Accessed 29 June 2016. www.qualitative-research.net/index.php/fqs/article/view/974.

Willard, Ann. 'Cultural Scripts For Mothering'. In *Mapping the Moral Domain* edited by Carol Gilligan, Janie Victoria Ward and Jill MacLean Taylor, 225–243. Cambridge MA: Harvard University Press, 1988.

Williams, Rowan. *Silence and Honey Cakes.* Oxford: Lion Books, 2003.

Women in Communion Blog. Accessed 30 April 2016. https://womenincommunion.wordpress.com.

Woodfield, Kandy, Gareth Morrell, Katie Metzler, Grant Blank, Dr Janet Salmons, Jerome Finnegan and Mithu Lucraft. 'Blurring the Boundaries? New Social Media, New Social Research: Developing a Network to Explore the Issues Faced by Researchers Negotiating the New Research Landscape of Online Social Media Platforms'. National Centre for Research Methods Methodological review paper (2013). Accessed 30 October 2015. http://eprints.ncrm.ac.uk/3168/1/blurring_boundaries.pdf.

Woodward, James and Stephen Pattison, ed. *The Blackwell Reader in Pastoral and Practical Theology.* Oxford: Blackwell, 2000.

Woolley, Alison. 'Women Choosing Silence: Transformational Practices and Relational Perspectives'. PhD diss., University of Birmingham, 2015.

Yip, Andrew K. T. and Sarah-Jane Page. *Religious and Sexual Identities: A Multi-Faith Exploration of Young Adults.* Farnham: Ashgate, 2013.

Zembylas, Michalinos and Pavlos Michaelides. 'The Sound of Silence in Pedagogy'. *Educational Theory* 54, no. 2 (2004): 192–210.

Index

Names in the index refer to authors cited in the main body of the text and in substantive footnotes. Authors only referenced in footnotes do not appear in the index.